T0314229

RESEARCH ACROSS BORDERS

Research across Borders

An Introduction to Interdisciplinary,
Cross-Cultural Methodology

CHRISTINA CLARK-KAZAK

UNIVERSITY OF TORONTO PRESS
Toronto Buffalo London

© University of Toronto Press 2023
Toronto Buffalo London
utorontopress.com

ISBN 978-1-4875-0647-6 (cloth) ISBN 978-1-4875-3423-3 (EPUB)
ISBN 978-1-4875-2437-1 (paper) ISBN 978-1-4875-3422-6 (PDF)

Library and Archives Canada Cataloguing in Publication

Title: Research across borders : an introduction to interdisciplinary, cross-cultural methodology / Christina Clark-Kazak.
Names: Clark-Kazak, Christina R., 1975– author.
Description: Includes bibliographical references and index.
Identifiers: Canadiana (print) 20230177360 | Canadiana (ebook) 20230177395 | ISBN 9781487524371 (paper) | ISBN 9781487506476 (cloth) | ISBN 9781487534233 (EPUB) | ISBN 9781487534226 (PDF)
Subjects: LCSH: Cross-cultural studies – Research. | LCSH: Cross-cultural studies – Methodology.
Classification: LCC GN345.7.C53 2023 | DDC 306.072/1 – dc23

Cover design: Michel Vrana, Black Eye Design
Cover image: iStock.com/FORGEM

We welcome comments and suggestions regarding any aspect of our publications – please feel free to contact us at news@utorontopress.com or visit us at utorontopress.com.

Every effort has been made to contact copyright holders; in the event of an error or omission, please notify the publisher.

We wish to acknowledge the land on which the University of Toronto Press operates. This land is the traditional territory of the Wendat, the Anishnaabeg, the Haudenosaunee, the Métis, and the Mississaugas of the Credit First Nation.

University of Toronto Press acknowledges the financial support of the Government of Canada and the Ontario Arts Council, an agency of the Government of Ontario, for its publishing activities.

 **Canada Council   Conseil des Arts
for the Arts   du Canada**

 ONTARIO ARTS COUNCIL
CONSEIL DES ARTS DE L'ONTARIO
an Ontario government agency
un organisme du gouvernement de l'Ontario

Funded by the   Financé par le
Government   gouvernement
of Canada   du Canada

For Mehroo Kazak (1947–2020), who lived across borders

Contents

Figures and Tables

Figures

Tables

Acknowledgments

This book has emerged from conversations with students and colleagues over more than fifteen years of teaching research methods at three different institutions: Saint Paul University, York University, and the University of Ottawa. Through my learning journeys, my thinking has been immeasurably shaped by my students and colleagues. I have also grown as a researcher by participating in the Refugee Research Network Methodology and Knowledge Production research group. I am grateful to Susan McGrath for providing the space for this work to take shape and grow, and to Jennifer Hyndman for her mentorship.

Research across Borders would never have moved from an idea to reality without the early encouragement and support of Mat Buntin, who was acquisitions editor at the University of Toronto Press at the beginning of this process. I am grateful for his belief in this project. I also acknowledge the dedication of Marilyn McCormack, Stephen Jones, and Rebecca Duce for shepherding this book through the editing and publication process. Anonymous reviewers provided thoughtful and detailed feedback, which strengthened this manuscript.

I gratefully acknowledge the following colleagues who offered research assistance and support: Gabrielle Verena Nkouatchet Matsodoum, Marko de Guzman, Amélie Cossette, Anahita Kazak, Leonne Valantin, and Daphnée Campeau. Leah Clark provided invaluable advice on textbook design.

This book went through multiple iterations and revisions as life took unexpected turns through the COVID-19 pandemic and several family emergencies. As always, my husband, Sam, and our children Anahita and Rustom were by my side as I navigated professional and personal challenges. I am grateful for their constant encouragement, love, and support.

1

Why Research across Borders?

LEARNING OBJECTIVES

By the end of this chapter, you will be able to:

- Explain the ways in which **borders** – even those which are **socially constructed** – define and constrain internationally focused research;
- Define **research** and explain the importance of research across borders;
- Identify methodological choices that affect research results; and,
- Explain how research across borders is unique.

KEY TERMS

Academic journals
Advocacy
Applied research
Basic research
Border
Category
Concepts
Control for

Critical analysis
Cross-cultural
Data
Discipline
Empirical
Epistemology
Ethics
Evidence-based policy-making

Indicator	Qualitative
Interdisciplinary	Quantitative
Knowledge production	Research
Lived experiences	Scholarly
Meta-	Secondary research
Methodology	Socially constructed
Methods	Sovereign state
Mind map	Theory
Pedagogical	Unit of analysis
Positionality	World view
Primary research	

INTRODUCTION

This book will introduce you to the key **concepts** and **methods** that you will need to understand and critically analyse the research that you read about in **scholarly** books and journals, as well as in media, government documents, and anywhere else where you encounter information. It will also help you to become a better researcher – whether you are gathering information from secondary sources, like government documents, or doing **primary research**, such as interviews. The book has been specifically designed for students who are taking courses and degrees in **interdisciplinary**, international programs, such as conflict studies, human rights, international studies, development studies, and migration studies.

In this chapter, we will discuss how research in these contexts is different than in more traditional disciplinary programs such as sociology, economics, history, or political science. We will also think about how cross-border, **cross-cultural** research may require specific ways of thinking about, and doing, research.

META-EXAMPLE: THREE TAKES ON STATE FRAGILITY

The idea of "fragile states" emerged in the early 2000s to describe countries whose governments are weak and that are at risk of not being able to perform all the functions of a **sovereign state**. But, "state fragility" is a complex concept. How can we measure it? This is an important methodological question.

Different research teams have developed different approaches – using different methods – for studying state fragility. Because of these different methods, they have come up with different results. In this example, we will compare three different methodological approaches.

The Fund for Peace (FFP) is an independent, non-profit organization headquartered in the United States. As indicated by its name, its primary objective is to promote peace. Recognizing that fragile states are often sites of violence and conflict, FFP has developed the Fragile States Index to try to measure fragility and hence to anticipate, and perhaps prevent, conflict. The Index draws on three different methods: content analysis (see chapter 11) of media articles; quantitative analysis of statistical data from the United Nations (UN) and other multilateral agencies; and qualitative review of key events in each country. The Index is composed of five clusters of **indicators**: cohesion indicators, economic indicators, social indicators, political indicators, and cross-cutting indicators.[1]

A team of researchers from Carleton University in Ottawa, Canada, has a similar project to measure fragility called "Country Indicators for Foreign Policy" (CIFP). Their methodology relies on a web-based country monitoring tool, which includes (1) "structural data" such as GDP per capita, political indicators, and human rights data compiled by international organizations; (2) events-based information analysis of dynamic data such as media stories; and (3) qualitative data from expert opinions.[2]

A third approach comes from the Organisation for Economic Co-operation and Development (OECD), an intergovernmental organization. The OECD measures fragility using five dimensions: economic, environmental, political, security, and societal. For each dimension, there are eight to twelve indicators, which are compiled from secondary data sources.[3]

While there are similarities across these three methodological approaches to fragility, the results are different as demonstrated by the top ten fragile countries in 2019 according to the different indices.

Table 1.1. Different methodological approaches to fragility

Country ranking	CIFP ranking[a]	FFP ranking[b]	OECD ranking[c]
1	Chad	Yemen	Yemen
2	Sudan	Somalia	South Sudan
3	Somalia	South Sudan	Somalia
4	Central African Republic	Syria	Central African Republic
5	South Sudan	Democratic Republic of Congo	Democratic Republic of Congo
6	Yemen	Central African Republic	Syria
7	Afghanistan	Chad	Chad
8	Democratic Republic of Congo	Sudan	Afghanistan
9	West Bank and Gaza	Afghanistan	Haiti
10	Eritrea	Zimbabwe	Burundi

[a] "Fragile and Conflict-Affected States in the Age of COVID 19: A 2020 Country Indicators for Foreign Policy Report," accessed 8 November 2022, https://carleton.ca/cifp/wp-content/uploads/2020-CIFP-Fragility-Report.pdf.
[b] "Fragile States Index Annual Report 2020," accessed 8 November 2022, https://fragilestatesindex.org/wp-content/uploads/2020/05/fsi2020-report.pdf.
[c] "States of Fragility 2022."

Activity 1.1: Analysing the Fragility Index

1. Highlight each country with a different colour to help you identify patterns across the three lists.
2. Identify similarities and differences across the rankings.
3. Are there any countries that are only on one list?
4. Can you identify the geopolitical entity that is not always formally recognized as a state? Why do you think it is included? Why is it not on the other lists?

This **meta-**example teaches a few important lessons, which will be unpacked in this chapter and throughout the book.

First, borders matter. Countries (or sovereign states) are often used – somewhat problematically, as discussed below – as the primary **unit of analysis** to compare phenomena, such as fragility, globally.

Second, **methodology** matters. Because the researchers in this example had different definitions of, and methods to measure, fragility, they got different results.

Third, research matters. The information on fragility that was generated through the research projects described in the example above not only were published in **academic journals**, they also had real life impacts on how international donors funded development projects. Indeed, FFP and OECD are not academic institutions, while the Carleton University project Fragile and Conflict-Affected States in the Age of COVID 19 A 2020 "Country Indicators for Foreign Policy Report," to demonstrate that the research findings were intended to be applied in the real world. This example shows that researchers inside and outside of universities do research. Sometimes, their objectives and approaches may be different because of their different perspectives on research.

THE POLITICS AND PRACTICE OF BORDERS

This book is centred on the idea of borders, because they are fundamental to research and **knowledge production**. Thomas Nail has defined the border as "a process of social division" that introduces "a division or bifurcation of some sort into the world."[4] Borders both include and exclude. We need to critically analyse these inclusion and exclusion processes and their impact on research.

In this book, we will think in particular about geopolitical borders between and within sovereign states, borders between academic **disciplines**, and social borders that create power inequalities. There are, of course, other borders that are important, but this book focuses on these ones as key factors to consider when doing research in internationally focused, interdisciplinary programs. Let's look at each one here.

Geopolitical Borders between and within Sovereign States. Within internationally focused programs, geopolitical borders of sovereign states often shape the way in which we think about and do research.

Methodologically, sovereign states or countries often serve as the key unit of analysis – that is the "what" or the "who" we are studying. Like in the fragility example at the beginning of this chapter, countries are taken-for-granted categories that provide comparative analysis of different issues – whether it be fragility, development, democracy, or gender equality – across the world. However, these boundaries are actually socially constructed. There is nothing normal or natural about countries' borders, many of which have been created and enforced through violence, colonization, repression, and displacement.

An example from the fragility lists above is the recent creation of the country of South Sudan in 2011, when it separated from Sudan. South Sudan is listed on all three lists of top ten fragile countries, while Sudan is not on the OECD list. In contrast, the CIFP list is the only one that includes in its fragility rankings the "West Bank and Gaza," also known as the Occupied Palestinian Territory. The State of Palestine is recognized by 138 UN member states and only has non-member observer state status in the UN. These examples demonstrate the politicization and socially constructed nature of geopolitical borders of sovereign states.

Moreover, while countries are technically at the same level of analysis, they are not necessarily easily comparable. Sovereign states vary vastly in terms of population, geographic size, economic weight, geopolitical power, government structure, and so on. Indeed, in the fragility index example above, the OECD **controls for** population variations when determining fragility. In terms of geographic area, the Democratic Republic of Congo (the second largest country in Africa) covers eighty-four times more area than Haiti, which shares an island with the Dominican Republic. If there is so much diversity in a list of top ten fragile countries, imagine the methodological challenges of comparing across many more countries globally.

Other geopolitical units of analysis can be as or more important. As Raka Shome asks, "How do we cross borders and barriers in a downward movement even within the same nation/region?"[5] Indeed, states or provinces in federal systems often have significant power over health, education, immigration, and other phenomena that we study. In the context of urbanization, cities play increasingly important roles. Some large cities have larger populations and economic weight than some countries. Also at a sub-state level, community and ethnic governance may have more influence over everyday life than formal government structures. The contemporary sovereign state is a relatively recent phenomenon in the history of the world. Because of artificial processes of state-building, especially through colonization and post-colonial nation-building, ethnic groups may be spread across several sovereign states.

In other cases, we need to scale up to think about regional dynamics and institutions. There are supranational geopolitical groupings, such as the European Union. Moreover, some global challenges, such as the environment or health issues, clearly surpass the control and influence of any one sovereign state. Many societies continue to organize themselves around world views and spiritual practices that transcend the state.

Despite these shortcomings, internationally focused research often takes countries as the point of reference. Practically and legally speaking, there are also real research consequences of national borders, even if they are contested and socially constructed. Researchers need appropriate documentation to move across borders – not just personal identity and citizenship documents, but also often permission from national research councils or government departments. Researchers also need to be aware of different laws in different jurisdictions. For example, the USA Patriot Act allows US government authorities to directly access data from individuals and companies based in the US, or with a link to the US, in any investigation to protect against suspected terrorism or clandestine intelligence activity. Because information in online cloud-sharing and social media platforms is often based in data centres internationally, this has consequences for people both within and outside the US. Similarly, as we will see in chapter 3, there are also different research ethics procedures in different countries and across different institutions.

Disciplinary Borders. In research, we also encounter borders that are not related to geographic or political entities. For example, much of the way research is managed and organized depends on academic discipline. As discussed in chapter 2, disciplines order and structure the way that knowledge is created, evaluated, and organized within academia. In this book, we will be focusing on research that crosses these disciplinary boundaries. In the example above, the fragility indices include economic, political, social, environmental, and other indicators. The complexity of international phenomena requires an approach that draws on many different disciplinary perspectives. However, as discussed in the next chapter, there are different ideas about how to cross these disciplinary borders.

Similarly, research is focused around analytical **categories**. These conceptual borders both include and exclude with consequences for research results. For example, the definitions of fragility above differ in how they conceptualize – and therefore measure – fragile states. A hallmark of all good research is clearly identifying how we define concepts, so that readers can understand and critique these conceptual borders. We will discuss concepts further in chapters 4 and 5.

Social Borders. Research is also affected by social boundaries related to **positionality** (see chapter 3). All societies organize themselves into hierarchical power relations based on various social factors, including socially constructed notions of race, age, gender, (dis)ability, class, religion, and many others. When doing research across borders, we need to understand these socially constructed borders and reflexively consider how we are positioned within these hierarchies. Danielle Jacobson and Nida Mustafa argue that "the way that we as researchers view and interpret our social worlds is impacted by where, when, and how we are socially located."[6] Margaret Kovach, an Indigenous scholar, calls this "researcher-in-relation" to describe the ways in which researchers define their work in terms of their personal experiences, their clan and tribe identities, their nationality, and their communities.[7]

Understanding our positionality can be complicated when working in cross-cultural contexts. Culture refers to the way life is socially organized through values, beliefs, behaviours, and symbols. Cree scholar Shawn Wilson argues, "All knowledge is cultural."[8] In the context of research across borders, we need to think carefully about how culture influences different **world views**. Different individuals and communities have different ways of being, doing, and knowing. This impacts how they generate, value, and share information and knowledge. It is therefore fundamental to research. In this book, I refer to cross-cultural research as research that occurs in contexts where more than one cultural reference point or world view is represented. Many cultures can co-exist within one sovereign state, and people can self-identify with different cultures, so cross-cultural research does not necessarily entail research across geopolitical borders. However, in many cases, crossing a geopolitical border also means engaging in cross-cultural research.

Cross-cultural and cross-border research also often entails linguistic borders. Not only are different languages and dialects spoken, but also there are often socio-linguistic differences in the ways in which different ideas are conceptualized and expressed in different languages.

Activity 1.2: Mind Mapping the Borders of a Research Topic

A **mind map** (sometimes called a brainstorm) is a visual representation of relationships between ideas. In this activity, you will create a mind map of a research topic to help you think about the ways that borders impact your research topic. An example is provided below. You can do this exercise with pen and paper or use an online mind map–making software, like this one at MindMup (https://www.mindmup.com/).

1. Write down a research topic that interests you. Place it in the centre of your mind map.
2. Identify the borders related to this topic and write these as parent and child nodes on your map. Think about:
   a. Geopolitical borders that define state and sub-state actors, institutions, and processes
   b. Disciplinary borders
   c. Social borders
3. What are points that divide?
4. Are there areas of convergence?
5. How would an approach "across borders" change the way you think about this topic?

METHODOLOGY MATTERS

The meta-example of fragility at the beginning of this chapter also shows that methodology matters. Methodology is the study of how to do research. In this book, we will explore three key elements related to methodology.

First, **epistemology** is the study of knowledge, including how knowledge is created, and what is valued and counted as knowledge. A researcher's epistemological approach will affect their research design. For example, in the meta-example above, all of the research is

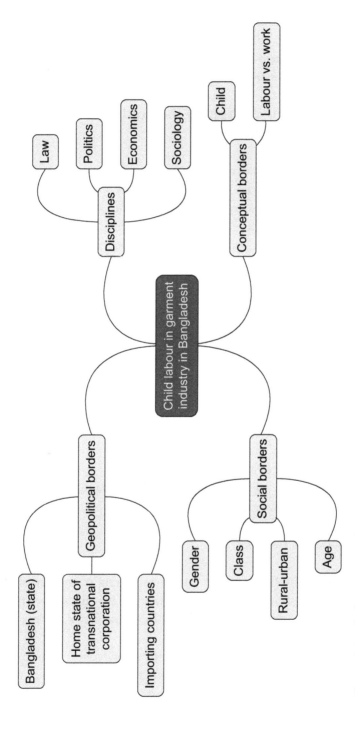

Figure 1.1. Mind map example – Child labour

from a positivist perspective because the researchers are trying to find general rules or principles about fragility. We will explore epistemology further in chapter 2.

Second, **ethics** are the moral principles that guide how we do research and the consequences of our research. One ethical question we can pose in relation to the fragility example above is the impact of fragility rankings on whether countries receive international development assistance and foreign investment. In other words, will a high fragility ranking dissuade donors and investors from working in a particular country? The ethical issues related to research will be discussed in more detail in chapter 3.

Third, methods are the tools and techniques of collecting and analysing information (often called **data**). As we saw in the example above, researchers can get different results depending on the methods they use. In this book, we will learn about several methods, including interviewing, observation, and textual analysis. Chapter 4 explains the kinds of research questions that can be answered using specific methods.

As students, you need to be aware of these different methodological, epistemological, and disciplinary approaches, so that you are better able to evaluate and critically analyse the results presented in secondary research you encounter. As researchers, we also need to be aware of how our methodological choices will have consequences for our results. We need to consciously choose our methods and be able to justify the choices we make.

As you will see throughout this book, methodological choices depend on the kinds of research questions we are asking, our epistemological approach (what we value as knowledge – see chapter 2), the available information on the topic we are studying, and the resources – time, money, and people power – that we have. All methodological choices involve trade-offs. This book will introduce you to these trade-offs so that you can make your own informed assessments and choices.

It will also allow you to better identify the trade-offs that researchers have made when generating information for academic and public studies. Understanding methodology will better enable you to **critically analyse** these studies. You will be better able to evaluate the quality of the information and the arguments presented. It will also empower you to ask the right questions.

Activity 1.3: Methodology Matters for Comparing Democracy across Borders

Democracy is a system of government characterized by Abraham Lincoln as "government of the people, by the people, and for the people." However, the institutionalization of democracy varies widely across different countries, posing methodological challenges when trying to compare across borders. Researchers have come up with different ways of measuring and evaluating democracy. In this activity, we will analyse three different approaches.

The Economist Intelligence Unit, the research arm of the Economist Group, which publishes *The Economist* news magazine, releases a yearly Democracy Index.[9] This index is based on sixty indicators under the following five categories: electoral process and pluralism; civil liberties; government functioning; political participation; and political culture. For each indicator, questions are posed to experts or through public-opinion surveys. The results are averaged to come up with a score for each indicator, aggregated into each category, and then to determine the overall score out of ten. Countries are then ranked and categorized as "full democracies" (overall score of 8.01–10); "flawed democracies" (overall score of 6.01–8); "hybrid regimes" (overall score 4.01–6); or "authoritarian regimes" (overall score 0–4).[10]

Researchers at the Polity IV project, funded by the US Central Intelligence Agency, also developed a **quantitative** index to categorize regime types within different countries from 1800 to 2013.[11] The composite score ranging from autocracy (-6) to democracy (+6) was calculated based on five dimensions: competitiveness of political participation; regulation of political participation; competitiveness of executive recruitment; openness of executive recruitment; and constraints on the chief executive.[12]

Another approach to evaluating democracy is proposed by the International Institute for Democracy and Electoral Assistance (International IDEA), an intergovernmental organization. IDEA uses quantitative indices to measure five attributes: representative government; fundamental rights; checks on government; impartial administration; and participatory engagement.[13] In addition, they have a **qualitative** self-evaluation process in which citizens, supported by external actors, reflect on questions grouped around seven "mediating values": participation, authorization, representation, accountability, transparency, responsiveness, and solidarity.[14]

Reflecting on these three examples:

1. Identify the key methodological similarities and differences of these three approaches. How would these influence the research results?
2. Think about the organization or institution conducting the research. How could their broader mandates influence their methodology?
3. In your own learning and research, do you find it more helpful to have information that is expressed as numbers and indices (i.e., a quantitative approach), or do you prefer an approach that is based on meanings and expressed in words (i.e., a qualitative approach)?

WHY DO WE NEED RESEARCH ACROSS BORDERS?

We do research all the time in our everyday lives. You would have likely researched different post-secondary programs before choosing the one you are enrolled in. You research different prices and customer reviews of products you buy.

In applied fields, such as conflict studies, human rights, development studies, and migration studies, we also encounter research undertaken by non-academic organizations, such as Amnesty International or Oxfam. Governments and intergovernmental organizations such as UN agencies also produce reports. In the fragility example above, the OECD, an intergovernmental organization, did research to come up with its ranking. We also find information in media reports. We need to be able to critically assess the accuracy of this information, especially as such research does not necessarily follow the same methodological and ethical protocols as research in academic settings. But, given the slower pace of academic research, sometimes this is the only information available on current events and issues. This book will help you evaluate these sources of information.

In academic contexts, research is similar, but it is more structured and governed by academic norms and conventions. So, we can define scholarly **research** (also called academic or scientific research) as a systematic study guided by clear definitions, a theoretical framework, and methodology. Primary research involves a researcher going out and collecting data – or information – that was not previously available. In this book, we will learn about data collection through interviews, surveys, and observation, for example. **Secondary research** is when a researcher analyses already existing data in new ways. All three examples of fragility above are secondary research, because the research teams relied on existing data to compile their index.

Research – whether primary and/or secondary – is a key component of academic life. Students and professors carry out research as part of their studies and their jobs. Generally speaking, academic research makes at least one of the following contributions to knowledge:

- **Empirical** contributions mean that the researcher finds new data (through primary research) or finds new relationships between information (through secondary research). The fragility example above is an empirical contribution through secondary research. An example of an empirical contribution through primary research would be to conduct interviews with people in South Sudan to find out their views on one of the fragility indicators, such as gender equality or transparency.
- Conceptual contributions are new ways of defining terms and thinking about social phenomena. For example, one of the key conceptual contributions of the twentieth century was the development of the concept of "gender" as socially constructed roles, in comparison to "sex," which was constructed as biological. The sex-gender binary has subsequently been critiqued by queer theorists, who have further contributed to our conceptual understandings of gender and sexuality.
- Theoretical contributions advance knowledge through new ways of understanding "systems of interconnected concepts that condense and organize knowledge about the social world."[15] **Theory** comes from the Greek word "theorein," which means to look at.

This is why we sometimes talk about a particular "theoretical lens" because theory affects the way we "see" or approach a particular topic. An example of a theoretical contribution is Amartya Sen's capability approach to human development. In contrast to purely economic theories, Sen argued that development should be viewed as a process by which people's choices and freedoms are expanded. We will return to this example in chapter 5.

- Methodological contributions provide new ways of doing research. For example, Participatory Action Research was developed by Robert Chambers in cross-cultural contexts of poverty in the 1980s (see chapter 10). For an introduction to his work, see his "Participatory Approaches to Data Gathering and Analysis" video (https://www.youtube.com/watch?v=kbl3VgrMbHw).

- **Pedagogical** contributions provide new ways of teaching and learning. For example, there has been a recent move to more experiential ways of teaching and learning. Researchers have written about the use of simulation or games in learning in international contexts.

In some cases, research makes more than one contribution to advancing academic knowledge.

But, is research for knowledge enough? In the international contexts where we are studying, research is also being undertaken to advance knowledge for many practical reasons. First, research can have implications for programing by providing information and analysis of the context in which projects are developed and delivered, as well as evaluations of what works and doesn't work in particular contexts. For example, researchers from Oxfam, the Feinstein International Center, and the British government collaborated on a research project to assess the effectiveness and efficiency of shelter projects following humanitarian emergencies.[16]

Second, research is undertaken for **advocacy** purposes. For example, international human rights organizations such as Amnesty International and Human Rights Watch regularly undertake research to document human rights abuses and to advocate for change.

Third, governments require research for **evidence-based policy-making**. This means that they need empirical data to inform what policies they decide to implement. For example, during the COVID-19 pandemic, governments used evolving information about the disease and how it spread to decide on public health measures.

In many university contexts, there is a distinction between **applied research**, which focuses on solving a practical problem, and **basic research**, which aims to increase knowledge without a direct practical application. In reality, a lot of research across borders is motivated by both factors, and often involves collaboration with non-academic partners, such as governments, international organizations, and civil society. We will return to this point in the next section and throughout this book.

Activity 1.4: Analysing the Rationale for Research on Gender Equality and Development

Shahra Razavi has written on "equity and efficiency arguments" for research on gender equality.[17] She shows how international development agencies and intergovernmental organizations use both utilitarian and normative arguments to promote gender equality. For example, the former UN Secretary General argued, "investing in women is not only the right thing" but also is "the smart thing to do."[18] In some cases, academic research has reinforced these "equity and efficiency arguments" through, for example, research that shows that increasing access to girls' education results in increased economic growth (as measured by GDP per capita) and better maternal and child health outcomes. In other cases, scholarly research has demonstrated that equity is not always economically efficient. In Razavi's article, for example, she points out that, in some contexts, gender *in*equality in wages results in higher economic growth, particularly in export-oriented industries that rely on inexpensive labour.

1. Imagine that you are working as a research and advocacy officer in a non-governmental organization promoting women's rights in the global south. What information would you need for practical programing, advocacy, and policy purposes?
2. Drawing on the information provided in the section above, as well as the research summary in this activity, think about some of the academic reasons for doing research on gender and development.
3. Identify some of the convergences and divergences in your answers above.

HOW IS RESEARCH ACROSS BORDERS UNIQUE?

This book is explicitly designed for students interested in research across borders. The context of our fields of study provide unique opportunities and challenges for several reasons.

First, as mentioned in the borders section above, our research often takes place across disciplines. The next chapter will provide more details on disciplines, which frame the way that academic knowledge is structured, valued, and taught. Unlike established disciplines, such as economics, political science, law, history, literature, or sociology, interdisciplinary fields do not necessarily have particular methodologies that have been developed to guide researchers. Rather, interdisciplinary fields draw on different disciplines and methodologies to enrich our knowledge of complex phenomena. There are both opportunities and drawbacks to this interdisciplinarity, which we will discuss in the next chapter.

Second, how knowledge is developed and transmitted and what counts as knowledge differs across different contexts. For example, the oral transmission of knowledge through storytelling is valued in many cultures. As a result of these cross-cultural differences, certain research methods may work better in some contexts than in others. In the example of orally based cultures above, life stories may be a rich source of information, but researchers may struggle to find written archives. Similarly, different cultures have different perceptions of what is moral and ethical, which means that research ethics need to be culturally sensitive, as we will discuss in chapter 3.

Third, international research takes place in contexts of global inequalities. Researchers based in rich countries have more access to resources – time, money, and labour – than those living in poor countries. People with direct experience of the phenomena researchers are studying – such as poverty, displacement, or environmental degradation – have important knowledge of the issues because of their **lived experiences**. However, they often have less opportunity to do research and/or to express this knowledge because of time and resource constraints. In some cases, research has been used to justify policies and ideologies – such as colonization – that create and reinforce inequalities.

Fourth, research across borders usually entails language and sociolinguistic differences. Researchers in such situations must not only find ways to communicate in different languages, but also be aware of different ways of expressing terms. There are also socio-linguistic challenges, such as minority language rights and the repression of certain languages. The use of English as an "international language" in policy contexts and academia means that those who think and write in other languages may be excluded from fully expressing themselves. We need to explicitly acknowledge the hegemony of English and proactively seek out knowledge and information in other languages, especially languages spoken in the areas we are studying.

Finally, as alluded to above, fields such as conflict studies, human rights, development and international studies have practical relevance. This is both an opportunity, but also a challenge. While researchers should strive to be policy relevant, they also need to maintain their independence. Because of the power relations in global inequalities, researchers need to be wary of policy-based evidence-making – that is, the co-option of independent research for political reasons.

There is also a debate within our fields of study about whether research for purely academic reasons – that is, basic research – is justifiable. Should all research be required to have both a practical application as well as an academic contribution to knowledge? Given the scale of global challenges, is it ok for researchers to only be interested in academic research? Conversely, if research is too practically oriented, do academics lose their independence? By collaborating with governments, intergovernmental organizations, and non-governmental organizations, can researchers become politicized and lose their critical-analysis perspectives?

CONCLUSIONS AND KEY TAKEAWAYS

This chapter has introduced the importance of research for academic and practical reasons in interdisciplinary, international contexts. It has shown how different methodological approaches yield different research results. As such, we – as researchers and users of knowledge – need to think about these methodological questions when critically analysing information we encounter in both university and everyday settings. Research across borders requires us to acknowledge borders – geopolitical, cultural, social, and disciplinary – and the implications of challenging and crossing them. It also entails a consideration of both the practical and the academic implications of the research we undertake.

QUESTIONS FOR DISCUSSION AND REFLECTION

1. In your program, what are the key borders that structure the way research is conducted and how knowledge is produced?
2. Thinking back to the research topic that you used for the mind map in Activity 1.2, identify examples of basic research versus academic research.
3. Is research for purely academic purposes justifiable and ethical given the scale of "real-world" challenges, such as global poverty, human rights abuses, and environmental degradation? Does all research across borders have to have a practical application?

FURTHER READINGS

Baldwin-Edwards, Martin, Brad K. Blitz, and Heaven Crawley. "The Politics of Evidence-Based Policy in Europe's 'Migration Crisis.'" *Journal of Ethnic and Migration Studies* 45, no. 12 (2019): 2139–55. https://doi.org/10.1080/1369183X.2018.1468307.

Drawson, Alexandra S., Elaine Toombs, and Christopher J. Mushquash. "Indigenous Research Methods: A Systematic Review." *International Indigenous Policy Journal* 8, no. 2 (2017). https://doi.org/10.18584/iipj.2017.8.2.5.

Jones, Briony, and Ulrike Lühe, eds. *Knowledge for Peace: Transitional Justice and the Politics of Knowledge in Theory and Practice.* Cheltenham, UK: Edward Elgar Publishing, 2021.

Landolt, Patricia, Luin Goldring, and Paul Pritchard. "Decentering Methodological Nationalism to Survey Precarious Legal Status Trajectories."*International Journal of Social Research Methodology* 25, no. 2 (2022): 183–95. https://doi.org/10.1080/13645579.2020.1866339.

Pelzang, Rinchen, and Alison M. Hutchinson. "Establishing Cultural Integrity in Qualitative Research: Reflections from a Cross-Cultural Study." *International Journal of Qualitative Methods* 17, no. 1 (2018). https://doi.org/10.1177/1609406917749702.

Pischke, Erin C., Jessie L. Knowlton, Colin C. Phifer, Jose Gutierrez Lopez, Tamara S. Propato, Amarella Eastmond, Tatiana Martins de Souza, et al. "Barriers and Solutions to Conducting Large International,

Interdisciplinary Research Projects." *Environmental Management* 60, no. 6 (2017): 1011–21. https://doi.org/10.1007/s00267-017-0939-8.

Rodriguez-Garavito, Cesar. "Scientists and Activists Collaborate to Bring Hard Data into Advocacy." Open Global Rights, 21 November 2017. https://www.openglobalrights.org/scientists-and-activists-collaborate-to -bring-hard-data-into-advocacy/.

Thaler, Kai M. "Reflexivity and Temporality in Researching Violent Settings: Problems with the Replicability and Transparency Regime." *Geopolitics* 26, no. 1 (2021): 18–44. https://doi.org/10.1080/14650045.2019.1643721.

Thambinathan, Vivetha, and Elizabeth Anne Kinsella. "Decolonizing Methodologies in Qualitative Research: Creating Spaces for Transformative Praxis." *International Journal of Qualitative Methods* 20, no. 1 (2021): 1–9. https://doi.org/10.1177/16094069211014766.

Web Resources

MindMup (mind-mapping software): https://www.mindmup.com/.
Participatory Action Research: https://www.youtube.com/watch?v =kbl3VgrMbHw.

How Is Knowledge Disciplined? The Opportunities and Challenges of Research across Disciplines and Epistemologies

LEARNING OBJECTIVES

By the end of this chapter, you will be able to:

- Understand and identify different epistemological and ontological approaches;
- Define "discipline" and understand the difference between multi-, inter-, trans-, and anti-disciplinary approaches;
- Identify the opportunities and challenges of using multiple disciplines in research; and,
- Identify debates and controversies around disciplines and epistemologies in applied fields of study in international contexts.

KEY TERMS

Causality
Critical epistemology
Decolonizing research
Disciplines
   Anti-disciplinary
   Interdisciplinary
   Multidisciplinary
   Transdisciplinary

Epistemology
Fields of study
Interpretivism
Literature
Ontology
Positivism
Variable

INTRODUCTION

Despite the growing number of **interdisciplinary** programs, such as international studies, conflict studies, diaspora studies, human rights, and international development, academia is still structured around disciplines. The majority of researchers are still trained in disciplinary programs. Funding structures, academic appointments and departments are dominated by disciplinary borders. This chapter will ask you to think about the opportunities and challenges posed by work within and across these disciplines. Given the methodological focus of this book, in this chapter we will think about the potential methodological pitfalls of interdisciplinary research, such as a "pick-and-mix" approach, a lack of depth of knowledge, and accusations of a lack of methodological rigour. We will explore strategies to address these potential weaknesses.

In this chapter, we will also see how these disciplines are linked to key epistemological traditions that discipline the way in which knowledge is created and valued. This is particularly important in international, cross-cultural contexts where knowledge is co-created or produced outside of academia and with communities with different world views. You will be challenged to think about the fundamentals of knowledge and research. How do we know what we know? What determines how knowledge is valued? These are important questions that frame the way we do research and use information – both in academic research and in our daily lives.

META-EXAMPLE: TERRORISM STUDIES WITHIN DISCIPLINARY AND EPISTEMOLOGICAL DEBATES

When you were deciding which university program to enrol in, you probably encountered different versions of the one you are ultimately in today. You may have noticed that these programs were called different things and presented in different ways. The main themes that you are studying – conflict, development, migration, human rights, etc. – may not have varied that significantly, but likely how the programs were packaged and taught were different. These differences may have influenced the choice you ultimately made.

In this example, I highlight current debates within terrorism research about how knowledge should be produced and structured. While there has been increased media and government attention to terrorism after the September 11, 2001, attacks in the United States and the subsequent "War on Terror," researchers have been studying terrorism for decades. Terrorism is an important topic in cross-border and cross-cultural contexts because it is the focus of international diplomatic efforts, of hundreds of billions of dollars in "counter-terrorism" initiatives, and of domestic law and policy. However, definitions and conceptualizations of terrorism vary significantly. Indeed, one of the key issues within the field – continually debated over decades of research – is the politicization of the term "terrorism," and the legal consequences of labelling a person or a group "terrorist." As the old adage goes, "One person's terrorist is another's freedom fighter."

Related to this debate is the degree to which terrorism research should be policy-relevant, and whether it is too close to governments and therefore results in bias, such as under-researching government-sponsored terrorism or the negative effects of state-led "counter-terrorism" measures. This relates to a key ethical issue about the ways in which information about terrorism can result in legal action against certain groups or individuals.

These debates have led to a split in the field between terrorism studies and critical terrorism studies (CTS). The latter argues for greater attention to power relations, ethical issues, and empirical data collection in researching terrorism.[1] For example, Stump and Dixit argue, "Whether or not terrorism exists is less important than *how* terrorists and terrorism are constructed in practice."[2] Some have gone so far as to suggest that codifying these ethics and methods within a discipline could help to resolve some of the underlying tensions within terrorism studies.[3]

This example illustrates several key points that will be explored in this chapter. First, how one views international issues depends on one's **ontology** – that is, what can be known and how. In internationally focused cross-cultural research we need to be conscious of how different world views influence ontological questions. In the terrorism example above, there is an ontological question about whether terrorism is something that can be known and measured, or whether we can only ever understand the ways that terrorism is labelled and interpreted.

Second, how one thinks about knowledge determines how one structures a program of study and a research project. In other words, we need to be able to identify **epistemology**. As we will see later in this chapter, different epistemological approaches to terrorism result in very different research questions and approaches.

Third, international programs tend to include more than one discipline and, in some cases, attempt to either codify their program within a discipline or argue for an approach that goes beyond disciplines. In the example above, terrorism has historically been studied from different disciplinary perspectives, including law, political science, psychology, sociology, and geography. However, there is a question about whether terrorism studies should become a discipline itself.

Finally, international research programs are predominantly based in the global north or the minority world. These world views inherently shape the ways in which international issues are taught and researched. They also result in power inequalities in the way in which knowledge is produced and shared. Traditionally, terrorism studies has been dominated by researchers in North America and Europe. In contrast, CTS proponents argue for greater decolonization of terrorism studies and for more diversity of perspectives from the global south. We will return to this point in the next chapter, when we discuss power relations in the (re)production of knowledge.

WHAT IS KNOWLEDGE? ONTOLOGICAL AND EPISTE-MOLOGICAL APPROACHES ACROSS BORDERS

At the heart of any research project or program of study is the pursuit of knowledge. But, what is knowledge? How do we know what we know? These ontological and epistemological questions have deep philosophical roots. They also have practical implications for the questions researchers pose, for the methods they use to produce information, and for whether that knowledge is accepted as "valid" or "true" within academia as well as in real life.

In this section, we will discuss four paradigms that shape ontology and epistemology: **positivism**, constructivism (also known as **interpretivism**), the critical approach, and Indigenous ways of knowing. There are other approaches, but these are the key ones that you are likely to encounter in research across borders. You need to be able to identify different ontologies and epistemologies as well as the consequences that these have on how the researcher views knowledge and what is considered to be "valid" research.

Positivism

Rooted in the thinking of the French philosopher Auguste Comte (1798–1857), positivists believe that scientific laws exist for human behaviour just like for natural phenomena. Comparable to the law of gravity, research in the positivist tradition attempts to establish laws that determine human behaviour.

In his seminal text, *The Rules of Sociological Method* (1895), French scholar Émile Durkheim argued that there are "social facts." These are ways of "acting, thinking, and feeling, external to the individual, and endowed with the power of coercion,"[4] which are expressed in society by way of patterns. Positivists are interested in studying these patterns of behaviour to predict how human beings will act in certain circumstances. They are particularly interested in cause and effect.

Ontologically, positivists believe that there is one singular truth and one reality. As a result, they strive to discover this truth through research. Taking their cue from natural sciences, positivists believe in the possibility of objective, value-free research. This means that positivist researchers attempt to minimize their impact on the research process and strive for detached objectivity.

Because epistemological approaches are rooted in philosophical understandings of knowledge, they can be abstract. Let us consider an example of a real research project on terrorism. In this chapter, I provide abstracts directly from articles. As researchers, we need to be able to identify epistemological approaches from abstracts because epistemology frames the methodological approach and choices that a researcher makes – from the design of the project all the way to publication. At the end of this section, there is an activity to test your ability to identify epistemological approaches in research you encounter. Indeed, I encourage you to do so in all the readings you are doing in different courses.

Here is an example of a positivist approach to researching terrorism:

Piazza, James A. "Rooted in Poverty?: Terrorism, Poor Economic Development, and Social Cleavages." *Terrorism and Political Violence* 18, no. 1 (2006): 159–77.

ABSTRACT

This study evaluates the popular hypothesis that poverty, inequality, and poor economic development are root causes of terrorism. Employing a series of multiple regression analyses on terrorist incidents and casualties in ninety-six countries from 1986 to 2002, the study considers the significance of poverty, malnutrition, inequality, unemployment, inflation, and poor economic growth as predictors of terrorism, along with a variety of political and demographic control variables. The findings are that, contrary to popular opinion, no significant relationship between any of the measures of economic development and terrorism can be determined. Rather, variables such as population, ethno-religious diversity, increased state repression, and, most significantly, the structure of party politics are found to be significant predictors of terrorism. The article concludes that "social cleavage theory" is better equipped to explain terrorism than are theories that link terrorism to poor economic development.

This article is positivist because it is trying to find a universal rule or explanation about the relationship between poverty and terrorism. Some clues or indicators that a research approach is positivist are:

- A hypothesis that predicts relationships between **variables**
- Testing **causality**
- An equation

- A prediction
- Large-scale, macro-comparative data across several countries or contexts

Not all of these have to be present, but the more there are, the more likely that the research is positivist.

Constructivism/Interpretivism

As implied in its name, constructivism (also called "interpretivism") takes as its starting point the idea that all knowledge is constructed. Ontologically, constructivists believe that truth is not absolute but is decided by individual judgement. Multiple realities can co-exist. While constructivism is sometimes seen as a reaction to the objectivist approach to positivism, it has its roots in humanism – going back to Portagora in 485–410 BCE, who said, "Man [sic] is the measure of all things."

More recently, Max Weber (1864–1920) emphasized *verstehen*: the empathetic understanding of behaviour. Constructivists reject the notion of universal laws of human behaviour; rather, they believe that knowledge is context-specific.

Here is an example of a constructivist approach to researching terrorism:

Brown, Katherine E. "Gender, Governance, and Countering Violent Extremism (CVE) in the UK." *International Journal of Law, Crime and Justice* (2019). https://doi.org/10.1016/j.ijlcj.2019.100371.

ABSTRACT

The paper draws upon ideas of decentred security, and governance and security assemblages, to explore the gendered nature of countering violent extremism. The paper focuses on the UK as an example of decentred CVE and concentrates on two areas. First, the paper looks at the evolution of modes of governing Muslim women in CVE initiatives.

> Second, the paper explores the tensions and frictions
> involved with the state and civil society using "formers"
> (men who were previously involved in violent extremism)
> to engage in countering violent extremism community and
> de-radicalisation work. The paper finds that a decentred
> security governance approach to understanding CVE reveals
> how CVE is productive of Muslim Women, of Muslim Com-
> munities and Violent Extremism. It also reveals CVE to oper-
> ate not only according to formal documents and programs,
> but through an assemblage of beliefs, traditions and prac-
> tices of everyday security.

Some clues or indicators that a research approach is constructivist are:

- The situation of a topic within historical, social, and political context
- Focus on meaning-making, ideas, perceptions, and interpretations
- Relativist definitions of a concept, rather than universalistic interpretations

Critical Epistemology

Like constructivists, researchers who adopt a critical epistemological approach also believe that knowledge is constructed, but they pay particular attention to power relations (based on class, race, gender, age, (dis)ability, etc.) within knowledge production and to the consequent value attached to different truths. Researchers adopting a critical approach believe that knowledge will thus be biased towards people who hold power and who may misuse knowledge production to reproduce oppressive structures and a particular version of reality.

Critical researchers therefore explicitly believe that social justice should underpin research and that new knowledge should be used to challenge – or, more dramatically, overthrow – oppressive social structures. Research is therefore not objective and value-free, but deliberately political and politicized. The critical approach is often linked to "radical" ideologies and theories, such as Marxism, feminism, and post-colonialism.

Based in critical epistemologies, there is a growing turn towards **decolonizing** knowledge within internationally focused programs to highlight how powerful "perspectives and worldviews get to count as knowledge and research and how these perspectives – repackaged as data and findings – are activated in order to rationalize and maintain unfair social structures."[5]

Returning to our terrorism example, here is an example of the critical approach:

Sharp, Joanne. "A Subaltern Critical Geopolitics of the War on Terror: Postcolonial Security in Tanzania." *Geoforum* 42, no. 3 (June 2011): 297–305.

ABSTRACT

Currently, hegemonic geographical imaginations are dominated by the affective geopolitics of the War on Terror, and related security practice is universalised into what has been called "globalized fear" (Pain, 2009). Critical approaches to geopolitics have been attentive to the Westerncentric nature of this imaginary, however, studies of non-Western perceptions of current geopolitics and the nature of fear will help to further displace dominant geopolitical imaginations. Africa, for example, is a continent that is often captured in Western geopolitics – as a site of failed states, the coming anarchy, passive recipient of aid, and so on – but geopolitical representations originating in Africa rarely make much of an impact on political theory.

This paper aims to add to critical work on the so-called War on Terror from a perspective emerging from the margins of the dominant geopolitical imagination. It considers the geopolitical imagination of the War on Terror from a non-Western source, newspapers in Tanzania.

Clues or indicators that this article is from a **critical epistemology** are:

- Critiques of hegemonic and ethnocentric perceptions
- Use of alternative, localized sources of knowledge
- Recognition of power relations within the production of knowledge

Pro Tip: It should be noted here that critical epistemology is still quite rare in social sciences and humanities. Sometimes students read too much between the lines and see critical epistemology everywhere. We need to distinguish critical epistemology from:

- Critical analysis: "thinking about thinking [. . .] analysing and evaluating what you think and why you think it."[6] *All scholars* do this. Indeed, this is one of the stated learning outcomes of most academic programs. We will talk more about critical analysis in chapter 4 on research design.
- The study of power more generally. Many researchers in cross-cultural and cross-border contexts are interested in power. The whole discipline of political science is arguably about the study of power. In chapter 3, we will talk about how all researchers need to be conscious of power relations as they relate to ethics. What distinguishes critical epistemology from more general studies of power is that the former is explicitly focused on *power in relation to the production of knowledge.*
- Criticism, in the everyday sense of the word. Just because a researcher critiques a particular policy, or organization, or program does not necessarily mean that they are doing so from a critical epistemological perspective.

Indigenous Epistemologies

While sometimes linked to decolonizing approaches and sharing some similarities with critical epistemology, Indigenous epistemologies predate minority world epistemologies that dominate research. "Indigenous knowledges are holistic and relational, interconnected and interdependent systems that encompass knowledge of the spirit, heart, mind, and body."[7] Indigenous epistemologies are diverse, but have common threads that have been summarized as the 5 R's: relationships, respect, responsibility, relevance, and reciprocity. Relationships are important to Indigenous knowledge production at several levels: the researchers' relationship to knowledge, to their research participants, and to the people who use their knowledge; the relationship between knowledge and the land and its peoples; and the relationships between ancestors' knowledge and current and future generations.[8] Respect is necessary in all of these relationships and requires researchers to "adapt to the research participants way of thinking about and doing things, not the other way around."[9] Indigenous epistemologies are place-based and rooted in particular world views developed over tens of thousands of years. Responsibility in knowledge production is about honouring the value of the information provided and ensuring that it does not harm people. Knowledge is cultural, so culturally based values need to guide research.[10] Relevance means that knowledge has to serve a purpose, not just in a utilitarian sense, but a sacred purpose in a holistic way. Reciprocity means that knowledge is constructed in a way that values and respects the contributions of different knowledge creators.

Proulx, Craig. "Colonizing Surveillance: Canada Constructs an Indigenous Terror Threat." *Anthropologica* 56, no. 1 (2014): 83–100. http://www.jstor.org/stable/24469643.

ABSTRACT

This article addresses the range and prevalence of continuing surveillance forms and practices imposed on Indigenous peoples wherein Indigenous peoples are constructed as potential insurgents, terrorists, and criminals collectively or individually threatening the security of the Canadian oligarchic state. Surveillance is used due to fears of Indigenous resistance to colonial projects (Thomas 1994:105) that challenge non-Indigenous peoples' knowledge and understandings of land, capitalism, and governance. I discuss how "securitization spreads out to connect diverse issues together" and how "the discursive framework of securitization therefore links issues in a selective way that reflects an *underlying political rationality*" (Gledhill 2008: 4–5, emphasis added). That underlying state rationality is colonialism.

Table 2.1. Summary of ontological and epistemological approaches

Paradigm	Ontology	Epistemology	Clues
Positivism	Single reality; truth is absolute	Universal rules or laws of human behaviour	• Equations • Hypothesis with variables • Cause-effect • Prediction • Large-scale, macro-comparative data analysis
Interpretivism/ Constructivism	There is no single truth; reality is constructed	Knowledge is constructed in particular contexts and processes	• Research is contextualized • Open research question • Focus on meanings
Critical	Truths and realities are constructed by those in power	Unequal power relations are (re)produced through knowledge creation	• Power relations in research project • Attention to alternative sources of knowledge • Research to challenge oppression
Indigenous	Truth is sacred and cultural	5 Rs: relationships, respect, responsibility, relevance, and reciprocity	• Land-based • Elders and knowledge keepers • Indigenous-based knowledge

Clues or indicators that research takes an Indigenous epistemological approach include:

- Cultural-specificity in knowledge production
- Reference to understandings of land
- Indigenous-based ways of knowing
- Attention to research relationships, reciprocity, relevance, responsibility, and/or respect
- Emphasis on the sacred as sources of knowledge
- Respect for Elders and traditional knowledge keepers

Activity 2.1: Identifying Epistemological Approaches

Consider the following images:

Figure 2.1. Different perspectives yield different results

$$\textbf{Happiness}(t) = w_0 + w_1 \sum_{j=1}^{t} \gamma^{t-j} \, \textbf{CR}_j + w_2 \sum_{j=1}^{t} \gamma^{t-j} \, \textbf{EV}_j + w_3 \sum_{j=1}^{t} \gamma^{t-j} \, \textbf{RPE}_j$$

$$+ \, w_4 \sum_{j=1}^{t} \gamma^{t-j} \max(\textbf{R}_j - \textbf{O}_j, 0) + w_5 \sum_{j=1}^{t} \gamma^{t-j} \max(\textbf{O}_j - \textbf{R}_j, 0)$$

Figure 2.2. Happiness equation[11]

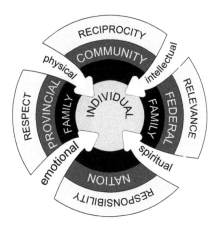

Figure 2.3. Circle of knowledge[12]

Engineering and
computational sciences

Biomedical,
behavioural,
and ecological sciences

Social
sciences

Physical and
mathematical sciences

Average citational
distortion (standard deviations)

0.6
0.4
0.2
0

The average distortion of countries mapped within transnational regions – Africa and the Middle East, Latin America and the Caribbean, Asia, North America, and Oceania – and by the type of field.

Figure 2.4. Map of knowledge production[13]

1. Categorize the images above in terms of the epistemological approach they represent.
2. Are there any points of convergence?
3. What epistemological paradigm best represents your view of knowledge?

RESEARCH ACROSS DISCIPLINARY BORDERS

Research in academic contexts has, over time, often become codified and institutionalized within specific disciplines, such as economics, sociology, history, geography, and psychology. While a comprehensive history of ideas is beyond the scope of this chapter, it is important to remember that disciplines have been created and have evolved within particular historical and social contexts. There has not always been the discipline that we now know as sociology, for example, and there are debates about when it was founded as a discipline and by whom. However, there is no doubt that today sociology is a discipline with its own academic programs and scholarly associations.

The evolution of disciplines is thus inevitably tied to the institutionalization of knowledge within academia. Universities, colleges, and degree-granting institutions define the boundaries of what is considered to be a discipline for training and research purposes.

Generally speaking, a discipline has the following characteristics:

- A specified topic or area of inquiry;
- A specialized "canon" or **literature** (an accumulated body of specialized knowledge and research, which scholars and students in a particular field are expected to have read);
- Particular theories and concepts that are widely understood and applied (or critiqued);
- Research methods and methodologies adapted to particular research questions and contexts in a discipline – for example, archival methodologies in history;
- Training and degree programs; and,
- Professional associations and other institutional presence, such as scholarly journals and research centres.

But, what about programs such as conflict studies, human rights, and international studies that are explicitly about working across these disciplinary boundaries? For example, to understand peace, one needs to think about the economic, political, psychological, social, historical, gendered, and so on dimensions. Each of these dimensions can be linked to a particular discipline, but to understand the phenomenon as a whole we need to draw on multiple disciplines. As Rosow argues, "An academic discipline becomes an institutional presence by establishing boundaries of knowledge."[14] Should research across borders attempt to cross these "boundaries of knowledge" through multi-, inter-, or transdisciplinary approaches or reimagine them by creating new disciplines? Or, should we take an anti-disciplinary approach and question the need for disciplines all together?

Multidisciplinarity combines multiple disciplinary approaches. Historically, this is the way that many research projects and educational programs have been conceived in the international, cross-cultural fields that we explore in this book. Here, the idea is that each discipline provides specialized knowledge, methods, and concepts that add up to a research project or a training program that provides breadth, but not necessarily depth. Indeed, this is the main critique of **multidisciplinary** approaches: it is an add-on approach that does not necessarily result in a whole that is greater than the sum of its parts.

For example: A multidisciplinary international studies program
would include courses on international economics, international politics, world history, global cultures, and so on.

Interdisciplinarity is the intersection and integration of disciplinary approaches. This approach posits that complex phenomenon can only be understood through the fusion of disciplines. As a result, interdisciplinarity draws on different disciplinary perspectives, but focuses on the content of the subject matter and can result in new ways of producing knowledge that fall between traditional disciplines. The potential pitfalls of this more innovative and transformative approach are that the resulting research and degrees are not recognized and "owned" by any discipline. They are a little bit of everything, but not "really" any particular disciplinary approach.

For example: An interdisciplinary international studies program
would include courses such as "Global Political Economy," which

would address "the intersection of politics and economics as goods, services, money, people, and ideas move across borders."[15]

Transdisciplinarity is the creation of a new, unified intellectual approach that goes beyond any one discipline. The transdisciplinary approach became popular at the turn of the twenty-first century in recognition that many complex international issues are "too big to know." The idea is that one needs to transcend traditional disciplinary boundaries in order to transform the way we think about such large topics. However, similar to the pitfalls of interdisciplinarity, the disadvantage of this is an "all and nothing" type of degree or research approach.

For example: A transdisciplinary course could be "Gender in Global Context."

Antidisciplinarity rejects disciplines all together and tries to find a new way of research and learning that goes beyond disciplinarity. It is thus similar to, but more radical than, transdisciplinarity. Drawing on the work of the French theorist Michel Foucault, this approach considers disciplines to be modern forms of power. In order to liberate research from the confines of this oppressive power, some advocate for abandoning disciplines all together.

For example: While International Relations is widely accepted as a subdiscipline of Political Science, International Studies programs often resist being codified into a discipline, suggesting instead that their value lies in their ability to see and analyse the world beyond disciplines.[16]

In this book, the term "interdisciplinarity" is used because it is the most common approach (or, at least, aspiration) in cross-border and cross-cultural fields, such as human rights, conflict studies, and development studies. However, a different approach may be used in your program.

Activity 2.2: Analysing Your Academic Program

1. Find the description of your academic program on its website and/or promotional materials. Based on this description, is it primarily multidisciplinary, interdisciplinary, transdisciplinary,

or anti-disciplinary? What are the clues or indicators of the disciplinary approach?

2. Look at the list of courses offered in your program, especially the required courses. Are there any courses that take a different disciplinary approach to the overall program? Are any courses – such as those that are cross-listed with your program – primarily situated in one discipline?

3. Look at the list of faculty members (or instructors) in your program. What is their disciplinary training? Do any of them have interdisciplinary degrees? Do they publish their research primarily in disciplinary journals, interdisciplinary journals, or both?

OPPORTUNITIES AND CHALLENGES OF RESEARCH ACROSS DISCIPLINES

I have highlighted some of the specific opportunities and challenges of different disciplinary approaches above, but they all share some common pros and cons. The advantage of all approaches that go beyond any one discipline is that they result in more nuanced understandings of complex global phenomena. They also allow for dynamic understandings of rapidly changing phenomena across borders. Practically speaking, "the problems of the world are not organized according to academic disciplines."[17] Without the confines of disciplinary restrictions, there is more flexibility to try new ways of thinking, doing, and researching.

Because interdisciplinary programs draw on and coexist with disciplines, students gain basic knowledge and appreciation of different disciplinary approaches. This is useful for identifying when more specialized knowledge, training, or expertise is required. For example, international migration issues are situated within overlapping and complex national and international laws. For these research topics, researchers often need to consult or collaborate with colleagues who are trained in law.

However, interdisciplinary training is criticized, often by those within disciplinary programs, for a few reasons. First, in some cases, interdisciplinary work takes a "pick and mix" approach – that is, at times there is an opportunistic use of concepts, theories, and methods that are taken out of context and are not necessarily appropriate without adaptation – to the study. Second, because interdisciplinary programs do not have specific training in the methods, concepts, and theories of any one discipline, it can lead to a criticism that research not only lacks a discipline, but also lacks discipline. At times, method-ological and conceptual rigour is sacrificed when too many different ideas are combined together. This is why it is important to have com-prehensive methodological training, even if it draws on different dis-ciplinary approaches, so that we understand when and how to apply different methods. Another key strategy is to adequately define one's terms and to situate these within different disciplinary conceptual debates; this will be discussed in chapters 4 and 5.

Interdisciplinarity is also critiqued from within interdisciplinary pro-grams. At one end of the spectrum, anti-disciplinary scholars argue that most interdisciplinary training doesn't go far enough and, therefore, it implicitly reinforces the centrality of disciplines to knowledge creation.[18] At the other end of the spectrum are those who advocate for the transfor-mation of **fields of study** into disciplines. They point out that academic structures and funding are still organized by disciplines. Therefore, they believe that the only way to ensure adequate resources, respect, and attention to an area of study is to codify it as a discipline. Others suggest that interdisciplinarity results in an unfocused curriculum with students consequently lacking both an in-depth understanding of any discipline *and* a core knowledge of the object of enquiry, such as human rights.[19]

CONCLUSIONS AND TAKEAWAYS

In this chapter, we have explored different ways of thinking about knowledge and research. We have seen how four different ontologi-cal and epistemological approaches result in fundamentally different ways of being, thinking, and doing. You need to be aware of these different approaches when you read research findings. You also need to think about where you position yourself within these different ontological and epistemological perspectives because you are more likely to value information that coincides with your ways of being and knowing. However, in cross-border and cross-cultural contexts, you are likely to encounter other ways of producing and valuing knowl-edge. You need to understand these perspectives and their ontological and epistemological underpinnings so that you don't simply dismiss information that is developed and presented in a different way.

We also learned about different ways to do research across disci-plines. Even within interdisciplinary programs, there are different approaches to disciplines and knowledge creation. It is important that you understand these different approaches, and the opportunities and challenges of doing research across disciplines.

QUESTIONS FOR DISCUSSION AND REFLECTION

1. Within which ontological and epistemological paradigm do you situate yourself? How does this impact your world view? What kinds of knowledge are you more likely to accept?
2. In what ways are Indigenous epistemologies particularly relevant to research across borders?
3. Given disciplinary structures within universities, what are the opportunities and challenges of pursuing an interdisciplinary degree?
4. In relation to your research interests, what are examples of multidisciplinary, interdisciplinary, and transdisciplinary approaches?

FURTHER READINGS

Abfalter, Dagmar, Julia Mueller-Seeger, and Margit Raich. "Translation Decisions in Qualitative Research: A Systematic Framework." *International Journal of Social Research Methodology* 24, no. 4 (2021): 469–86. https://doi.org/10.1080/13645579.2020.1805549.

Bergen, Nicole. "Narrative Depictions of Working with Language Interpreters in Cross-Language Qualitative Research." *International Journal of Qualitative Methods* 17, no. 1 (2018). https://doi.org/10.1177/1609406918812301.

Bright, Jonathan, and John Gledhill. "A Divided Discipline? Mapping Peace and Conflict Studies." *International Studies Perspectives* 19, no. 2 (2018): 128–47. https://doi.org/10.1093/isp/ekx009.

Cargas, Sarita, and Kristina Ederbach. "Rethinking Multidisciplinarity within Human Rights Education." Open Global Rights, 3 September 2020. https://www.openglobalrights.org/rethinking-multidisciplinarity-within-human-rights-education/.

Chimni, Bhupinder S. "The Birth of a 'Discipline': From Refugee to Forced Migration Studies." *Journal of Refugee Studies* 22, no. 1 (2009): 11–29. https://doi.org/10.1093/jrs/fen051.

Garcia, Gina A., and Jenesis J. Ramirez. "Proposing a Methodological Borderland: Combining Chicana Feminist Theory with Transformative

Mixed Methods Research." *Journal of Mixed Methods Research* 15, no. 2 (2021): 223–41. https://doi.org/10.1177/1558689820954023.

Gerber, Nancy, Elisabetta Biffi, Jacelyn Biondo, Marco Gemignani, Karin Hannes, and Richard Siegesmund. "Arts-Based Research in the Social and Health Sciences: Pushing for Change with an Interdisciplinary Global Arts-Based Research Initiative." *Forum Qualitative Sozialforschung/Forum: Qualitative Social Research* 21, no. 2 (2020): 30. https://doi.org/10.17169/fqs-21.2.3496.

Harris, La Donna, and Jacqueline Wasilewski. "Indigeneity, an Alternative Worldview: Four R's (Relationship, Responsibility, Reciprocity, Redistribution) vs. Two P's (Power and Profit): Sharing the Journey towards Conscious Evolution." *Systems Research and Behavioral Science* 21, no. 5 (2004): 489–503. https://doi.org/10.1002/sres.631.

Mac Ginty, Roger. "Complementarity and Interdisciplinarity in Peace and Conflict Studies." *Journal of Global Security Studies* 4, no. 2 (2019): 267–72. https://doi.org/10.1093/jogss/ogz002.

MacLeod, Miles, and Michiru Nagatsu. "What Does Interdisciplinarity Look Like in Practice: Mapping Interdisciplinarity and Its Limits in the Environmental Sciences." *Studies in History and Philosophy of Science* 67 (2018): 74–84. https://doi.org/10.1016/j.shpsa.2018.01.001.

Seehawer, Maren Kristin. "Decolonising Research in a Sub-Saharan African Context: Exploring Ubuntu as a Foundation for Research Methodology, Ethics and Agenda." *International Journal of Social Research Methodology* 21, no. 4 (2018): 453–66. https://doi.org/10.1080/13645579.2018.1432404.

Tuck, Eve, and K. Wayne Yang. "Decolonization Is Not a Metaphor." *Decolonization: Indigeneity, Education & Society* 1, no. 1 (2012): 1–40.

Tucker, Karen. "Unraveling Coloniality in International Relations: Knowledge, Relationality, and Strategies for Engagement." *International Political Sociology* 12, no. 3 (2018): 215–32. https://doi.org/10.1093/ips/oly005.

Youngman, Mark. "Building 'Terrorism Studies' as an Interdisciplinary Space: Addressing Recurring Issues in the Study of Terrorism." *Terrorism and Political Violence* 32, no. 5 (2020): 1091–105. https://doi.org/10.1080/09546553.2018.1520702.

Web Resources

Indigenous Epistemologies and Pedagogies: https://opentextbc.ca/indigenizationcurriculumdevelopers/chapter/topic-Indigenous-epistemologies-and-pedagogies/#:~:text=Personal%20and%20holistic,spiritual%20development%20are%20also%20valued.

World Indigenous Nations Higher Education Consortium: https://winhec.org.

3

Ethics, Power, and Positionality

LEARNING OBJECTIVES

By the end of this chapter, you will be able to:

- Define and identify the key ethical principles of **voluntary, informed consent**; **confidentiality** and **privacy**; and **"do no harm"**;
- Understand the role of institutional **research ethics boards**;
- Discuss the complexities of applying ethical principles in cross-border and cross-cultural contexts;
- Explain and critically analyse positionality and **reflexivity** in contexts of intersecting power relations; and,
- Identify ethical guidelines developed for research in specific contexts of (de)colonization and forced migration.

KEY TERMS

Academic integrity
Anonymity
Anonymized
Assent

Attribution
Beneficence
Big data
Confidentiality

Consent – voluntary, informed

Do no harm

Ethics

   Ethics of care

   Procedural ethics

   Professional ethics

   Relational ethics

   Scholarly ethics

Falsify evaluations

Gatekeepers

Heisenberg effect

Literature reviews

Maximizing benefits

Minimizing harm

Over-research

Plagiarism

Positionality

Privacy

Pseudonyms

Reflexivity

Research

Research ethics boards

Suppression of data

INTRODUCTION

Many of us are interested in fields like human rights, conflict studies, and migration studies because we want to learn how to make a positive difference in the world. But, research also has the potential to cause great harm to individuals and communities. In this chapter, we will discuss ethical principles and processes that have been established to try to minimize harms and maximize the benefits of research.

The chapter introduces the core ethical values of voluntary, informed consent; confidentiality and privacy; and "do no harm." While these seem fairly straightforward, we will see how the application of these norms in different international research contexts can be challenging. We will also learn about how intersecting power relations – at individual, institutional, national, and global levels – give rise to ethical dilemmas. Related to these intersecting power relations, we will discuss the notion of positionality and the ways in which a researcher's positionality may change across borders.

Finally, this chapter highlights ethical guidelines developed for research with people in particular cross-cultural situations, such as forced migration and Indigenous communities. It will also demonstrate the complexity of ethics approval processes when different countries, institutions, and disciplinary programs are involved.

META-EXAMPLE: MILGRAM'S OBEDIENCE
EXPERIMENT

In this chapter, I use one of the most well-known examples of questionable ethics because it illustrates several important points that we
will discuss. Stanley Milgram's obedience experiment is an infamous
example of questionable ethics that ushered in many of the **procedural
ethics** protocols that are used in North America and other contexts
today. While this example is used in most standard research methods
courses, I have chosen to re-use it here because it has implications for
research across borders. In particular, Milgram was interested in people's deference to authority – a recurring question in studies on diverse
international topics, such as genocide in Rwanda and child soldiering.
Moreover, the positivist approach to experiments with Americans to
understand what happened in Nazi Germany poses questions around
the cultural construction of ethics and research.

Milgram, a psychologist at Yale University in the United States, conducted a research experiment to try to understand why people defer to
authority, even when those in authority instruct them to commit atroci-
ties. The context was the post–Second World War period when defen-
dants in the Nuremberg War Crimes trials used obedience to authorities as an excuse or justification for their participation in the Holocaust.

Milgram recruited respondents and told them that the experiment was
about how people learn. He asked them to play the role of a "teacher,"
while a trained actor played the role of a "student." For each wrong
answer, the "teacher" was asked to administer what they thought were
stronger and stronger electrical shocks. In response, the actor playing the
"student" in the other room would cry out in pain and beg the "teacher"
to stop. If the "teacher" expressed reservations about continuing with
the experiment, the researcher would encourage them to continue.

Milgram found that 65 per cent of the research respondents playing
the role of "teacher" administered the highest level of electrical shock,
which had the potential to kill the "student." Many of the "teachers"
became visibly distressed during the experiment.

You can watch excerpts from the experiment at https://www
.youtube.com/watch?v=xOYLCy5PVgM&t=4s (some viewers may find
the content disturbing).

This experiment is ethically questionable because it involved
deception – participants were not told the real reason for the study or

what they were asked to do. Moreover, it caused extreme distress and psychological harm in some participants, who thought they had killed or seriously injured the "student."

This example highlights key issues that we will explore in this chapter. First, this experiment and other research that posed ethical questions are the rationale for the development of procedural ethics in many universities. While such ethics processes vary from one place to another, they tend to revolve around three main principles: voluntary, informed consent; confidentiality; and do no harm. These principles will be discussed in greater detail below.

Second, the fact that the experiment took place in the United States but was intended to understand deference to authority in very different contexts – including Nazi Germany – raises questions about cultural specificity in research design as well as different world views in research ethics.

Third, this example demonstrates the importance of recognizing power and privilege in research processes. Professor Milgram was a well-known academic at a prestigious university. When he told participants what the study was ostensibly about, they tended to trust in his authority. Ironically, this experiment – which is about deference to authority – also shows a fundamental problem in many research studies: lack of attention to the power, privilege, and authority researchers hold, and the impact of this on the study. This chapter will discuss these issues of positionality, reflexivity, and what is known as the **Heisenberg principle**.

WHAT IS ETHICS?

When you watched the video about the Milgram experiment, you likely felt uncomfortable at some points. This alerts you to a "gut feeling" or a visceral sense that "something is wrong." At its core, ethics is about what is moral, or what is right and wrong. If you discussed the experiment with others in your class, you likely would have identified different elements that made you feel uncomfortable. You and your colleagues may also have different views about whether some level of deception and emotional discomfort was justified in order for Milgram to have information about a greater problem – deference to authority that leads ordinary people to kill. In other words, you may have had different perceptions on whether the ends justified the means. These differences of opinion exist because ethics is socially constructed. Notions of "right" and "wrong" vary across world views and individual and communal belief structures. Ethics also evolves over time.

In this course, we are interested in ethics as it applies to research. There are four key distinctions we will discuss in this book: scholarly ethics, procedural ethics, professional ethics, and relational ethics.

Scholarly Ethics

First, **scholarly ethics**, sometimes called **academic integrity**, are moral norms that apply to how we work and do research in academic settings. You are likely familiar with **plagiarism**, which means passing off other people's words and ideas as your own. It also relates to appropriate **attribution** of previous work, including your own. So, if you re-use arguments, ideas, or text, you need to cite yourself. It is a good idea to learn about how and when to cite properly, as this is the foundation of scholarly ethics. Some resources are included in the section at the end of this chapter.

Scholarly ethics also applies to the falsification or **suppression of data**. This means that researchers are not allowed to make up the results of their research. They are also not allowed to ignore information that does not support their world view, argument, or hypothesis.

Related to this, students and researchers should not **falsify evaluations**. This includes cheating on tests, buying or copying assignments, or falsifying credentials, such as degrees or certificates, and medical notes or death certificates to allow for accommodations in assignments and exams.

Students also are not allowed to work together on projects that are not clearly group projects.

Each institution has its own academic integrity policy. You should familiarize yourself with what is and is not allowed in your university or college, as there is some variation across different contexts. Ignorance of a policy is not a defence for committing academic fraud. In many cases, penalties for plagiarism can include a zero on the assignment; failing the course; additional training; and/or expulsion from your program or university.

Table 3.1. Examples of academic dishonesty

Kinds of academic dishonesty	Examples
Plagiarism	Copying all or part of another person's work without attributing them
	Re-using all or part of your own work (this is self-plagiarism)
	Paraphrasing without acknowledging the source of the idea
	Inserting verbatim quotes without quotation marks, even if the source is acknowledged
Falsification of data	Changing the results of an experiment or study
	Making up information
	Suppressing or omitting data that do not support your argument, theory, or hypothesis
	Citing articles you have not read
Falsification of evaluations	Cheating
	Falsifying medical, death, or legal documents to get extensions, exemptions, or other accommodations
	Impersonating someone else
	Buying essays
	Getting unauthorized access to exam questions prior to the exam
	Signing attendance sheets on behalf of someone else
Unauthorized group work or co-authorship	Working as a group for an individual assignment
	Getting editing help that substantively changes your essay

Activity 3.1: Academic Integrity Tutorial and Quiz

If your institution provides training on scholarly ethics (also called academic integrity or plagiarism), please do it now. If not, complete one of the suggested trainings at the end of the chapter. Your instructor may require proof of completion of this training.

PROCEDURAL ETHICS FOR RESEARCH WITH HUMAN SUBJECTS

In addition to scholarly ethics, there are procedural ethics for research with human subjects. These include policies and processes that are usually administered through a specific research ethics board (REB), also called an institutional research board (IRB). Not all institutions have them, but if you are conducting primary research with human beings, you should double check your institution's requirements as well as any requirements in partner institutions or organizations. In some cases, you will not be allowed to submit an assignment or publish a paper based on this primary data if you do not have an ethics certificate. As discussed below, research across borders often entails multiple procedural ethics from different institutions in different countries.

Activity 3.2: Training on Procedural Ethics

Most institutions that require procedural ethics clearance either provide their own training or refer researchers to nation-wide training. If your institution provides training, please complete it now. If not, please refer to the list at the end of this chapter and take the online training that is most applicable to your country or situation.

RELATIONAL ETHICS

Relational ethics are also sometimes known as **ethics of care**. These are norms that shape the way you interact with research participants, collaborators, and colleagues. They go beyond procedural ethics both in scope and in timeframe. They will be explored further in the section below.

PROFESSIONAL ETHICS

Professional ethics guide work in certain professions, including journalism, medicine, social work, and law. This book does not address these directly. However, you should be aware of them, especially if your program is aligned with a particular profession. For example, human rights is often informed by law.

KEY ETHICAL PRINCIPLES AND DILEMMAS OF APPLICATION ACROSS BORDERS

While there is variation across different contexts because of the socially constructed aspects of morality, there is some consensus on key ethical principles in research. We will learn about them here, and then see how it may be challenging to apply them in practice, especially in cross-cultural, multilingual, and international contexts.

Voluntary, Informed Consent

This ethical principle has three different components:

Voluntary: means that people agree to participate in research out of their own free will, with no pressure to take part in the research and no penalties for refusing to participate.

Informed: means that participants understand the purpose and scope of the study as well as the risks and benefits of participation.

Consent: means that research participants agree to participate in research, and that this agreement is recorded in some way – either on paper or verbally. In most contexts, minors under a certain age and individuals with impaired cognitive abilities are not legally recognized as having the capacity to consent. In these cases, a third party – a parent, guardian, or official responsible for their care – consents, while **assent** is provided by the minor or other individual deemed not to have the capacity to consent. Both consent and assent are required for research to proceed.

Voluntary, informed consent should be continual. Research participants should be able to withdraw their consent at any time.

When laid out in such clear-cut terms, it appears that voluntary, informed consent would be straightforward to apply in research projects. However, in the reality of cross-border contexts, several dilemmas may arise.

First, unequal power relations can undermine the voluntariness of consent. As will be discussed later on in this chapter, research across borders takes place within local and global inequalities. Researchers need to carefully think about their positionalities within these power hierarchies and how they may impact the degree to which people feel free to refuse to participate in research. Obviously, when people in authority facilitate research as **gatekeepers**, or conduct research themselves, this can call into question the voluntariness of consent. For example, people who have been displaced from their homes sometimes live in refugee camps, access to which are controlled by governments, United Nations agencies, and non-governmental organizations. People in refugee camps often depend on these organizations for food aid, basic necessities, social services, and/or refugee status. Therefore, if such organizations "authorize" a researcher to conduct research in the camp and/or if these organizations conduct research themselves, refugees may feel obligated to participate.

Second, disproportionate monetary compensation for participation may call into question voluntary consent. Because participation in research takes time and may result in travel or childcare costs, researchers may feel an ethical obligation to provide some sort of remuneration for research participation. However, if this compensation is substantial, people can sometimes decide to participate in research for the money, rather than because they want to be part of the study. This poses ethical questions. For example, when relatively well-off researchers do research in impoverished contexts, how much monetary compensation for participation is the right amount?

Third, covert observation and deception are sometimes explicitly part of a research design because the topic is sensitive or socially unacceptable. For example, some argue that Milgram's experiment – explained in the meta-example at the beginning of this chapter – would not have worked without deception. If those who were recruited to play the "teacher" had been told that the study was really to test their deference to authority, they would have been less likely to administer the "shocks." Also, if they had known that the "shocks" were not real, then the experiment would not have really tested their willingness to seriously harm or kill someone. This example shows how methodological considerations are sometimes in tension with ethical standards. Where the right balance lies is a matter of personal discretion and perception and of localized ethical norms.

Fourth, online research, especially that which relies on social media information, poses challenges for voluntary, informed consent. While this data is "public" to a certain degree, access to some information, such as Facebook or LinkedIn posts, for example, requires a login and in some cases requires researchers to be "friends" with the poster in order to access private sites. While social media has great potential for research across borders at low costs, it also then presents ethical issues because users are posting information for purposes other than data collection and are not explicitly consenting to the use of this information in research. We will explore this further in chapter 9.

Similarly, voluntary, informed consent is often not practically possible when researchers use third party data, including **big data**. Big data refers to the information generated by digital sources, including internet searches, emails, texts, and social media. Research that relies on administrative case files, which are accessed through third party organizations, also pose problems about consent. Even if the information is **anonymized** (see below), the fact remains that the individuals whose personal information is shared did not consent. For example, Benham and Crabtree discuss the growing trend of international donors expecting direct access to information gathered in the context of service provision without the explicit consent of the individuals who access these services.[1]

Fifth, in research projects that involve participant observation, continual, voluntary consent is limited. As discussed in chapter 9, participant observation relies on a researcher participating in the community and gathering insights from this participation. This means that researchers play multiple roles in such contexts and research respondents may be unclear when they are interacting with a "researcher" and when the person is playing another role. This poses a dilemma for the researcher in terms of data gathered during these "grey area" interactions.

Sixth, informed consent requires participants to understand the risks and benefits of their involvement in research. However, it is impossible for the researcher to be able to anticipate all of the ways in which the study may impact reality. This is particularly the case in cross-border research that intends to effect real change, as discussed in chapter 1. For example, studies have shown that human rights research and advocacy to "name and shame" governments that use torture may have unintended negative impacts on civil and political rights in these countries.[2]

Seventh, research projects involving both assent (by minors and those with cognitive disabilities) and consent (by a parent or guardian) pose particular challenges in cross-cultural contexts where researchers may not be aware of the intersectional power relations. In some cases, once a responsible adult has given consent, a dependent under their care may feel obliged to agree. In other cases, the dependent wants to participate, but the responsible adult refuses. Given the social construction of inter-generational relationships and notions of vulnerability, researchers need to be attentive to differential world views in interpretation of assent and consent. Moreover, in some cases, such as unaccompanied minors who have migrated without their parents or guardians, there is no clear responsible adult to provide consent. The legal definition of "minor" also varies across different legal jurisdictions.

Finally, the widespread use of standardized consent forms in many procedural ethics processes is problematic due to the technocratic language in such forms. Even if they are translated into the first languages of participants, as mentioned above, the meanings of terms like "voluntary, informed consent" and the potential complicating factors are not always clear. Moreover, in some contexts, especially where administrative processes are used to oppress people, research participants may be wary of signing forms. In other cases, where forms are part of administrative processes like applying for asylum or registering for financial assistance, people may think that they need to sign the research form to get access to these other services. Written consent forms are also problematic for research contexts where people cannot read and write or where, culturally, consent occurs more frequently through oral processes or ceremonies. In these cases, research ethics boards may allow verbal consent, but this is not always possible due to the ethnocentric nature of these processes.

Activity 3.3: Analysing Voluntary, Informed Consent

Consider the following hypothetical case study:

A professor is proposing a research project on the experiences of international students studying at her institution. The professor plans to contact current international students in her classes to invite them to take part in the study. Participants will be compensated $50 for their time for a three-hour in-depth interview and will be required to sign a consent form, available only in English. If she cannot obtain enough data, she plans to use her own observations from her classes, including students' grades.

1. Identify *three* issues that may undermine the *voluntariness* of consent in this case study.
2. Identify at least one example of something that may undermine *informed* consent.
3. Identify one proposed research activity that would definitely violate voluntary, informed consent.

PRIVACY, CONFIDENTIALITY, AND ANONYMITY

Everyone has the right to protect the privacy of their information. However, research often entails asking people about their experiences and opinions. How can this be reconciled? In research ethics, there are three distinct but interrelated concepts:

Privacy means that research participants have the right to control their own personal information.

Confidentiality is the responsibility of the researcher(s) to protect research respondents' information.

Anonymity is one way of protecting confidentiality by ensuring that no one – not even the researcher(s) – can trace back information to any particular research participant. Anonymity is obviously not possible in small-scale, qualitative studies where researchers know which information comes from individual participants. In these cases, data are anonymized – that is, all identifying characteristics are removed from the information and participants are assigned numbers or **pseudonyms**.

As with voluntary, informed consent, most researchers understand and agree with the principles of privacy, confidentiality, and anonymity (where possible). However, in applying these principles in research across borders and world views, several challenges arise.

First, protecting people's privacy may be challenging in practice. In cultures that centre on communal spaces and collective story-telling, it may be difficult to have one-on-one interviews with individuals in private. Similarly, adults may insist on being present when researchers are interacting with children and young people. However, privacy is both an ethical and methodological imperative if the research seeks to uncover unequal power relations, human rights abuses, discrimination, or socially sensitive topics like sex work, substance use, infidelity, or divorce. Researchers may have to find creative solutions to ensure privacy while not drawing undue attention to the research. For example, when I was doing research with young Congolese refugees in Uganda, one person disclosed sexual exploitation. In order to gather more information on this topic, I visited the person while she worked at a hair salon. I waited until there were no clients present and then continued with the interview. When someone entered the shop, we switched to other topics of conversation.

Second, research across borders may also take place in highly controlled and monitored contexts, like refugee camps, schools, prisons, detention centres, and government buildings. Researchers may have to undergo regular security searches, where their research materials – notebooks, laptops, and so on – could be searched. In such situations, the protection of personal data is particularly important. It is a good idea to use code names and to back up information regularly (on a cloud or flash drive, by sending photos by mobile phone and then deleting them, or by photocopying and sending by fax or mail), in case the material is confiscated all together. In extreme cases of surveillance, researchers may choose not to take any notes at all while in the "field," but rather wait to write up all their information after they leave a restricted area. This obviously precludes verbatim quotes, but may be the only way to protect privacy and confidentiality of data.

Third, researchers who are working with undocumented populations or on topics that involve criminality or illegality should be conscious of the limits of the legal protection of their data. Moreover, some disciplines – such as social work – and some jurisdictions require that a researcher report cases of self-harm and harm to authorities. Unlike other professions such as medicine and law, researchers are not protected by client privilege. If they are subpoenaed, they will have to hand over their data to the courts or face criminal charges. For consent to be truly informed (see above), researchers should mention these limits to confidentiality and the potential risks when asking people to participate in research. For example, Singhal and Bhola undertook a systematic review of community-based research on self-harm in Asia and concluded that researchers need to explicitly state in consent processes the steps that will be taken in the event of self-harm disclosure, including the seriousness of the self-harm intents. They also flagged specific ethical issues related to online data collection and varied legal definitions of "minor" and "harm" across legal jurisdictions.[3]

Fourth, researchers need to be aware of limits to privacy when conducting research online. As mentioned in chapter 1, the USA Patriot Act empowers the US government to access, without a permit, information stored in the US, including electronic data. Even if your research is physically based outside the US, the information may be virtually held in the US. Similarly, large information technology companies, such as Zoom, Survey Monkey, and Facebook, have service agreements that allow them to use private information that is shared on these platforms, including in surveys and interviews, for research purposes. Governments increasingly engage in social media surveillance and interference to gather intelligence, often without the knowledge of users or researchers.[4]

Fifth, some research methods, such as focus group discussions (see chapter 8) and participatory research (see chapter 10), inherently limit privacy because they involve multiple research respondents at the same time. When using these methods, particularly in cross-cultural contexts where researchers may not be fully aware of all the power dynamics, it is important that research respondents collectively agree on the ground rules for the research activities and on what they can and cannot share outside of the research context. In some cases, it may be culturally sensitive to organize focus groups around specific positionalities, such as age or gender.

Finally, some research methods, such as narratives and life stories (see chapter 6), do not lend themselves to privacy and confidentiality because the point is to share detailed experiences of individuals. Even if some identifying characteristics are removed, people who know the person in the life story will likely be able to identify them. Similarly, co-production of knowledge through shared authorship also jeopardizes privacy unless authors use pen names, which undermines the notion of ownership.

Activity 3.4: Identifying Confidentiality and Anonymity Issues in a Hypothetical Case Study

Consider this hypothetical case study:

Australia has a policy of mandatory immigration detention for all asylum seekers. Access to these detention centres is strictly controlled. A doctoral student was denied access to the detention centres for his PhD research, but he managed to secure interviews with three musicians from a non-governmental organization called Freedom Songs, who were the only people allowed to access the detention centre in order to provide music lessons for detained young people. During these interviews, the musicians disclosed information about how refugees' rights are abused in the detention centre. The PhD student would like to include this information in his thesis and attribute it to the musicians, but even if he anonymizes their names, people who know the situation would be able to identify them, as they are the only ones who had access to the detention centre during the time period covered.

1. Identify at least one issue related to *privacy* in this hypothetical case study.
2. Identify at least one issue related to *confidentiality* in this hypo-thetical case study.
3. Identify a distinction between *anonymity* and *anonymization* in this case study.
4. If you were the PhD student, would you include the information on rights abuses in the detention centre? Why or why not?

MINIMIZE HARM AND MAXIMIZE BENEFICENCE

A final key principle of research ethics relates to minimizing harm and maximizing benefits. The central concepts here are:

Minimizing harm means anticipating and mitigating the risks of research and research findings for participants. Due to the severe consequences that can arise in research on human rights, conflict, and other contexts, some researchers propose extending this principle to "do no harm." This latter principle, found in medicine, means that researchers should not engage in any activity that will negatively impact participants.

Maximizing benefits involves ensuring that the greatest number of people benefit from the research and that the research has the most beneficial impact. This principle also means that the benefits of research cannot be denied to participants. For example, in the infamous Tuskegee Syphilis Study, the US Public Health Service conducted a clinical study of syphilis in African-American men from 1932 to 1972. Even after penicillin became a standard cure in 1947, the men in the study were not treated for syphilis because it would "interfere" with the results of the study. This is a flagrant example of denying benefits.

Beneficence is a term from applied ethics that is sometimes used, particularly in medical research, to encapsulate the essence of minimizing harm and maximizing benefits of research.

As with the other ethical principles, the application is complicated when researching across borders. First, it is often difficult to accurately predict and control the full effects of research, especially in dynamic international contexts and given the practical relevance of much of the research in our fields (see chapter 1). Moreover, research findings can be co-opted to support particular agendas, policies, or ideologies, even if that is not the researcher's intent. For example, Navin and Dieterle demonstrate how food sovereignty research and advocacy has been used to promote the interests of food producers in the global north, sometimes in ways that are "actively harmful to FS [food sovereignty] in poorer societies."[5]

Second, and relatedly, research is often dependent on funding and, therefore, sometimes responds to government priorities and media attention. This can lead to over-research of some topics and under-research of others; both ends of the spectrum undermine the beneficence principle. **Over-research** refers to "a combination of the sheer repetition, frequence, and often redundance of research [. . .] as well as a sense that research fails to bring any tangible or substantive change or benefit."[6] Linked to the efforts to be relevant, discussed in chapter 1, researchers, at times, tend to gravitate to "flavour of the month" research topics. This results in over-researched topics and research participants. For example, after the genocide in Rwanda, there was a heightened interest in this topic. Similarly, given the scale of the Syrian refugee movements since 2015, many researchers have focused on this population for study. However, recognizing the potential risks of research and its costs to participants also means limiting the number of studies on the same topic and involving the fewest number of participants as necessary. To reduce the risks of over-research, researchers can ensure that they do adequate **literature reviews** to find out what is already written on the topic (see chapter 4) and also to collaborate more on joint projects and on data-sharing – where that does not violate confidentiality.

The flip side of the "over-researching" problem is under-researching topics and communities, who, consequently, do not have an opportunity to participate. Similarly, in power asymmetries related to positionality, discussed later in this chapter, certain individuals and groups may be under-represented in research on a topic or community. To partially address this problem, "All efforts should be made to include a diversity of perspectives in research studies, with specific recruitment strategies and methodology to include differential perspectives and research needs based on age, gender, sexuality, ability, class, race, education, literacy, and language."[7]

Third, the increased use of big data and information technologies in cross-border research poses particular questions for minimizing harm. In particular, these methods have the potential to predict conflict, large-scale movements of people, natural disasters, famine, and so on, thereby potentially providing early warnings to alleviate suffering. However, they can also be used for ill – that is, for starting these conflicts and/or trapping people in contexts of violence, poverty, or immobility. For example, European governments could use big data as part of externalization and push-back policies to anticipate, and then block, asylum seekers from reaching their territories.[8]

Fourth, in contexts of surveillance, criminalization, and repression of individuals and groups, research can sometimes be used to undermine rights. For example, individuals who have participated in studies on sexual and gender-based violence have sometimes faced retribution by their violent partners,[9] while trafficked individuals have experienced reprisals from traffickers and organized crime.[10] Research that is critical of governments, big business, and other powerful actors may result in reprisals – not only against the individuals who participated in research (if data are not adequately anonymized), but also against the whole community (especially in cases where confidentiality is protected, because no one can identify participants, everyone is suspected). For example, there has been a reported increase in violence and killings of environmental activists.[11]

Fifth, as alluded to above, in contexts of extreme poverty, violence, mass displacement, environmental degradation, and other structural problems, some researchers across borders argue that minimizing harm does not go far enough. They advocate for doing *no harm*, and, in some cases, *preventing* harm. From critical and Indigenous epistemological perspectives, the argument is that research needs to actively engage in challenging and dismantling oppressive structures. It is not enough to simply stand by and witness; indeed, researchers become complicit in structural problems if they do not try to effect change. However, positivists would suggest that the researcher's role is to act as a neutral observer.

Whatever one's epistemological perspective, too often research participants in cross-border research express concerns about persistent inequalities in the benefits of research:

> That kind of parasitic relationship is that researchers are – I feel that researchers, they come get our data, then waste our time. There is no mutual benefit, the benefit is on one side. Those guys collect the data, and for us at the end of it we don't see any change. We expect to at least get some benefit back, but there is no benefit. You get your data, you go – maybe use it for your own benefit and you leave us hanging. So, I feel only one party is benefitting and the other one is not benefitting. So that's why I say it's kind of a parasitic relationship.[12]

Activity 3.5: Analysing Multiple Ethical Issues in a Hypothetical Case Study

Consider the following hypothetical case study:

A researcher conducted interviews with young people who participated in violence during the civil war in Sierra Leone. During an interview with one former child soldier, he revealed that he had committed a war crime while he was the leader of a military unit. The Special Court in Sierra Leone has a mandate to prosecute all those who committed war crimes during the civil war, including child soldiers. Therefore, the professor decided not to include data related to war crimes in her research findings in case she were called to testify at the Special Court. However, during the peer review process for an article that the professor wrote based on her research findings, one reviewer suggested that in her study the professor was portraying the child soldiers simply as victims. The reviewer asked whether there were any other data that could provide a more complex picture of child soldiers as both victims and perpetrators of war.

1. Identify one ethical challenge related to voluntary, informed consent in this case study.
2. Identify one ethical challenge related to confidentiality in this case study.

3. Identify one ethical challenge related to minimizing harm in this case study.
4. Identify one way in which scholarly ethics and research ethics may be in tension in this example.

PROCEDURAL ETHICS IN CROSS-BORDER AND CROSS-CULTURAL RESEARCH

As mentioned at the beginning of this chapter, procedural ethics involve formal ethics approval processes and institutions. Because of the socially constructed nature of ethics, research across borders may result in different norms and approaches to procedural research ethics. Some countries, such as France, do not have institutionalized ethics processes. In other cases involving multiple institutions and countries, researchers may have to navigate a myriad of different ethics procedures across organizational and national boundaries – sometimes in different languages. It is important that you understand the procedural ethics requirements in your home institution, in any partner institutions (for example, if you go on exchange to a different university, or if you are affiliated with another university or research centre when doing research in a community), and in all countries in which you are doing work. These requirements will be context-specific and may change even in the course of one research project, given the evolving societal and legal dynamics related to ethics.

Due to the specific historical and legal circumstances in certain contexts, and thus differential and heightened risks posed by research in these areas, specific guidelines have been developed for research relating to Indigenous issues and forced migration. Many of these guidelines are national or context-specific. A partial list is provided in the resources section as a starting point for further ethical awareness in these and analogous contexts.

While procedural ethics provide important frameworks for protecting the key ethical principles highlighted above, they are limiting in at least three important ways.

First, most institutional ethics only apply to research with human beings (sometimes called "human subjects"). Let's break this down:

- **Research**: For the purposes of procedural ethics review, research is usually defined as data collection for scientific purposes. This means that data collection for evaluation, administrative, or pedagogical purposes is usually not subject to ethics review. For example, course evaluations at your institution are generally not subject to procedural ethics review because the information is intended to inform teaching and factor into decisions on the course instructor's employment, and is not intended as data for a research project.

- **With human beings**: Ethics boards are concerned with researchers' interaction with other human beings (and with animals, but that is generally not relevant in our contexts). This means secondary research and primary research with textual data is generally not subject to procedural ethics review.

However, just because secondary research does not entail direct contact with human beings and is thus not subject to formal procedural ethics review, this does not mean that researchers are exempt from thinking through the ethical consequences of their work. Most research on global issues aspires to be policy relevant and, therefore, has the potential to impact individuals and groups directly or indirectly. For example, the fragility indices presented in chapter 1 do not require institutional ethics review because they rely on existing secondary data. However, a country's fragility ranking could determine the amount of development assistance it receives from donor countries. Because there is usually no formal ethics review of these secondary research projects, the responsibility falls to the researcher to identify and respond to potential ethical dilemmas in this work.

Second, "procedural ethical processes are different from ethics-in-practice: the day-to-day ethical issues that arise during research conduct."[13] As discussed above, it is in the *application* of ethical principles in the actual doing of research where researchers often confront ethical dilemmas. Procedural ethics processes do not necessarily equip researchers to face these "ethically important moments."[14] Ethical codes and procedural ethics provide a moral framework, but may not be practical enough to address the everyday ethical decisions that researchers must make in their ongoing research projects and relationships.

Third, procedural ethics codify particular socially constructed ways of thinking about ethics. However, when conducting research across borders and world views, it is important to ask who decides "what is normal," whose norms will be used, and what normative standards may be applied.[15] Ethics are embedded in power relations and ways of knowing and being. In some cases, there could be a tension between procedural ethics conceived within a particular institutional context and the ways in which morality is constructed in the research context. For example, many ethics boards have particular processes and protocols for assessing research with groups whom they deem "vulnerable," such as children or people whose rights have historically been violated, such as Indigenous or incarcerated people. However, vulnerability is context-specific and dynamic. Moreover, procedural ethics restrictions on "vulnerable" groups can dissuade researchers from working with individuals and communities, thereby excluding their experiences and views from research. This undermines the principle of beneficence.

This leads to the fourth limitation with procedural ethics. In many cases, the role of institutional ethics boards is to limit, at least partially, the legal liability of the institution(s).[16] As a result, these committees can be conservative and can focus their attention on the technicalities of the review process rather than on the broader moral or ethical questions of the research. Moreover, while many procedural ethics boards include at least one community representative, they do not necessarily have the full knowledge of the substantive issues and the contexts in which research takes place, especially research across borders and world views.

RELATIONAL ETHICS

Because of the limitations of procedural ethics, some researchers advocate for relational ethics to complement formal ethics processes. Relational ethics situates moral decision-making within research relationships, including power asymmetries within these relationships. It therefore centres a relational social ontology, similar to Indigenous epistemologies. Some researchers have drawn on medical ethics to think about relational ethics as an ethics of care. "The ethics of care [...] sees persons as relational and interdependent, morally and epistemologically."[17]

Key elements of relational or care ethics are:

- Relationships: Researchers need to be aware of the way they behave with other people in relationships and within contexts of unequal power structures. Research should build on mutually beneficial interdependence, even within power asymmetries. Investing in relationships mitigates the risks of extractive research.

- Responsibility: As Lawson argues, "A care ethics approach to research design also asks us to take seriously the ways in which our work is *'for* others.'"[18] Beyond the risk mitigation strategies required by procedural ethics (as discussed above), a relational ethics of care requires researchers to acknowledge and take responsibility for all consequences of the research, including those that were unintended or unexpected.
- Connection and reciprocity: Acknowledging the ways in which human beings and our actions are interconnected, a relational approach to ethics privileges reciprocity. This is the idea of not only "giving back" to research participants, but also allowing them to probe our lives and experiences, the way we do in our research.
- Emotions: In contrast to the positivist ideal of the neutral, objective researcher, proponents of relational care ethics value emotions, "to enable morally concerned persons in actual interpersonal contexts to understand what would be best."[19] This approach validates "gut reactions" as ways to tune into one's moral compass and to implicitly know what is right and wrong.

This relational approach to ethics resonates with Indigenous epistemologies. As discussed in chapter 2, many of the key elements cited here – relationship, responsibility, and reciprocity – are central to Indigenous ways of knowing and doing.

POWER, POSITIONALITY, AND REFLEXIVITY

Within both relational and procedural ethics, attention is paid to power relations and how these impact moral behaviour and decision-making. These differential power relations also have methodological implications. The German physicist Werner Heisenberg observed that the very act of observing particles changes their behaviour. This Heisenberg principle comes from the natural sciences, but is also relevant for researchers in the humanities and social sciences. If even sub-atomic particles react to observation, how much more impact will research have when observing human beings? Check out the layperson's explanation in the TV show *NUMB3RS* (http://www.youtube.com/watch?v=e8pwMKVYQkA).

Primary research involves interaction between human beings. This interaction takes place within existing social structures and power relations. When thinking about power relations in research, two concepts are particularly important:

Positionality is an explicit understanding of the researcher's position within intersecting and dynamic power relations. It requires both attention to broader structures of inequality, and also how we as researchers (re)produce or challenge these structures in our research relationships.

Reflexivity means proactively thinking about our positionality. It is about being aware of who we are, as researchers and as human beings: our personal characteristics, our beliefs, and our role within the research and within broader social relationships. It also means thinking about how these different personal and professional characteristics may affect the way we do research, but also how research respondents interact with us. Finlay argues that reflexivity is "a politics of location and a practice of positioning" leading to "analytical accountability."[20]

Reflexivity and positionality are especially important when working in cross-cultural and cross-border contexts, where researchers have to learn other ways of being and knowing. It may take some time before researchers understand the nuanced and context-specific social structures and how their position within these structures will impact their research and ethical considerations like consent.

Not only are individual identity markers – such as race, nationality, class, linguistic profile, ethnicity, ability, age, gender, and so on – important, but professional affiliations and alliances will also influence power relations within research processes. If a researcher is, or perceived to be, associated with a group or an organization who has a stake in the context, this will impact the quality and kind of data the researcher has access to.

In cross-cultural and muti-lingual contexts, researchers may also need to navigate these power relations with gatekeepers (see chapter 7), research assistants, and interpreters. The more people who are involved in the research project, the more complex these intersecting power relations become. There are different ethical and practical issues of being an "insider" or an "outsider"[21] to the research population, with some – such as peer researchers (see chapter 10) – straddling these roles.

The increasing use of first person in academic articles – while still avoided by some researchers, especially positivists – reflects a growing acknowledgement of the role and impact of researchers in the research process. While this is more commonly found in constructivist and critical approaches, positivists are also interested in the Heisenberg principle as they attempt to conduct objective research.

Activity 3.6: Positionality Mapping

This section is written by Danielle Jacobson and Nida Mustafa and is based on their 2018 article.[22]

Positionality is an important concept used in qualitative research that involves reflecting on who you are as a person and the impact this has on the research process. This includes consideration of how you interact with the world around you and how those around you interact with you. There are countless facets that make up our positionality. Some of these include our race, gender, sex, class, religion, citizenship, ability, age, and sexual orientation. Reflecting on our social identities and on how these identities influence our reciprocal interactions with the social world are often perceived as abstract and challenging tasks. Therefore, we have created the "Social Identity Map."

How to use the Social Identity Map as a tool to practice explicit positionality:

1. Fill in the first tier of boxes by identifying your class, citizenship, ability, age/generation, race, sexual orientation, cis/trans status, and gender.

   • Add any other aspects of your social identity that are particularly relevant for you today.
   • See an aspect of your social identity that you are not comfortable reflecting on in this moment? Leave it out. Consider reflecting instead on why this aspect elicits discomfort.
   • Your social identity and its representation on this map will change over time. If you leave something blank today, you can change your map later on.

2. Fill in the second tier of boxes by reflecting on how these facets of your social identity affect your life. There is no one way to complete this task. Go with what is intuitive to you.

   • How do these facets affect how you interact with the world around you (this may include the way you interpret or react to particular scenarios)?
   • How do these facets affect how others view and interact with you (this may include the way that others interpret or react to you)?
   • What values and/or norms are linked to particular aspects of your social identity?

3. Fill in the third tier of boxes by reflecting on how the facets of your social identity intersect.

   • What emotions are tied to your experiences of particular facets of your social identity?
   • What privilege or oppression do you experience related to your social identity?

4. Go beyond the confines of the map.

- Certain aspects of social identity (i.e., class, citizenship, etc.) and the ways in which these aspects are expressed (i.e., gender, sexuality, etc.) may change over time. This map can be updated to reflect the ways in which you change and grow.
- Although the map provides boxes to give structure and direction to those new to reflecting on their social identity, identities do not neatly fit into a box. Feel free to:

  - Cross out aspects of the map that do not work for you at this time.
  - Add aspects that are missing for you on the map.
  - Draw new shapes, lines, connections, symbols, and words to reflect your identity.

Mapping social identity is a beginning step toward better understanding positionality in the research context. This map acts as a concrete tool that can be used to reflect on who you are and how this influences the research process. The map also has important implications for reflecting on our world view and experiences more broadly, as it allows us to take a moment in time to look inwards, reconnect with ourselves, and position our lives in relation to our ever-evolving social world.

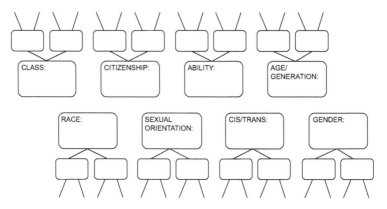

Figure 3.1. Blank positionality map. Jacobson and Mustafa, "Social Identity Map."

CONCLUSIONS AND KEY TAKEAWAYS

Ethical considerations in research provide moral reference points for the ways researchers behave in research contexts. The key principles of voluntary, informed consent; respect for privacy; and "do no harm" need to be adapted and applied depending on the power relations in any particular context, especially in research across borders and world views. While institutionalized procedural ethics can help researchers to identify how to apply these principles, they are not present in all institutions and in all countries, and they do not apply to all research projects. Ultimately, it is up to researchers to continuously reflect on the ways that their research may benefit – and harm – the people whose lives are impacted, both directly and indirectly, by their studies.

QUESTIONS

1. Do researchers have an ethical obligation to prevent harm, or simply to minimize or avoid harm? What are the methodological opportunities and challenges of your position?
2. Somewhat surprisingly, despite the "do no harm" ethic ingrained in peace and conflict work, there are no internationally recognized ethical standards for researchers in this field. John Brewer, in the article referenced below, suggests that this gap be urgently closed. In your view, what would be the key elements of a code of ethics in peace and conflict studies?
3. What would a rights-based approach to research ethics look like? How would it be similar to and different from procedural ethics and relational ethics approaches?
4. What professional ethics are related to your field of study? Find the documents that are more relevant to your area of research and compare them to the research ethics principles described in this chapter. How are they the same and different?

FURTHER READINGS

Brear, Michelle R., and Rebecca Gordon. "Translating the Principle of Beneficence into Ethical Participatory Development Research Practice."

Journal of International Development 33, no. 1 (2021): 109–26. https://doi
.org/10.1002/jid.3514.

Brewer, John D. "The Ethics of Ethical Debates in Peace and Conflict
Research: Notes towards the Development of a Research Covenant."
Methodological Innovations 9 (2016). https://doi.org/10.1177
/2059799116630657.

Campbell, Susanna P. "Ethics of Research in Conflict Environments." *Journal
of Global Security Studies* 2, no. 1 (2017): 89–101. https://doi.org/10.1093
/jogss/ogw024.

Celestina, Mateja. "Between Trust and Distrust in Research with Participants
in Conflict Context." *International Journal of Social Research Methodology* 21,
no. 3 (2018): 373–83. https://doi.org/10.1080/13645579.2018.1427603.

Griffin, Gabriele, and Doris Leibetseder. "'Only Applies to Research
Conducted in Sweden … ': Dilemmas in Gaining Ethics Approval in
Transnational Qualitative Research." *International Journal of Qualitative
Methods* 18 (2019). https://doi.org/10.1177/1609406919869444.

Keikelame, Mpoe Johannah. "'The Tortoise under the Couch': An African
Woman's Reflections on Negotiating Insider-Outsider Positionalities
and Issues of Serendipity on Conducting a Qualitative Research Project
in Cape Town, South Africa." *International Journal of Social Research
Methodology* 21, no. 2 (2018): 219–30. https://doi.org/10.1080/13645579
.2017.1357910.

Komil-Burley, Mateja. "Conducting Research in Authoritarian Bureaucracies:
Researcher Positionality, Access, Negotiation, Cooperation, Trepidation,
and Avoiding the Influence of the Gatekeepers." *International Journal of
Qualitative Methods* 20 (2021). https://doi.org/10.1177/1609406921996862.

Montreuil, Marjorie, Aline Bogossian, Emilie Laberge-Perrault, and Eric
Racine. "A Review of Approaches, Strategies and Ethical Considerations
in Participatory Research with Children." *International Journal of Qualitative
Methods* 20 (2021). https://doi.org/10.1177/1609406920987962.

Parashar, Swati. "Research Brokers, Researcher Identities and Affective
Performances: The Insider/Outsider Conundrum." *Civil Wars* 21, no. 2
(2019): 249–70. https://doi.org/10.1080/13698249.2019.1634304.

Raghuram, Parvati. "Race and Feminist Care Ethics: Intersectionality as
Method." *Gender, Place & Culture* 26, no. 5 (2019): 613–37. https://doi.org
/10.1080/0966369X.2019.1567471.

van der Geest, Sjaak. "Lying in Defence of Privacy: Anthropological and
Methodological Observations." *International Journal of Social Research
Methodology* 21, no. 5 (2018): 541–52. https://doi.org/10.1080/13645579
.2018.1447866.

World Health Organization (WHO). "Indigenous Peoples and Participatory
Health Research." https://www.mcgill.ca/cine/files/cine/partreresearch
_english.pdf.

Web Resources

SCHOLARLY ETHICS – TUTORIALS
Ten Golden Rules for Academic Integrity: https://academicintegrity
.uoguelph.ca/academic-integrity/ten-golden-rules-academic-integrity.
APA Plagiarism: https://apastyle.apa.org/style-grammar-guidelines
/citations/plagiarism.
Toronto Metropolitan University, Academic Integrity Resources: https://
www.torontomu.ca/academicintegrity/students.
Turnitin Plagiarism Test: https://www.turnitin.com/static/plagiarism-quiz/.
University of Oxford: https://www.ox.ac.uk/students/academic
/guidance/skills/plagiarism.

RESEARCH ETHICS – TUTORIALS
Tutorial Course on Research Ethics: http://www.pre.ethics.gc.ca/eng
/education/tutorial-didacticiel/.

INDIGENOUS RESEARCH
Assembly of First Nations. "First Nations Ethics Guide on Research and
Aboriginal Traditional Knowledge": https://www.afn.ca/uploads/files
/fn_ethics_guide_on_research_and_atk.pdf.
Guidelines for Ethical Research in Australian Indigenous Studies: https://
aiatsis.gov.au/research/ethical-research/guidelines-ethical-research
-australian-Indigenous-studies.
Tri-Council Policy for Research Involving the First Nations, Inuit and
Métis People of Canada: http://pre.ethics.gc.ca/eng/policy-politique
/initiatives/tcps2-eptc2/chapter9-chapitre9/.
World Health Organization (WHO). "Indigenous Peoples and Participatory
Health Research": https://www.who.int/ethics/Indigenous_peoples/en
/index1.html.

FORCED MIGRATION
"Ethical Considerations: Research with People in Situations of Forced
Migration": https://refuge.journals.yorku.ca/index.php/refuge/article
/view/40467.
International Association for the Study of Forced Migration Code of Ethics:
http://iasfm.org/blog/2018/11/30/adoption-of-iasfm-research-code-of
-ethics/.

GENERAL RESOURCES AND TOOLS
Heisenberg Principle, *NUMB3RS*: http://www.youtube.com/watch?v
=e8pwMKVYQkA.
Your Rights in Research: https://ccrweb.ca/sites/ccrweb.ca/files
/rightsinresearch-en-finalformatted2018.02.21.pdf.

Designing a Research Project across Borders

LEARNING OBJECTIVES

By the end of this chapter, you will be able to:

- Distinguish between a research topic, a research puzzle, and a research question or hypothesis;
- Identify tools and strategies that will help you to formulate a research question or hypothesis;
- Explain the methodological implications of posing a question that implies causality;
- Describe and identify qualitative, quantitative, participatory, and mixed approaches to research;
- Define research design;
- Understand the kinds of questions that can be answered by different kinds of methods; and,
- Identify the key components of any quality research study.

KEY TERMS

Causality   Dependence relationship
Correlation (or covariation)   Falsifiable
Critical analysis   Hypothesis

Literature	Mixed
Academic (or scholarly),	Participatory method
published literature	Peer reviewed
Grey	Qualitative
Popular	Quantitative
Published	Question
Literature review	

INTRODUCTION

In chapter 1, we discussed some of the reasons why researchers – both within and beyond academia – conduct research across borders. In this chapter, you will learn more about how researchers move from identifying a problem or puzzle to formulating a question and research design. This will be helpful for you as emerging researchers who need to investigate questions for courses and programs. The tools and concepts in this chapter will also help you to evaluate research you encounter in academia and real life. You need to understand the fundamentals of asking research questions and designing projects before you are able to do research yourself and assess the quality of research findings.

META-EXAMPLE: EVALUATING PEER-TO-PEER VOLUNTEERING AMONGST POST-SECONDARY STUDENTS IN CANADA

In my undergraduate research methodology course, a non-governmental organization (NGO) graciously collaborated with my students and me on an experiential learning opportunity. This NGO works with university and college students across Canada who volunteer in internationally oriented programs for young people. They wanted to know how this peer-to-peer volunteer experience affected student volunteers' competencies, capacities, goals, and motivations to engage in international development issues. Their challenge to my class was twofold: (1) undertake individual secondary research on a research **question** related to the topic; and (2) design, in groups, a proposed research project for data collection with former volunteers to understand the impact of their volunteer experiences.

For the secondary research, students were required to propose a research question and then find ten **academic, published** sources on this question. This was an iterative process. Students zeroed in on one aspect of the overarching topic that interested them – such as competencies or motivation – and formulated an initial research question. They thought about the keywords in that question and, with the assistance of a librarian, searched for academic sources. If there were too few relevant sources, they broadened their question; if there were too many, they narrowed it. They also used the bibliographies of relevant sources to find other studies that addressed their research question. Reading these articles also helped them to refine their question, particularly in relation to broad concepts like "capacities" or "goals." For example, one student chose to focus exclusively on the relationship between youth-to-youth volunteering and young volunteers' employment goals.

Working in groups of six to eight, students then proposed a research design for primary data collection. Due to time constraints and lack of procedural ethics approval, they did not undertake this data collection themselves. Rather, they developed a video pitch and a two-page summary document that outlined their research question, analytical framework, and proposed methods. In designing this research proposal, they drew on the secondary literature that they had individually developed, adopting and adapting relevant methods from similar previous studies. During the group project, students had to negotiate how they could narrow down the overall challenge into a workable research proposal. During this process, they learned the challenges of operationalizing and measuring concepts like "capacities" as well as the difficulty of determining the impact of volunteering, especially given the self-selection bias of volunteers (those who volunteer are likely to be more motivated to begin with) and many other factors that could contribute to volunteers' career and life trajectories.

This meta-example reveals several important points that will be discussed in more detail in this chapter.

First, all good research projects address a research problem or puzzle. Problem-based research does not necessarily have to be motivated by a specific operational need, as in this example, but there needs to be a clear challenge that is addressed.

Second, this research puzzle needs to be formulated into a specific research question or hypothesis. This is an iterative process based on the available literature and knowledge of the topic; available resources (time, money, people power); access considerations (including linguistic, administrative, and geopolitical borders); and ethics.

Third, research design involves thinking carefully about the kinds of information different methods generate and whether this information can answer the research question. In particular, research puzzles that involve causality or impact are difficult to answer definitively. In this example, the NGO wanted to know if volunteering had a positive impact on university student volunteers. It is difficult to attribute positive outcomes solely to volunteering given the many other factors that influence volunteers' lives.

Fourth, research is a creative process. Unlike some other research methods books, I contend that there is no magic formula or simple, linear process to follow for a "perfect" research project. This is particularly the case in dynamic cross-border and cross-cultural research, where it is impossible to predict exactly how the research will unfold. However, there are key elements to all good research projects: definition of key terms; an analytical framework; references to existing knowledge; and an explanation of methodology.

A RESEARCH PROBLEM OR PUZZLE

Most of us are able to list, fairly quickly off the top of our heads, topics that we would be interested in researching or learning more about. For example, you may be interested in adaptation to environmental change in the Pacific; or changing gender roles in conflict; or differential access to primary education; or young people's participation in peace processes.

These topics are important brainstorming starting points, but they need to be refined to provide a particular angle of enquiry to frame your research project. In the meta-example above, the research topic is peer-to-peer university student volunteering. This is a starting point, but it is too broad for a research project. Indeed, a quick Google Scholar search on this topic results in thousands of relevant results, ranging from empathy in medical students, to sexual consent, to stopping fake news.

At the other end of the spectrum, sometimes we come into a research project with a preconceived conclusion or argument and are simply looking for information to "back it up." While it is, of course, reasonable to test hypotheses (see below), we need to start off with a spirit of enquiry, not a predetermined idea of what we are going to find. In the example above, when I first discussed the research project with the NGO, their idea for a challenge was, "To demonstrate that university students' volunteer work changes their lives." This is an assumption that needs to be proven, not a research problem.

So, many researchers suggest that we begin with a research puzzle – a problem or a conundrum that frames our research and gives it meaning. This puzzle is at the core of the so-called "so what?" test. Why do you want to spend your time and resources to investigate this puzzle? What does it mean – to you personally, but also to your wider field or discipline of study and to the world around you? Christopher Day and Kendra Koivu suggest a puzzle-based approach is based on a "logic of discovery."[1] To return to our meta-example, the research puzzle is how to evaluate the impact of peer-to-peer volunteering on university student volunteers. At its heart, this research puzzle – like many others – is about causality.

UNDERSTANDING CAUSALITY AND CORRELATION

Many of us are attracted to programs like conflict studies, human rights, and development studies because we are interested in addressing the root causes of global inequalities and insecurity. Others are interested in assessing the impact or utility of particular programs or policies. Given that these big "why" questions are at the heart of many globally focused interdisciplinary programs, we need to understand the difference between correlation and causality.

Correlation (also called covariation) means that two variables (see chapter 5) or phenomena are related to one another. It is a necessary, but insufficient, condition for proving causality. For example, many analysts have observed that peace and economic development tend to occur at the same time.

Causality means that there is a **dependence relationship** between variables where one is causing another to change. Causality is one of the most contested methodological and epistemological issues in research across borders. It is often difficult to prove definitively that one variable is causing a change in the other, especially when considering a complex global phenomenon where multiple factors are occurring within dynamic contexts. For example, there are ongoing debates about whether countries need a certain level of economic development in order to have peace. In this example, economic development would be the independent variable that is affecting the level of peace in a country. Others argue that the causal relationship is the other way around: wars are costly, so it is war that is causing countries to be poor.

See the video "International Relations" (https://www.youtube.com /watch?v=9tXsWOIIF2o), which provides further explanations and some great examples from international studies.

Activity 4.1: From Topic to Puzzle

In this activity, we will use Day and Koivu's puzzle-based approach to help you move from a topic of interest to a puzzle that can focus your research.

First, identify a research topic that you are interested in. Write it down.

Second, think about *why* this topic interests you. Select from one of the following options identified by Day and Koivu:[2]

- "Is it a real-world event or process?" [empirical]
- "Is it a set of theories or theoretical debates about these events?" [theoretical]
- "Is it a particular method that measures these events?" [methodological]

Third, depending on the choice you make above, think about the following questions:[3]

For *empirical* puzzles:

- "Is there something unusual or unexpected?"
- "Is the event or process similar to, or different from, other examples in different places?"
- "Does it represent a sudden change or variation over time?"

For *theoretical* puzzles:

- "Is there an existing literature [see below] that can be applied to a new phenomenon?"

- "Are there different literatures not in dialogue with one another but could be?"
- "Is there an unreconciled disagreement between explanations for a phenomenon?"

For *methodological* puzzles:

- "Is there a method that could provide a better way to measure a given concept?"
- "Is there a technique that could provide an alternative way to understand a given phenomenon?"

Fourth, using the information gathered from the questions above, reformulate your research topic into a research puzzle.

RESEARCH QUESTIONS AND HYPOTHESES

While a research puzzle provides an overall framework for creative discovery, it needs to be articulated in a clear research question or hypothesis in order for a specific research design to be identified. In this section, we will walk through some of the factors to consider when formulating a research question or hypothesis.

First, a note on terminology. While there are epistemological debates about the use of questions versus hypotheses (see chapter 2), a hypothesis is basically the predicted answer to a research question. In this chapterand throughout the book, I will be using the term "research question" because it is more inclusive. However, because you will encounter it in articles you read, you need to understand terminology related to hypotheses.

A **hypothesis** is a "statement that specifies or describes the relationship between two variables in such a way that the relationship can be tested empirically."[4]

- For example, you may have encountered the notion of "democratic peace." According to this research, the hypothesis (H) is: Democratic states never (or rarely, depending on the theorist!) go to war with each other.
- Hypotheses need to be **falsifiable**. One needs to be able to disprove a hypothesis. In this example, (1/H) is: Democratic states *do* go to war with each other.

- The null hypothesis (H_o): There is no relationship. It is assumed true until proven otherwise. To continue with our example, democratic states are as likely to go to war with each other as states with other kinds of political/government structures.

So, how can we move from a research puzzle to articulating a specific research question? This section will guide you through some key considerations in formulating a research question – whether it be for primary research involving data collection or secondary research based on existing data and resources.

One of the first things to consider is what you are personally interested in. Academic fads come and go. a topic that is at the top of the political agenda or in the media circuit today may no longer be relevant in a few weeks or years. Good research is hard work: at times, it will be difficult to get information, or you may encounter methodological and ethical challenges. What will sustain you during these difficult moments is the belief that your research question is important. Sometimes students wonder whether a topic is too personal if they are directly affected by it. Beyond the epistemological debates about whether or not "objective" research is possible (see chapter 2), the main consideration here is to be open to views that directly contradict your personal experiences. And, like all good research, your project needs to be embedded in the conceptual and theoretical debates in the academic literature (see below and chapter 5).

A second important consideration is whether scholarly research can answer the question. Because international questions are often about deep-rooted inequalities and injustices, students sometimes lean towards normative questions. But, these cannot always be easily answered by academic tools and approaches. For example, a question such as "Should gender-based violence embedded in cultural practices be allowed to continue?" does not lend itself to scientific enquiry. Rather, one could ask: "What are the origins of gender-based violence embedded in cultural practices in community x?"

Relatedly, a third consideration, which was discussed briefly in chapter 3, is whether the question poses ethical issues. First, it is important to avoid over-researched questions. Second, you need to think about the methods that will be required to answer the question and about whether these methods involve deception or coercion, which could pose ethical dilemmas. Finally, if you are researching a topic that involves criminality or illegality, you will need to carefully consider how you will ensure confidentiality and what the limits are to this confidentiality in the case of (self-)harm or criminalized activities.

Fourth, you need to be realistic about the time, the financial resources, and the human resources you have available to answer the question. One common mistake is trying to tackle a question that is too broad or large for the scope of a term paper or a dissertation. In cross-border contexts, one needs to think about the financial costs of travelling to another country. Similarly, you should carefully consider your language proficiency and whether you have the linguistic skills required to gather and analyse data in another language. Even if your research project is based on secondary data and literature, it is better to have at least a working, reading knowledge of the language spoken in the country in which you are doing your work, so that you are able to read daily newspapers for context and academic studies by scholars from that country.

A related point is the methodological tools that you have at your disposal. In general, it is difficult to answer causality questions without a large-scale quantitative study with control groups. Even if your research project does not involve primary data collection or analysis, you will need to be comfortable enough with basic quantitative methodology and statistics in order to critically analyse and assess the findings presented in other studies. When causality is difficult to research and prove, reformulate the research question so it is more descriptive.

For example, consider this research question: "Has the Safe Third Country Agreement between Canada and the US resulted in fewer asylum claims in Canada?" To prove a cause (Safe Third Country Agreement) and effect (fewer asylum claims) relationship, a researcher would need to control for many other variables that impacted the number of asylum claims, such as political events in the countries of origin as well as differences across decision-makers within Canada's refugee determination system. It is also difficult to disprove because 1/H implies a **counterfactual**. A possible reformation that still retains the focus of the question but eliminates causality is "How has the nature of asylum claims in Canada changed in the context of the Safe Third Country Agreement?"

Related to this is whether you will be doing primary research or relying on secondary literature. If it is the latter, you want to avoid a topic that is too current, since there is a publication lag of one to two years for academic, published literature on which your analytical framework should be based (see below). If you are doing primary research, then you need to be able to justify the contribution that your study will make – whether this be empirical, conceptual, theoretical, methodological, and/or pedagogical.

A final consideration is if there are any assumptions in the research question and whether these are substantiated by empirical evidence.

> For example, what policy measures has the US government taken to respond to increased illegal migration? This question contains several assumptions:
>
> 1. That there is migration that can be deemed "illegal." The scholarly literature questions this and instead prefers the terms "irregular" or "undocumented."
> 2. That irregular migration is indeed increasing. This would require empirical evidence, which may be difficult to obtain (as discussed in chapter 5) because the phenomenon is, by definition, not documented.
> 3. That the US government is indeed responding to irregular migration through policy measures.

Activity 4.2: Formulating a Research Question

Start with the research puzzle you arrived at through Activity 4.1. Think about each of the factors identified above and revise your question, accordingly, using the following guiding questions:

1. What is your research puzzle?
2. What is personally, professionally, or academically interesting to you about this puzzle? What motivates you to be interested in this puzzle? Try to formulate these key interests and drivers into one or two possible questions.
3. Are there normative assumptions in your answer to question two above? If so, how could you reformulate these so that the question is better suited to an academic study?

4. Think about the ethical implications of asking this question. Revise accordingly.
5. Is your question realistic? If the topic is too broad, think about one aspect of the theme, or narrow it down to a particular case study – a city, a country, a region, an organization, or group of individuals – that you could focus on.
6. Does your question imply causality? If so, do you have the data and methodological knowledge to answer it? If not, how could it be reformulated so that it is descriptive, rather than causal?

RESEARCH DESIGN: CONNECTING QUESTIONS, METHODOLOGY, AND DATA

Once a researcher has a good idea of their key question, they need to turn their attention to research design: "a strategic framework for action that serves as a bridge between research questions and the execution or implementation of the research."[5] While this section will focus on research design for primary data collection, even those researchers who will be undertaking secondary research need to understand the basics of research design, so that they are better able to evaluate the quality of the information they find in secondary sources.

One key methodological decision in research design is to think about the overall approach to research. In this section, I describe the key approaches, using examples from real research projects focused on student volunteering in international programs, as inspired by the meta-example. In chapter 5, we will expand on **qualitative and quantitative measurement.**

A qualitative approach is one that relies primarily on verbal descriptions and explanations to qualify human behaviour. Researchers use words, images, and non-numeric symbols as data.

For example, to respond to the research question in the meta-example on volunteering, one student found a study on young people participating in a community refugee project. This research was based on in-depth interviews with eighteen young people and ten of their friends or family members. "The participants were asked to describe the reasons they joined the project, why they stayed on, what they liked most/least about the project, how the project influenced their lives, and what they would change about the project."* This is a qualitative approach because the researchers asked participants to describe in their own words their motivations and experiences of volunteering.

* Makhoul, Alameddine, and Afifi, "'I felt that I was benefiting someone,'" 914.

A quantitative approach uses numeric analysis and data, including statistics. By turning information and variables into numbers, researchers can compare large amounts of data and find statistical relationships between variables.

For example, during the secondary research on volunteering described in the meta-example above, students in my methods course found a study where researchers compared student volunteering in five countries.* In each country, the researchers conducted anonymous surveys with at least 600 students and asked them to rate their motivation on a five-point scale. They then aggregated this information across the students to compare the relative proportion of altruistic versus individualistic motivation across the five studies.

This is a quantitative approach because the researchers are using numbers to quantify motivation and then using statistics to compare levels across the five countries.

* Smith et al., "Motivations and Benefits of Student Volunteering."

Participatory approaches involve those who are most affected by the research in designing, conducting, and analysing the research. External researchers act as facilitators and catalysers to support and amplify the knowledge of people who have experienced the phenomenon under study.

Pro Tip: participant observation is not a **participatory method**. In participant observation, as we will discuss in chapter 9, it is the researcher who is participating in the activities of the community they are observing. It is not the community members who are participating in the conception and implementation of the research. Indeed, in some cases, participant observation has been used to gather intelligence on a community for military or colonization purposes.

An example of a participatory approach from the meta-example on student volunteering is a proposal by one of the groups for a research project led and implemented by post-secondary students, involving both those who volunteered and the peers who were "recipients" of the volunteer work.* The group proposed a simulation that generated data through students' experiences in a real-world scenario. Few of the studies in the secondary literature took a participatory approach. As will be discussed in chapter 10, this is symptomatic of a broader trend in cross-border and cross-cultural research, where those most impacted by an issue are least likely to be involved in designing and implementing a study.

* Richards et al., Proposition MÉSI.

Finally, in reality, many researchers combine different approaches within the same study. In particular, it is important to stress that quantitative methods are not necessarily inherently more "objective" than qualitative methods. As we saw in chapter 1, quantitative studies can get different results depending on the methods and measurements researchers use. Moreover, as discussed in chapter 3, positionality and the Heisenberg principle will affect all research: quantitative, qualitative, participatory, and **mixed**. It is possible to combine different methodological approaches – simultaneously, or in sequence. A researcher may use qualitative approaches to describe and interpret quantitative approaches. In contrast, sometimes quantitative analysis is used to aggregate qualitative results. Participatory approaches use qualitative and/or quantitative methods for data collection.

For example, students in my methods course found a study that combined in-depth focus groups and interviews involving mostly qualitative data with a large-scale survey that generated primarily quantitative data.* The focus groups and interviews allowed participants to formulate responses in their own words. These expressions were then integrated into the survey, where respondents selected pre-established choices, so that the results could be compared quantitatively across all those who took part.

* Holdsworth and Brewis, "Volunteering, Choice and Control."

Table 4.1. Methods and data generation

Methods	Data generated
Interviews	Reported behaviour
	Opinions
	Feelings
	Explanations for reported or observed behaviour
Surveys	Same as interviews, plus:
	Ranking of opinions, feelings, etc.
Focus groups	Same as interviews, plus:
	Interaction between participants
	Points of debate/discussion
Observation	Observed behaviour
	Contextual information
	Observed events

Some courses and textbooks focus on qualitative or quantitative methods, but I suggest that no method is inherently qualitative or quantitative. For example, in the same interview, a researcher may explore qualitatively a participant's feelings, opinions, or experiences, but also ask them to quantify these feelings on a scale of 1 to 5. Instead, I suggest that we focus here on the types of information or questions that can be answered by particular methods. I summarize these in table 4.1.

Activity 4.3: Identifying Research Approaches

1. Read the following abstracts of four different studies on *maquila* (also known as *maquiladora*): low-cost and low-wage factories

that benefit from duty- and tariff-free movement of goods. These abstracts are reproduced below verbatim because it is important to be able to distinguish different methodological approaches in study summaries that you will encounter in research databases.

2. Then, identify each research design as primarily quantitative, qualitative, participatory, or mixed.

3. Identify a data collection method mentioned in each abstract. What kind of information did the researcher gain from this method?

De Hoyos, Rafael, Maurizio Bussolo, and Oscar Núñez. "Exports, Gender Wage Gaps, and Poverty in Honduras." *Oxford Development Studies* 40, no. 4 (2012): 533–51. http://dx.doi.org/10.1080/13600818.2012.732562.

This paper identifies and estimates the reduction in poverty attributable to the improved opportunities that international trade integration offered to women in Honduras. The expansion of the export-oriented *maquila* sector has brought gender equality both in terms of employment and labour earnings. A simulation exercise shows that, at a given point in time, poverty in Honduras would have been 1.5 percentage points higher had the *maquila* sector not existed. Of this increase in poverty, 0.35 percentage points is attributable to the wage premium paid to *maquila* workers, 0.1 percentage points to the wage premium received by women in the *maquila* sector, and 1.0 percentage point to employment creation.

Mendez, Jennifer Bickham. "Gender and Citizenship in a Global Context: The Struggle for *Maquila* Workers' Rights in Nicaragua." *Identities: Global Studies in Culture and Power* 9, no. 1 (2002): 7–38. https://doi.org/10.1080/10702890210364.

This article analyses the strategic deployment of rights and citizenship discourses by a Nicaraguan women's organization (MEC) and the struggle that this group has faced in reconciling the use of these discourses with its aim of bringing about changes in the conditions faced by women workers in the Free Trade Zone (FTZ). Contestations regarding notions of citizenship are explored, and I discuss Nicaraguan state agents' and (to a lesser degree) *maquila* factory owners' use of notions of citizenship, and how they both coincide and conflict with neoliberal social and economic projects. The case of this Nicaraguan organization's discursive engagement with state actors sheds light on the question: How do ideologies linked to transnational social movements filter into regional and national discourses and become transformed by local actors? In addition, this case has important implications for the larger issue of changing state sovereignty within a global context. A contextualized approach to the strategic use of (human) rights and citizenship calls attention to the complex and situationally specific dilemmas and opportunities involved in adapting this "frame" to work for oppositional objectives. Furthermore, viewing rights and citizenship as always situational calls us to move away from narrow conceptualizations of structural transformation to a more complex and nuanced vision.

Huesca, Robert. "Social Aspects of Labor Organizing: *Maquiladora* Workers in a Grassroots Development Effort." *Journal of Developing Societies* 19, no. 2–3 (2003): 227–67. https://doi.org/10.1177/0169796X0301900205.

Beginning in the mid-1960s, Mexico encouraged the development of industrial assembly plants known as *maquiladoras* along its northern border and in selected areas of the interior. Although it began as a stopgap measure to employ men returning from the US bracero worker program, the Border Industrialization Program soon became Mexico's principal development initiative for the border region. Since then, numerous scholars have evaluated the success of the plants by examining their impacts on the economy, the environment, and labor. This study adds to this research literature by assessing the impact of the *maquiladora* program from the perspective of the assembly line workers. It describes and analyses the activities of a grassroots, participatory development effort to organize *maquiladora* workers for more than 20 years. Participatory approaches to development are defined and described in terms of the problems and challenges that animate this field of research. The findings demonstrate how participatory efforts at organizing constitute one of the few avenues available to workers to resist factory exploitation and improve their general well-being. The study confirms some of the shortcomings of participatory development theory, such as its conceptual ambiguity, significant time commitment, and general cumbersomeness, but it provides justifications for its continuance.

Mendez, Jennifer Bickham. "Organizing a Space of Their Own? Global/Local Processes in a Nicaraguan Women's Organization." *Journal of Developing Societies* 18, no. 2–3 (2002): 196–227. https://doi.org/10.1177/01697 96X0201800209.

This article analyses the internal organizational processes within a Nicaraguan women worker's organization, the Working and Unemployed Women's Movement or "María Elena Cuadra" (MEC), to explore the ways in which place-centred, locally constituted political identities articulate with transnational flows of ideas and discourses to shape actors' collective practices. MEC's changing organizational practices reflect the influence of strategies and practices employed in the mass organizations of the FSLN [Frente Sandinista de Liberación Nacional] and transnational flows of discourses and ideas about issues such as feminism, personal and political autonomy, and the relationship between individuals and a collective. I explore the impact of members' experiences within the Sandinista mass organizations on MEC's organizational practices and analyse MEC's uneasy relationship with feminist organizations and northern-based NGOs. While transnational linkages have opened new opportunities for groups like MEC, certain relations of inequality, such as those based on neocolonialism, persist. The case of MEC sheds light on the complex ways in which power operates through and within transnational organizational relations.

KEY ELEMENTS IN ANY RESEARCH PROJECT

Regardless of one's methodological approach, or whether research is primary or secondary, all good research projects contain the following key elements.

First, as discussed above, a study needs a clearly defined research question or hypothesis.

Second, a researcher needs to identify key terms. Unlike dictionary definitions, the conceptual framework contains both operational and conceptual definitions that help to measure phenomenon (as will be explained in chapter 5).

Third, a research project needs a theoretical framework in order to guide the analysis. Here, it is important to note that this theory is separate from the hypothesis. A hypothesis is a projected answer to a research question, while the theoretical framework is a "research tool" (*outil de recherche*) that allows researchers to "filter and organize" (*filtrer et organiser*) information.[6] As mentioned in chapter 1, the theoretical framework is a lens through which the phenomenon under study is conceptualized and analysed. Indeed, the theoretical and conceptual frameworks are linked and must be consistent. These will be discussed in chapter 5.

Fourth, all solid research contains a methodology section. This will vary depending on the research question and the extent of the empirical contribution. However, all researchers should spell out how they conducted their research, even if it is primarily theoretical.

Finally, research projects need to be situated within the broader literature. It is important to show how your research is positioned in relation to other studies that have been conducted on the topic or to related questions. Reading related research helps to narrow down your research question; to understand relevant concepts, definitions, and theories; to learn from data that has already been generated on the topic; and to identify gaps or shortcomings of the existing research. In other words, a good **literature review** helps researchers to build on knowledge and information.

> *Pro Tip*: While you are searching and reading studies related to your research, it is a good idea to organize them in a bibliographic database. At the end of this chapter, you will find links to Zotero, a free online software that helps you organize your references. Zotero or another referencing software will help you to keep all your references in the same place, allow you to search within your database, and will save you time when you go to format your citations when writing and sharing your work.

Generally speaking, academic studies privilege **published, scholarly literature**. Let's break this down:

Published literature is produced by an entity whose mandate is to publish. This includes publishing companies, academic presses, newspapers, and other companies with a formal mandate to publish.

In contrast, **grey literature** is published outside of publishing and distribution channels. This includes documents that are produced by governments, non-governmental organizations, and think tanks.

So, the published versus grey distinction is fairly easy to discern. One simply looks at the bibliographic reference information to see who produced the document. If the entity who produced the document is a publishing house, it is published; if it is any other organization or institution, it is grey literature.

> *Pro Tip*: While a university press is a publisher, a university and its affiliated research centres are not. So, a book or journal article published by Oxford University Press is published, while a working paper from Oxford's Refugee Studies Centre is grey literature.

The second distinction – scholarly versus **popular** – is not as clear-cut. What makes a document scholarly or academic? Generally speaking, it is research that includes the key elements in this section – that is, the definitions of terms; the citations of sources; a conceptual and theoretical framework; and a methodology section. Also, scholarly literature is usually **peer reviewed**. This means that at least two professionals with knowledge of the topic have read the document and recommended that it be published.

Here are some examples of different kinds of documents:

Table 4.2. Examples of grey versus published and academic versus popular documents

Academic

Grey	**Examples:** Theses Working papers Conference presentations	**Examples:** Books published by academic presses Academic journal articles, including those that are open access	Published
	Examples: Websites Government documents Report from NGO Blogs	**Examples:** Newspaper articles Books published by non-academic presses	

Popular

Pro Tip: A researcher needs to distinguish between documents they are using as literature and those that are data. Literature refers to documents that have some level of analysis and argumentation. In contrast, documents – like historical records, laws, international conventions, censuses, and newspaper articles – can be important sources of data. Like all data, these latter need to be interpreted, using an analytical framework. Textual analysis will be discussed in chapter 11. The academic, published literature is often helpful in identifying the concepts and theories that can be key components of this analytical framework.

In academic work, published, scholarly literature is generally preferred. Why? Primarily, because this work is subjected to quality control twice: first, because it is peer-reviewed; and second, because it is copy-edited and fact-checked by a publishing company. However, there are critiques to privileging academic, published works. First, this process is long. The publication lag is generally at least one to two years. This means that topical research questions do not have much

Figure 4.1. Critical thinking. "UBC Learning Commons, Questions a Critical Thinker Asks," accessed 8 November 2022, https://learningcommons.ubc.ca/student-toolkits/thinking-critically/. Reproduced with permission.

scholarly, published literature available. Second, focusing on academic knowledge produced by publishers could exclude important perspectives from people who have less access to formal publishing opportunities. Researchers from a critical epistemological perspective, in particular, take issue with the way in which knowledge hierarchies reinforce values attached to dominant ways of knowing and doing. They argue that power relations within these publication processes exclude critical voices and perspectives, resulting in this knowledge being under-represented in the literature.

Ultimately, you have to decide on the quality of the information and the documents that you use in your research. This chapter, and the knowledge you gain through reading this book and taking your course, will help you to develop critical analysis skills to evaluate information you encounter in your research. Critical analysis is not simply about critiquing. Rather, it is about asking the right questions about all data and arguments you encounter to ensure the quality of the information. "Critical thinking consists of an awareness of a set of interrelated critical questions, plus the ability and willingness to ask and answer them at appropriate times."[7] As mentioned in the introduction, it is especially important to engage in critical analysis of arguments with which you agree because of confirmation bias.

Figure 4.1 on page 91 summarizes some key questions for critical thinking.

CONCLUSIONS AND KEY TAKEAWAYS

This chapter has introduced you to the main elements of research design. These include identifying a research puzzle and formulating it into a specific research question or hypothesis. You need to understand the methodological consequences of research involving causality and correlation as well as the implications of research across linguistic, geopolitical, and cultural borders. This chapter has helped you to identify the key components you need in your research and what you should expect to find in quality studies upon which you should base your work: namely, a conceptual and theoretical framework; methodological clarity; and acknowledgment of existing knowledge. Research is a creative process. The tools and principles in this chapter are not intended as prescriptive rules, but rather as resources to transform your ideas into meaningful, innovative knowledge to be shared.

QUESTIONS FOR REFLECTION AND DISCUSSION

1. To what extent does interdisciplinary research necessitate mixed methods?
2. How does critical analysis vary across borders? Are different questions needed?
3. What are the particular opportunities and challenges of privileging academic, published literature in cross-border research?

FURTHER READINGS

Day, Christopher, and Kendra L. Koivu. "Finding the Question: A Puzzle-Based Approach to the Logic of Discovery." *Journal of Political Science Education* 15, no. 3 (2019): 377–86. https://doi.org/10.1080/15512169.2018.1493594.

Hall, Johana, Mark Gaved, and Julia Sargent. "Participatory Research Approaches in Times of Covid-19: A Narrative Literature Review." *International Journal of Qualitative Methods* 20 (2021). https://doi.org/10.1177/16094069211010087.

McAvoy, Libby. "Centring the 'Source' in Open Source Investigation." Open Global Rights, 21 January 2021. https://www.openglobalrights.org/centering-the-source-in-open-source-investigation/.

Peltier, Cindy. "An Application of Two-Eyed Seeing: Indigenous Research Methods with Participatory Action Research." *International Journal of Qualitative Methods* 17, no. 1 (2018). https://doi.org/10.1177/1609406918812346.

Stoecker, Randy, and Elisa Avila. "From Mixed Methods to Strategic Research Design." *International Journal of Social Research Methodology* 24, no. 6 (2021): 627–40. https://doi.org/10.1080/13645579.2020.1799639.

Tomaszewski, Lesley Eleanor, Jill Zarestky, and Elsa Gonzalez. "Planning Qualitative Research: Design and Decision Making for New Researchers." *International Journal of Qualitative Methods* 19 (2020). https://doi.org/10.1177/1609406920967174.

Web Resources

Causality versus Correlation: https://www.youtube.com/watch?v=9tXsWOIIF2o.

Critical Thinking Toolbox: https://learningcommons.ubc.ca/student-toolkits/thinking-critically/#.

Zotero: https://www.zotero.org/.

Zotero Training: https://uottawa.libguides.com/how_to_use_zotero.

5

Measurement across Borders

LEARNING OBJECTIVES

By the end of this chapter, you will be able to:

- Explain the importance of measurement in research across borders;
- Identify conceptual and operational definitions;
- Distinguish between quantitative and qualitative measurement;
- Understand the opportunities and challenges of obtaining comparable statistical data across different countries; and,
- Develop critical analysis reflexes when encountering measurement.

KEY TERMS

Analytical framework   Measurability
Concept   Theory
Definition   Validity
  Conceptual   Variability
  Operational   Variable

INTRODUCTION

As discussed in chapter 4, a key methodological principle in all good research projects is to define your terms. This sounds pretty straightforward. However, in academic research, it is not as simple as looking up dictionary definitions. Rather, the fundamental question is how one is measuring complex concepts, such as security and development, especially given different world views and contexts globally. Even specific concepts like "child soldiers" are subject to debate, particularly in cross-border contexts with different political agendas and different ways of defining and counting the phenomenon under study. This chapter will introduce some key methodological principles related to measurement and will raise some questions to keep in mind when critically analysing international, cross-cultural research.

META-EXAMPLE: THE 300,000 QUESTION – A CAUTIONARY TALE

In 1996, Rachel Brett and Margaret McCallin published a book titled *Children: The Invisible Soldiers*. It was one of the first publications about the issue and was widely cited, especially one statistic: that there were 300,000 child soldiers worldwide. For decades, governments, the UN, and non-governmental organizations repeated this figure as if it were "fact." But, how could the number of child soldiers possibly stay the same year after year? Surely, as wars started and others ended, the number would fluctuate. And, the children themselves would grow older (and, therefore, no longer be children), be demobilized, be newly recruited, or die.

Why did people continue to use this number? Because there was no better alternative. Indeed, even in the original book, Brett and McCallin state, "The total number of child soldiers in each country, let alone the global figure, is not only unknown *but unknowable*."[1] There are many reasons why it was – and still is – difficult to get an accurate number of child soldiers. First, as will be discussed below, there are conceptual debates about who is a child, who is a soldier, and who is a child soldier. Second, international law prohibits the use of children as soldiers, so armed forces and groups are reluctant to admit that there are children in their ranks. Third, child soldiers live and work in conflict zones, which are hard for researchers to access (see also chapter 7).

The 300,000 figure was the authors' best guesstimate; an attempt to give a sense of the magnitude of the problem. But it was cited as "fact" without the important qualification that the number of child soldiers is *unknowable*.

Many of the topics that we study in cross-cultural and cross-border contexts are difficult – if not impossible – to measure. But, research is all about providing, at least attempting to, an approximation of complex phenomena. This is why definitions and measurement are key methodological issues.

In this chapter, we will draw on this example to explore a few key issues in relation to measurement across borders.

First, we will distinguish amongst everyday, conceptual and operational definitions. We will think about the ways in which taken-for-granted meanings may vary across cultural, linguistic, and geopolitical contexts and about how important it is for researchers to clearly define terms in a way that contextualizes and localizes these diverse perspectives.

Second, we need to think carefully about the abstraction and reduction of a complex phenomenon into variables, especially when these variables are then used for macro-comparative data analysis across very different cultural, economic, and geopolitical contexts.

Third, we need to understand how conceptual frameworks are linked to theory. While some of the issues that we study – such as children in armed conflict – arise out of practical or policy puzzles (see chapter 4), researchers need to think carefully about what Oliver Bakewell calls "research beyond the categories."[2] A solid analytical framework allows for critical reflections on data that go beyond "categories of practice"[3] (see below). Both conceptual and operational definitions need to be clearly aligned with the theoretical approach to enable a coherent framework for analysis.

DEFINITIONS: THE POETICS AND POLITICS OF LABELLING

Because definitional questions are so central to measurement, they are a building block of solid methodology. All researchers need to clearly define their terms. Continuing with the example of child soldiers, introduced earlier in this chapter, we will distinguish between many different kinds of definitions: everyday, conceptual, and operational.

Everyday Definitions

The topics that we study in international contexts are also usually a part of policy discussions, programing interventions, and media stories. In the course of our everyday lives outside of academia, we will have often heard terms and will have our own ideas of what they mean, sometimes based on our own experiences. These everyday meanings and definitions form part of what Brubaker and Cooper[4] call categories of practice.

In the child soldier example, many people, when they hear the word "child soldier," picture a small boy with a big gun. This boy is often racialized and in a country in the global south. These are the types of images that are also common in the media and are sometimes even portrayed on the covers of academic books.

Another category of practice when thinking about child soldiers is the ways in which governments, intergovernmental institutions, and non-governmental organizations define child soldiers. In some cases, these are codified in policies or laws. For example, in 2007, a group of states adopted *The Paris Principles: Principles and Guidelines on Children Associated with Armed Forces and Groups*, with the following definition of "child soldier": "A child associated with an armed force or armed group refers to any person below eighteen years of age who is, or who has been, recruited or used by an armed force or armed group in any capacity, including but not limited to children, boys, and girls used as fighters, cooks, porters, spies, or for sexual purposes."[5]

A final "everyday meaning" is found in dictionary definitions. The *Oxford English Dictionary* (OED) does not have a definition of "child soldier." It defines "child" as "A young person of either sex, usually one below the age of puberty; a boy or girl;"[6] and "soldier" as "One who serves in an army for pay; one who takes part in military service or warfare."[7]

While these popular, everyday definitions are helpful in understanding the way an issue is perceived, they are not generally accepted in scholarly research. This is because they are not always technically accurate. For example, the "boy with a gun" conception overlooks girls and children who play non-combatant roles, as per the policy definition above. The OED definition of "child" is not the same as the international legal definition, which is based on chronological age (under eighteen) rather than biological markers (puberty).

Moreover, everyday definitions do not provide the analytical framework necessary to measure the concept in quantitative or qualitative terms. Researchers must resist the urge to turn to Google or the dictionary as their first port of call and, instead, immerse themselves in the academic literature (see chapter 4) on the topic in order to understand conceptual and operational definitions.

Conceptual Definitions

This literature will help to identify the **conceptual definitions** – and debates – about a topic. **Concepts** are linked to **theory** – the way one views a topic (see chapters 1 and 4, and below) – and thus provide the analytical framework at the heart of measurement and the methods to achieve this measurement.

Conceptually, the term "child soldier" has three interlinked ideas: "child," "soldier," and "child soldier." Therefore, we would need to look at the academic literature on all three terms to understand the conceptual debates that underpin different definitions and measurements of the phenomenon of children participating in armed forces and groups. While a full exploration of the conceptual debates goes beyond the scope – and purpose – of this chapter, we will highlight some key findings here.

First, as alluded to in chapter 2, the conceptual debates are framed differently depending on the discipline. This is why it is important to make sure a diversity of disciplines is represented when we are researching complex, international issues. In the literature on child soldiers, we find contributions from law, sociology, anthropology, social work, psychology, economics, political science, and others.

For example, from a legal perspective, the conceptual debates revolve around the interpretation of key international and domestic laws and norms. A child is defined in the UN Convention on the Rights of the Child as a person under the age of eighteen. In contrast, the sociological and anthropological literature on childhood focuses mostly on social roles and relationships. Here, scholars critique the chronological definitions found in legal documents as inherently ethnocentric, important only in contexts organized by chronological time.

They point to other physical markers – such as puberty – and social markers – such as formal education and marriage – as more important ways to define childhood and adulthood in other contexts. There is also a large body of literature in the disciplines of medicine, psychology, and social work, which describes variations in human development based on genetics, environment, and social context.

As researchers and students working in cross-cultural and cross-border contexts, it is important to understand these different disciplinary perspectives on key concepts.

Second, the scholarly literature demonstrates the politicization of all three concepts. The distinction between childhood and adulthood determines access to formal political processes, such as voting and political representation. The size of a country's armed forces is a political and a security question. Since child soldiering is technically prohibited under international law, countries and non-state armed groups are sensitive about accusations of child soldiers in their ranks. Many of the topics we study in international contexts are sensitive, and the scholarly literature helps to uncover this politicization.

Finally, the academic literature highlights the complexity of the topic, and the consequent difficulties in measuring the phenomenon. In our child soldier example, the more we read, the more likely we are to question widely cited "facts" like the 300,000 number. In other words, understanding the conceptual debates sharpens our critical analysis skills.

Operational Definitions

Conceptual definitions thus provide important methodological and analytical foundations for research. However, in order to translate these abstract conceptual definitions into quantitative and qualitative measurement, we need to have clear operational definitions. To come up with operational definitions, it is useful to ask yourself the question "How will I know [insert concept] when I see it?" As Loseke explains, operationalization is "the process of deciding what particular data will indicate the presence of a particular concept."[8]

Operational definitions need to flow from the conceptual definition. For example, if a researcher's conceptual approach critiques the chronological definition of childhood, they cannot then rely on an operational definition of children as people under the age of eighteen. The operational definition would have to be linked to other physical (for example, puberty) or social (for example, education, marriage, or employment) markers.

Our definitions will then inform our data collection methods, as demonstrated in chapter 4. If we are interested in what people think or believe, or in their reported behaviour, then interview or survey data are useful (see chapter 8). If our operational definitions require information on actual (rather than reported) behaviour, then we need to include observation (see chapter 9). If the definitions require information on how people or phenomena are described and talked about, then textual analysis is important (see chapter 10).

Activity 5.1: Everyday, Conceptual, and Operational Definitions of "Armed Conflict"

1. Think about an everyday definition of armed conflict; for example, what you would find in a newspaper article.
2. How do you, as a researcher and a learner, define armed conflict?
3. Now, identify the conceptual and operational definitions in the following extract from the *UCDP/PRIO Armed Conflict Dataset Codebook*:

> We follow the definitions used by the Uppsala University Conflict Data Project: An armed conflict is a contested incompatibility that concerns government and/or territory where the use of armed force between two parties, of which at least one is the government of a state, results in at least 25 battle-related deaths.
>
> The separate elements of the definition are operationalized as follows:
>
> (1) Use of armed force: use of arms in order to promote the parties' general position in the conflict, resulting in deaths. (1.1) Arms: any material means, e.g. manufactured weapons but also sticks, stones, fire, water, etc.
>
> (2) 25 deaths: A minimum of 25 battle-related deaths per year and per incompatibility.
>
> (3) Party: A government of a state or any opposition organization or alliance of opposition organizations. (3.1) Government:

The party controlling the capital of the state. (3.2) Opposition organization: Any non-governmental group of people having announced a name for their group and using armed force.

(4) State: A state is: (4.1) an internationally recognized sovereign government controlling a specified territory, or (4.2) an internationally unrecognized government controlling a specified territory whose sovereignty is not disputed by another internationally recognized sovereign government previously controlling the same territory.

(5) Incompatibility concerning government and/or territory: The incompatibility, as stated by the parties, must concern government and/or territory. (5.1) Incompatibility: the stated generally incompatible positions. (5.2) Incompatibility concerning government: Incompatibility concerning the type of political system, the replacement of the central government, or the change of its composition. (5.3) Incompatibility concerning territory: Incompatibility concerning the status of a territory, e.g. the change of the state in control of a certain territory (interstate conflict), secession, or autonomy (internal conflict).[9]

4. Do you agree with these conceptual and operational definitions? Why or why not?

Operationalizing Concepts as Variables and Questions of Measurement

The child soldier example as well as the armed conflict activity above demonstrate the power – and the potential pitfalls – of operationalizing concepts as **variables**. "A variable is a type of concept, one that varies in amount or quality. A variable is something that it is possible to have more or less of, or something that exists in different 'states' or 'categories.'"[10] Variables help to translate abstract concepts – such as armed conflict – into something that can be observed and measured. Indeed, O'Sullivan et al. define a variable as "A measurable characteristic that can have more than one value."[11]

For example, in the armed conflict database described in Activity 5.1 above, one variable is "conflict type." In this database, the variable "conflict type" has four values: "interstate," "extrastate," "internal," and "internationalized internal."[12] Another variable, "intensity," is coded in three categories:

1. Minor: More than 25 battle-related deaths per year for every year in the period.
2. Intermediate: More than 25 battle-related deaths per year and a total conflict history of more than 1,000 battle-related deaths.
3. War: More than 1,000 battle-related deaths per year for every year in the period.[13]

Generally speaking, when a researcher chooses variables, they need to consider the following aspects:

- **Validity** is the degree to which the variable actually measures or represents the concept. For example, in the armed conflict database referenced above, some critique the use of quantitative measures of conflict-attributed deaths as the variable to represent "intensity." There is on-going debate about whether only those deaths that are "documented" and directly attributable to conflict adequately represent intensity, or whether indirect deaths that are due to the deterioration of health infrastructure and access, for example, should also be included.
- **Variability** – the variable must have different states or properties. For example, the intensity variable cited above is measured in three different states – "minor," "intermediate," and "war."
- **Measurability** – there has to be a way to observe and measure the amount or quality of a variable. For example, the intensity variable is measured by the number of battle-related deaths in a given year. In order to be counted, a death has to have been documented by an appropriate authority and be directly attributable to a specific conflict.

In terms of measuring variables, it is important to remember that measurement can be qualitative or quantitative. As discussed in chapter 4, quantitative measures attempt to quantify human behaviour, phenomena, structures, and relationships through the use of numbers, symbols, and statistics. Quantitative measurement is helpful to provide precise calculations, which can be comparable across contexts.

For example, in chapter 1, we saw the way that fragility could be measured and ranked. While quantitative measurements may be perceived to be "objective," they are not inherently so. As demonstrated by the child soldier example, at times quantitative measures are "best guesses" and not supported by a strong methodology. At other times, as demonstrated by the fragility example in chapter 1, different methodological approaches result in different quantitative measures.

In contrast, qualitative measures use verbal descriptions and explanations. They attempt to qualify human behaviour, phenomena, structures, and relationships through the use of words. The advantage of qualitative measurement is that it can capture complexity and nuance. The disadvantages are that there is limited comparability across qualitative measurement and that qualitative analysis is generally more time-consuming than quantitative analysis. While qualitative measures are sometimes perceived to be "subjective," they are no more so than quantitative measures.

Indeed, measurement is underpinned by definitional questions that are often subject to great debate. How one defines and operationalizes a concept will ultimately determine how one measures it. These definitional questions, therefore, bring a level of subjectivity and variation to *all measurement* – both quantitative and qualitative.

By reducing these complex human phenomena across borders to variables, the nuance and contextualization can be lost. In other words, the different parts do not necessarily "add up" to the whole phenomenon. The section below will highlight some of these challenges of measurement across borders.

Challenges of Measurement across Borders

Research across borders encounters multiple challenges of measurement that are both inherent in any research project and specific to international, cross-cultural, and interdisciplinary work. When operationalizing concepts, researchers encounter challenges when translating ideas into variables that can be measured quantitatively and/or qualitatively.

First, there are questions of meaning. As mentioned above, definitions inform measurement. However, in cross-cultural contexts, different world views may result in a multitude of meanings for the same thing. For example, as demonstrated in relation to "child soldier" above, the concept of childhood and who is a child is socially constructed. It therefore varies across cultural and geopolitical borders and intersects with religion, gender, ethnicity, (dis)ability, and so on. In some cases, languages do not have words for certain concepts. For example, "gender" is difficult to translate in many languages. In contrast, some languages have many words for a single word in other languages.

Second, the multidimensionality of many cross-border phenomena, such as development, colonization, racism, or environment, make them difficult to measure consistently. Researchers face the challenge of trying to find measurement tools that are comprehensive enough to cover the many different aspects of a global issue, while, at the same time, ensuring that it is practically possible to measure. This leads to methodological challenges and differences, as we saw in previous chapters in relation to fragility and democracy, for example, and in this chapter in relation to armed conflict (above) and development (below).

Third, measurement in cross-border research is complicated by imprecision and variability. Different national and sub-national governments often have different ways of measuring and collecting information. In some cases, state-level statistical organizations do not have the resources or the capacity to gather accurate information. In contexts of war, some parts of the country may be inaccessible for data collection. In other cases, measurement is subject to political interference or politicization.

These measurement challenges have implications for the validity and trustworthiness of the information collected. They also put into question the ability to accurately compare information globally across very different contexts.

Linking Theory and Concepts

The child soldier example above demonstrates that analysing real-world phenomena requires aligning conceptual and operational definitions with a clear theoretical framework to allow for coherent and consistent measurement across borders. Who "counts" as a child soldier depends on theoretical approaches to children and armed conflict as well as the roles that are deemed to be military. Indeed, there are debates about whether young people participating in violent organized crime should be included in statistics on child soldiers.

As Loseke notes, "Theories are interconnected concepts that condense and organize knowledge about the social world."[14] Etymologically, the word "theory" comes from the Greek *theōrein*, "to consider, speculate, or look at."[15] As a way of "looking at" a particular issue, theory is, therefore, instrumental in conceptualization and measurement as well as data analysis. While students often make the mistake of relegating theory to one section at the beginning of a paper, the theoretical framework should be consistently applied at all stages of research. This should be an iterative process, with adaptations to theory as needed, based on the measurement process and findings from data. Taken together, the theoretical approach along with the related concepts are referred to as the **analytical framework**. This is because theory, concepts, and measurement assist in interpreting and making sense of data and real-world events.

Because theory is, by definition, abstract, let's take a concrete example to show how theory is connected to measurement. Since the 1990s, one of the most influential theories of development is the "capabilities approach," developed by Amartya Sen.[16] In contrast to development theories that focus primarily on economic indicators, such as the Gross Domestic Product or income (the famous $1/day threshold for poverty), Sen argued that development should focus on expanding human "capabilities and thus enlarge the freedoms people have to lead valuable and flourishing lives."[17]

Unlike economic growth models, the capabilities approach is abstract and not obviously measurable. How can one move from the theory through concepts to variables? Interestingly, this has been done not only by academic researchers, but also by intergovernmental development agencies, such as the United Nations Development Program (UNDP) in their influential annual *Human Development Report* and through their Millennium Development Goals and, subsequently, the Sustainable Development Goals. In other words, theory can have practical implications for measurement, policy, and practice.

The theoretical idea of human capabilities was translated into practice in the following ways.

First, there was a theoretical shift from state- and economy-centred approaches to human-centred thinking about development: "The new idea of helping people, or individuals, out of dire poverty replaces the old idea of supporting countries that are historically disadvantaged in the global context."[18]

Second, Sen's theoretical approach to capabilities was translated into a concept. For example, it was conceptualized as follows in the UNDP *Human Development Report* from 2001: "The most basic capabilities for human development are to lead long and healthy lives, to be knowledgeable, to have access to the resources needed for a decent standard of living and to be able to participate in the life of the community."[19] This is a conceptual definition because it contains several components that remain abstract, such as knowledge and "a decent standard of living." While these concepts are clearly aligned with the capabilities theory, it is not immediately clear how a researcher could measure them.

Third, this conceptual definition was therefore operationalized into four clusters of variables – and international development goals – centred on (1) health and well-being; (2) education; (3) standard of living; and (4) participation.

There are, of course, critiques of the capability approach as well as of the way it has been adopted, adapted, and (mis-)applied to the Development Goals and other large-scale mainstream development policies. Indeed, the translation of any theory into practice inevitably leads to revisions to the theory and, in some cases, results in measurement and practical applications that differ from the original vision. As discussed throughout this chapter, measuring a complicated global phenomenon is inherently difficult, but our challenge as researchers is to try – and to document both the successes and the shortcomings of our conceptual and operational definitions.

Activity 5.2: Analysing a Theoretical and Conceptual Approach to Human Security

Now it's your turn to analyse how theory is connected to conceptual and operational definitions. In this activity, we will use the example of human security, developed by the Global Partnership for the Prevention of Armed Conflict (GPPAC). This example demonstrates that even non-academic researchers use theories, concepts, and measurement.

1. Watch this video: "What Is Human Security" (https://www
   .youtube.com/watch?v=BH5Jy1fTlvw).
2. Summarize the theory of human security proposed by GPPAC.
3. Identify the conceptual definition of human security.
4. Identify an operational definition from one of the three parts of
   the conceptual definition identified in question 3.
5. Answer the following questions: To what extent do you think this
   operational definition adequately aligns with both the conceptual
   definition and the theory of human security? Would you suggest
   any changes or additions to this operational definition?
6. Think about the measurement challenges identified in the section
   above in relation to this theoretical and conceptual approach to
   human security. What are some potential issues that the researchers would need to address?

CONCLUSIONS AND KEY TAKEAWAYS

In this chapter, we discussed the opportunities and challenges of measurement across borders. We saw how definitions and measurements
can become politicized and be taken out of context. Solid research begins
with a theoretical framework, which provides the lens through which
complex global phenomena are conceptualized and then operationalized as variables. Conceptual and operational definitions will inform the
way we approach the topic and how we do research about the topic. We
therefore need to carefully choose and deliberately define the terms we
use to describe and measure complex concepts, such as war, development, and migration. This is particularly the case in cross-cultural and
multilingual environments where "words used to label concepts carry
with them entire systems of meaning."[20] We also need to be clear about
the limitations inherent in any measurement process and avoid over-
simplifying cross-border phenomena that are sometimes "unknowable."

QUESTIONS FOR DISCUSSION AND REFLECTION

1. What are some common terms in your field of study? Think about
   the different everyday, conceptual, and operational definitions of
   these terms.

2. Should researchers attempt to quantify cross-border issues that are "unknowable," such as transnational crime, undocumented migration, and child soldiering? What is the purpose of these numbers?

3. Think about some culturally specific words that don't translate into English as noted in this article: "10 of the Best Words in the World (That Don't Translate into English)" (https://www .theguardian.com/world/2018/jul/27/10-of-the-best-words-in -the-world-that-dont-translate-into-english). What do these words tell you about qualitative localized meanings in these contexts?

4. What is gained and lost in the operationalization of human security theories and the capabilities approach explored in this chapter?

FURTHER READINGS

Bennett, Kevin J., Tyrone F. Borders, George M. Holmes, Katy Backes Kozhimannil, and Erika Ziller. "What Is Rural? Challenges and Implications of Definitions That Inadequately Encompass Rural People and Places." *Health Affairs* 38, no. 12 (2019): 1985–92. https://doi.org /10.1377/hlthaff.2019.00910.

Collins, Christopher S., and Carrie M. Stockton. "The Central Role of Theory in Qualitative Research." *International Journal of Qualitative Methods* 17, no. 1 (2018). https://doi.org/10.1177/1609406918797475.

Grek, Sotiria, and Christian Ydesen. "Where Science Met Policy: Governing by Indicators and the OECD's INES Programme." *Globalisation, Societies and Education* 19, no. 2 (2021): 122–37. https://doi.org/10.1080/14767724 .2021.1892477.

Walter, Maggie, and Michele Suina. "Indigenous Data, Indigenous Methodologies and Indigenous Data Sovereignty." *International Journal of Social Research Methodology* 22, no. 3 (2019): 233–43. https://doi.org/10 .1080/13645579.2018.1531228.

Yousefi Nooraie, Reza, Joanna E.M. Sale, Alexandra Marin, and Lori E. Ross. "Social Network Analysis: An Example of Fusion between Quantitative and Qualitative Methods." *Journal of Mixed Methods Research* 14, no. 1 (2020): 110–24. https://doi.org/10.1177/1558689818804060.

Web Resource

Armed Conflict Dataset Codebook: https://www.prio.org/Global/upload /CSCW/Data/UCDP/v2/codebook_v2_0.pdf.

Case Studies in Global Context

LEARNING OBJECTIVES

By the end of this chapter, you will be able to:

- Define and identify case studies;
- Describe and identify different epistemological approaches to case studies and their methodological implications;
- Analyse the opportunities and challenges of selecting cases at the same unit of analysis across borders;
- Understand the opportunities and limitations of case studies in cross-border research;
- Explain the pros and cons of case selection of single and multiple case studies; and,
- Understand the ways in which life stories are used in research across borders and across cultural contexts.

KEY TERMS

Analytic generalization	Life story or narrative
Case studies	Longitudinal
Life history	Unit of analysis

INTRODUCTION

The use of case studies is a common methodological approach in cross-border, cross-cultural research. Because of the complexity of the phenomena under study, using cases – or examples – helps researchers to "drill down" to the specifics of a particular context and/or to compare across these different cases. A **case study** is an in-depth, often **longitudinal**, examination and analysis of one or more units of analysis. The latter can be individuals, events, entities (such as organizations, social groups, neighbourhoods, cities, countries, or regions), policies, decisions, programs, and so on.

This chapter will introduce case studies as a methodological approach and show how the role of case studies in research design depends on the researcher's epistemological approach. In essence, the researcher's approach to case studies varies depending on whether the case(s) is intended to demonstrate broader trends or to contextualize and enrich understanding of the particular case(s). In this chapter, we will discuss the rationale for single versus multiple case studies and think about the opportunities and challenges of comparing cases across borders and world views.

Pro Tip: Some students find it useful to replace the word "case study" with "example."

META-EXAMPLE: "EXPORTING" MICROCREDIT AND IMPLICATIONS FOR GENDER

In 2006, Professor Muhammad Yunus and the Grameen Bank he founded were jointly awarded the Nobel Peace Prize "for their efforts to create economic and social development from below."[1] The Grameen Bank, established by Yunus in Bangladesh, was based on the idea of microcredit (sometimes called microlending): small loans to people who did not have the financial means to provide collateral for the loans. Microcredit loans are unsecured financially – although sometimes there are group incentives to repay – and are accompanied by training in financial literacy and entrepreneurship.

Based on the success of the Grameen Bank, which saw high levels of loan repayment, as well as the publicity afforded by the Nobel Prize, microcredit programs were introduced in many other contexts where poverty had historically prevented access to credit, limiting the entrepreneurship of people living in poverty. However, in some cases, these microcredit programs did not see the same levels of successful repayment and/or did not improve, and in some cases worsened, the financial outcomes of borrowers.[2] What explains the variation across these case studies?

There is also debate about the impacts of the microcredit programs on gender equality. The majority of Grameen Bank recipients were women. "Advocates of microcredit programs argue that the empowerment of women as economic actors will benefit women by enhancing their economic and political power and, in doing so, will make the societies in which they live more equitable politically and more competitive economically."[3] However, the gendered outcomes of microcredit programs vary across case studies. They also vary depending on women's positionality, experiences, and stories.

This meta-example demonstrates several important points about case studies, which we will explore throughout this chapter.

First, how a researcher uses one or more case studies in their research design depends on their epistemological approach. In the first section below, I show how different researchers have approached microcredit work and the implications for their methodology and research conclusions.

Second, the **unit of analysis** depends on one's perception of borders (see chapter 1) and the conceptual framework (see chapter 5) within which the research is framed. Whether one chooses a case at the individual, community, country, or regional level also depends on the research question. In the last section, we will talk about life stories as case studies at the individual level.

Third, and related to the two previous points, is the question of whether examples of "success" can be exported across borders. The microcredit example is symptomatic of many other development approaches and policies that work well in one place, and therefore provide the impetus for replication in others. Thus, research based on case studies has broader implications for policy and practice.

EPISTEMOLOGICAL APPROACHES TO CASE STUDIES ACROSS BORDERS

Using case studies is a methodological approach, not a data collection method. Therefore, how a researcher conceptualizes case studies and uses them in their research design depends on the epistemological approach. In general, there are differences amongst positivists who use case studies to demonstrate patterns or principles; constructivists who use case studies to explore the complexities and richness of phenomena; critical researchers who attend to power relations in the construction of case studies and their use to undermine or perpetuate power asymmetries; and Indigenous world views that are place-based and thus contextualize case studies within specific, localized ways of being and knowing. Let's look at each one of these in turn, with an example from the microcredit literature.

Positivist Approach to Case Studies

Positivist researchers use case studies in order to test hypotheses. These hypotheses can come from the existing literature – that is, using a previously tested hypothesis on one or more new cases. Or, researchers can propose a new hypothesis with one or more exploratory case studies if there is not enough existing literature.

Through a case study (or studies), a positivist researcher is aiming at **analytic generalization**: "previously developed theory is used as a tem-

---

For example, researchers empirically tested the hypothesis that microcredit improves well-being by focusing on a case study of an urban microcredit program in Zambia. They found that "borrowers who obtained a second loan experienced significantly higher average growth in business profits and household income. Inflexible group enforcement of loan obligations resulted in some borrowers, especially amongst those who had taken only one loan, being made worse off."*

* Copestake, Bhalotra, and Johnson, "Assessing the Impact of Microcredit," 81.

plate with which to compare the empirical results of the case study."[4] Similar to the logic of scientific experimentation, the idea is that if two or more cases are shown to prove a certain hypothesis (and especially if they refute the counter-hypothesis), then replication can be claimed.

As Yin explains, "Analytic generalization may be defined as a two-step process. The first involves a conceptual claim whereby investigators show how their case study findings bear upon a particular theory, theoretical construct, or theoretical (not just actual) sequence of events. The second involves applying the same theory to implicate other, similar situations where analogous events also might occur."[5] In the example above, researchers first tested the degree to which microcredit improved well-being for participants in a particular Zambian program. The next step in analytical generalization would be to compare this to other, similar programs in Zambia and in other countries to see if the same conditions produced similar well-being outcomes.

> *Pro Tip*: Case studies can only be used for analytic generalization, not statistical generalization, which requires random sampling (see below on case selection and chapter 7 on sampling).

Positivists use case studies as examples that, together, make up patterns of human behaviour. The idea is to try to build up a series of cases that show trends or general principles. Postitivist researchers are not interested so much in the specifics of the case per se, but rather in what the case says about broader social laws and comparability across international contexts.

Constructivist Approach to Case Studies

In contrast to the analytical generalizability to which positivists aspire through case studies, constructivist researchers use case studies to demonstrate the richness and the context-specificity of complex global phenomenon. Instead of "reducing cases to instances of a general law,"[6] the constructivist approach to case studies attempts to connect cases to others to show linkages. In this way, cases inform theory through iterative, inductive approaches, rather than starting with a hypothesis that is proved or disproved by the case(s). Moreover, recognizing the reflexivity (see chapter 3) and intersubjectivity of both the researcher and the participants, constructivists recognize the uniqueness of each case study's construction. In this way, constructivists believe that comparability across case studies is inherently limited.

> For example, Isabelle Guérin undertook long-term field-work with people involved in microcredit programs in rural South India to understand their "lived experience of micro-credit as debt." Rather than attempting to assess the impact of microcredit on participants' economic outcomes and well-being, this study explored "how microcredit is used, experienced, signified, and interrelated to other forms of debt." Compared to the positivist example above, this study is more descriptive and contextualized.*
>
> * Guérin, "Juggling with Debt, Social Ties, and Values."

Critical Approach to Case Studies

From a critical epistemological approach, case studies are embedded in power asymmetries in the production of knowledge. Like constructivists, researchers from a critical epistemological perspective do not aim to prove or disprove a particular hypothesis, or to generalize. Instead, case studies serve to expose, and attempt to address, inequalities in research.

> For example, researchers worked with ten landless labourers in a village they named Arampur (Bangladesh) to explore experiences with microcredit through community-based oral testimony.* They trained the labourers in research and developed a "cooperative research agenda that mapped to specific concerns within the village" (Cons

and Paprocki, 637). The purpose was not simply to understand the power relations within microcredit programs, but
also to enable community-based responses.

* Cons and Paprocki, "Contested Credit Landscapes."

Indigenous Epistemologies and Case Studies

Case studies rooted in Indigenous approaches to knowledge privilege relationship-building within particular culturally specific practices and spaces. The value of the case study approach lies in the
preservation of knowledge and in reciprocal efforts of knowledge
exchange.

For example, a case study of Warmi Sayasunqo, an Indigenous microcredit organization in the Andean Altiplano of
Argentina, explored "the ways in which efforts to reconcile
debts come to configure both the microcredit practices of
Warmi as well as struggles over Indigenous rights and recognition in Argentina."* The research showed that "Warmi
leadership envisioned their obligation to borrowers in
terms of identity recuperation and community strengthen-
ing" within social relationships (Schuster, 47). The authors
suggest that "reconciliation through lending keeps bor-
rower and creditor on intimate terms, which serves as a
valuable counterpoint to transaction-based audit processes" (47).

* Schuster, "Reconciling Debt," 47.

Activity 6.1: Comparing Approaches to Case Studies

Read the following two examples of projects that use multiple case
studies on internal conflicts.

1. Explain the difference between the positivist and constructivist approach to case studies using these examples.
2. Think about how researchers from critical and Indigenous epistemologies would conduct case study research on this topic. How would their approaches be similar and different from these examples?

EXAMPLE: MINORITIES AT RISK PROJECT*

Established by Ted Robert Gurr in 1986 and now based at the University of Maryland, the Minorities at Risk Project analyses the status and conflicts of more than 284 communal groups around the world. Underlying the data collection for these case studies is a positivist attempt at comparability and generalizability. There are also explicit attempts to mitigate against selection bias (see the case study selection section below).

EXAMPLE: BEYOND INTRACTABILITY CASE STUDIES**

An example of the constructivist approach to case studies can be seen in Beyond Intractability. This is a research project that acts as a repository of knowledge on conflict in various contexts. The researchers' approach to case studies is inherently inductive and context-specific. They also privilege submissions from "citizens of the countries about which they wrote and/or peacebuilders who had worked in these countries" (Beyond Intractability, par. 2). The idea is to privilege intimate and in-depth knowledge about particular places and conflicts, rather than try to generalize across different contexts.

* Minorities at Risk Project, accessed 10 November 2022, http://www.mar.umd.edu.
** Beyond Intractability, accessed 10 November 2022, https://www.beyondintractability.org/library/case-studies.

CASE STUDY SELECTION

The selection of case studies is a key methodological question in case study approaches. Case study selection varies depending on one's research question, on whether other cases are already covered in the existing literature, on the scope of the research, and on the epistemological approach.

Single Cases. Choosing a single case study is one way of narrowing down the scope of a research question or hypothesis (see chapter 4). By limiting the research to one example, the researcher can devote more time and resources to in-depth examination.

A single case study can be used for one or more of the following methodological reasons:

- Revelatory case: the researcher has access to a previously under-studied population or phenomenon. For example, in the early stages of microcredit, the Grameen Bank was a revelatory case because it presented a "new" way of thinking about microcredit.
- Longitudinal case: the same case is studied over a long period of time to see how conditions change.
- Extreme or unique case: the example reveals rare circumstances or characteristics that are not widespread or that have the potential to provide a new way to test a hypothesis (positivist) or to understand a phenomenon (constructivist or critical).
- Research relationships: The case study builds on existing relationships with a particular community (Indigenous approach).

Multiple Cases. The selection of multiple cases poses several methodological questions.

First, a researcher needs to ensure that they have the time and resources to study each case in the same level of depth. Generally speaking, the more cases in a study, the less detail there is on each one. Quantity will result in a reduction of quality.

Second, case studies need to be selected at the same unit of analysis. However, there is debate about whether some units lend themselves to comparability. For example, as discussed in chapter 1, in international contexts, countries are often used as the unit of analysis. But countries vary greatly by size (e.g., Republic of Nauru vs. Russia), population (e.g., Liechtenstein vs. China), geography, economic development, political organization, and so on. Moreover, in federal states, sometimes sub-national governments have jurisdiction over certain issues, such as education or healthcare. In the microcredit examples above, while each country is included in the title of the article, the unit of analysis is actually sub-national.

The unit of analysis in case studies can also be:

- Village or community
- City
- Organization
- Project
- Individual

Third, case selection is vulnerable to accusations of selection bias, or what is colloquially known as "cherry picking." Unlike random sampling (see chapter 7), cases are selected for specific reasons. A researcher needs to have a logical, research-based explanation for why each case is chosen and for the limits of comparability across the cases. This is particularly important in positivist approaches, where the researcher is attempting analytical generalization.

For example, Gwendolyn Tedeschi identifies two potential sources of selection bias in microcredit impact assessments.[7] First, there is self-selection bias: "the possibility that microentrepreneurs who borrow may have unobservable traits, such as more entrepreneurial ability, that would make them more likely to have higher levels of the impact variables, even without access to credit."[8] This is problematic if the unit of analysis is the individual. We will return to this question in chapter 7 on sampling. Second, if the unit of analysis is the community (as in the examples above), "undocumented village-level differences, such as prices, infrastructure, or cultural attributes may influence the demand for and use of credit."[9] This relates back to issues of comparability across units of analysis, as discussed above.

Activity 6.2: Analysing Case Studies in Microcredit Research

1. For each of the case study examples of microcredit research above, identify the unit of analysis.
2. What are the advantages and disadvantages of using this unit of analysis?

3. Could the research presented above be compared? Why or why not?

4. What are the potential sources of selection bias in the examples above? In which studies are they more important? Why?

LIMITS OF CASE STUDIES

Indeed, for positivists, the limited generalizability of case studies is one of the main weaknesses of this methodological approach. As George and Bennett argue, "case study researchers generally sacrifice the parsimony and broad applicability of their theories to develop cumulatively contingent generalizations that apply to well-defined types or subtypes of cases with a high degree of explanatory richness."[10]

Here, it is important to return to the caution that case studies can only ever result in analytic generalization, rather than statistical generalization. As we will see in chapter 7, statistical generalization requires random sampling. But, case studies are not randomly sampled; they are chosen for specific characteristics, as explained in the section on case study selection above. Indeed, as Tedeschi points out, micro-credit programs are located in communities based on need and programatic reasons, rather than through a random selection. Therefore, even if one chose such programs randomly, there would still be an inherent bias.

Because case studies cannot be used for statistical generalization, they can also not be used to prove causality. This then poses questions about the ways in which "success stories" in one context are often "exported" across borders. If we cannot definitively prove causality, the justification for such replication is therefore called into question.

Case studies are sometimes dismissed as anecdotal evidence, especially when compared to macro-comparative statistics, where statistical relationships can be measured. However, case studies do allow for in-depth understanding and analysis of the unit of study.

LIFE STORIES

When the unit of analysis is the individual, the case study may involve one or more life histories or narratives. A **life history** is a "retrospective account by the individual of his [or her] life in whole or in part, in written or oral form, *that has been elicited or prompted by another person.*"[11] A **life story or narrative** is a broader term that does not necessarily involve chronology implied by life "history."

Scholars in international contexts have historically documented the lives and experiences of "great people" who famously changed the course of history. However, there is a recent trend towards life stories of ordinary people. These stories can be powerful ways to illustrate the complexity of lived experiences of forced migration, poverty, conflict, and other multidimensional phenomena. Because they are in-depth, they can provide rich contextual details that deepen understandings.

Life stories resonate with world views that validate oral history and honour ancestors. For example, in many Indigenous cultures, one always starts by introducing one's place, family, group, and position within that group. Narratives are also central to many Indigenous methodologies. As Coast Salish scholar Jo-ann Archibald explains, "The words *story* and *work* together signal the importance and seriousness of undertaking the educational and research work of making meaning through stories, whether they are tradition or lived experience stories. Seven principles comprise storywork: respect, responsibility, reverence, reciprocity, wholism, interrelatedness, and synergy."[12]

In global, cross-cultural contexts, several factors need to be taken into consideration when engaging in life story research. First, as discussed in relation to case selection more broadly above, the experiences of one or a few individuals cannot represent everyone's experience of complex phenomena. Representivity is limited, so findings from these case studies cannot be generalized to all people living in that context. Second, because life stories provide detailed information about the individual(s), anonymity cannot be guaranteed, even if the researcher uses a pseudonym. Careful consideration about the possible consequences of the research findings, including reprisals against the individual and people in their families and communities, is essential. Third, who owns the life story? While it is obviously the respondent's story, traditionally, researchers are the ones who have most benefited from the dissemination of the life story. This has sometimes resulted in accusations of appropriation, especially given unequal power relations in the production of knowledge and global inequalities. In some cases, co-authorship is used to address this issue. Finally, a related issue is representation – both for the subject of the life story and the people in their networks. What happens when people do not like the way they have been portrayed in the narratives? We will return to some of these points in chapter 12 on dissemination.

CONCLUSIONS AND KEY TAKEAWAYS

Case studies provide rich, detailed insights. Their strength is the depth and breadth of analysis, rather than their ability to generalize. Positivists use case studies to test hypotheses to see if they hold true across different cases. Researchers from constructivist, critical, and Indigenous epistemologies use case studies as examples to illustrate a context-specific phenomenon. Research across borders complicates the selection of units of analysis as well as the comparability of cases across very different geopolitical, economic, cultural, and social contexts.

QUESTIONS FOR REFLECTION AND DISCUSSION

1. What unit of analysis is most common in your field of study? What are some of the strengths and weaknesses of using this unit of analysis? How would research be different if another unit of analysis were chosen?
2. Life stories cannot be generalized. What purposes could they be used for in your area of study? What are some of the methodological and ethical challenges of using life stories?
3. International policymakers often want to find an example of a "good practice" that can be replicated in other communities and countries. How can case studies be used to support this work? What are some of the limitations?

FURTHER READINGS

Archibald, Jo-ann. "An Indigenous Storywork Methodology." In *Handbook of the Arts in Qualitative Research: Perspectives, Methodologies, Examples, and Issues*, edited by J. Gary Knowles and Ardra L. Cole, 371–93. Los Angeles: Sage Publications, 2008.

Harrison, Helena, Melanie Birks, Richard Franklin, and Jane Mills. "Case Study Research: Foundations and Methodological Orientations." *Forum Qualitative Sozialforschung/Forum: Qualitative Social Research* 18, no. 1 (2017): 19. https://doi.org/10.17169/fqs-18.1.2655.

Onghena, Patrick, Bea Maes, and Mieke Heyvaert. "Mixed Methods Single Case Research: State of the Art and Future Directions." *Journal of Mixed Methods Research* 13, no. 4 (2019): 461–80. https://doi .org/10.1177/1558689818789530.

Robards, Brady, and Siân Lincoln. "Uncovering Longitudinal Life Narratives: Scrolling Back on Facebook." *Qualitative Research* 17, no. 6 (2017): 715–30. https://doi.org/10.1177/1468794117700707.

Walton, Janet B., Viki L. Plano Clark, Lori A. Foote, and Carla C. Johnson. "Navigating Intersecting Roads in a Mixed Methods Case Study: A Dissertation Journey." *Journal of Mixed Methods Research* 14, no. 4 (2020): 436–55. https://doi.org/10.1177/1558689819872422.

Web Resources

Beyond Intractability: https://www.beyondintractability.org/library/case -studies.

Minorities at Risk Project: http://www.mar.umd.edu.

7

Sampling, Access, and Representation across Borders

LEARNING OBJECTIVES

By the end of this chapter, you will be able to:

- Define and identify key terms related to sampling;
- Explain the principles of representivity and generalizability in sampling, and identify them in cross-border research;
- Understand the difference between random and non-random sampling;
- Identify key random and non-random sampling methods and their advantages and disadvantages;
- Analyse methodological challenges related to sampling in international, cross-cultural contexts;
- Identify opportunities and challenges to accessing populations in cross-border, cross-cultural contexts; and,
- Understand how language and interpretation are related to sampling.

KEY TERMS

Access
Confidence interval

Confidence level
Generalizability

Population
Probability sampling
Representivity
Sample
Sampling
   Cluster or Area random
     sampling
   Convenience sampling

Non-random sampling
Quota sampling
Random (or probability)
   sampling
Respondent-driven sampling
Simple random sampling
Snowball (or chain) sampling
Sampling frame

INTRODUCTION

Because of logistical constraints, such as time and money, it is usually not possible to conduct research with every person, institution, document, or object that is related to your research question. Therefore, researchers use sampling to identify a subset of the phenomenon or group they are studying.

This chapter introduces the key methods of random and non-random sampling and then explains how methodological challenges may arise in international, cross-cultural contexts, such as sampling mobile populations, people who do not have formal legal status, and people living in conflict zones. It highlights power relations in accessing populations who are subject to control by gatekeepers, such as local authorities, governments, and international organizations.

It also raises other issues that may inhibit access in international contexts, such as security, immigration controls, seasonal weather patterns, and periods of intense political activity, such as election campaigns. Linguistic barriers will be addressed, as well as the pros and cons of using interpreters.

Pro Tip: Make sure you understand sampling terminology, as some words have a technical meaning that is different from everyday understandings.

Population: The totality of the elements representing the topic under study. In sampling, the population is *not necessarily human*. The population can be human beings, but can also be documents, countries, conflicts, organizations, and/or other inanimate units of analysis.

Sample: A subset of the population that is selected to be in the study.

Sampling: The process by which a researcher selects units of the population to be in the sample. Sampling can either be random or non-random.

Sampling frame: A list of elements in the population from which a sample is drawn.

Here is an example: Imagine that we are interested in studying how publicly funded elementary schools in the US register students who are not US citizens. In this case, the population is elementary schools in the US. It would be very costly and time-consuming for a researcher to visit every elementary school in the country. So, we would need a sampling frame, such as a list of public schools provided by the National Center for Education Statistics. From this sampling frame, we could use **random sampling** to select a subset of public elementary schools to make up our sample.

META-EXAMPLE: PUBLIC HEALTH RESEARCH WITH PEOPLE WITHOUT FORMAL MIGRATION STATUS

Researchers in the US wanted to conduct a study with undocumented Latinx immigrants who were living in the US to assess the impact of this precarious immigration status on mental and physical health outcomes. This information was intended to improve their health and provide recommendations for programing, advocacy, and policy. However, identifying, accessing, and recruiting participants for the study proved difficult due to "heightened immigration enforcement, [. . .] poor understanding of the research process, reluctance to disclose legal status, fear of stigmatization and/or retaliation, and demanding lifestyles and work schedules."[1] In public health, as in positivist approaches, simple random sampling is considered the "gold standard" for generalizing results. However, this kind of random sampling requires a sampling frame – or a list of all units in the population – that is obviously not possible with people who are not officially documented.

How could the researchers get an adequate sample without a list of the total population in "extremely conservative areas with substantial Immigration and Custom Enforcement (ICE) presence, and strong opposition/punitive actions against UIs [undocumented immigrants]"?[2] In this study, they used **respondent-driven sampling** (RDS). This is a sampling methodology where initial participants are asked to assist in recruiting other potential participants. Because it uses "a mathematical model of the social networks that connect participants in a study,"[3] it is considered statistically representative, so the results can be generalized to all undocumented Latinx in the areas studied.

While technically representative, to what extent can RDS – or any sample, which is by definition a subset of a population – truly represent the diversity of experiences of people living in fear of deportation? Moreover, there are ethical issues in relying on respondents to identify other respondents, including power relations which can undermine consent. In this example, each participant was given $10 for each person they recruited who completed the study. This means that there were incentives to convince people to participate, potentially undermining voluntary, informed consent. Ethical questions also remain because people who referred participants know who took part in the study, calling into question confidentiality and making anonymity impossible. Given that people without official immigration papers are at risk of deportation, the methodological benefits of RDS need to be weighed against the risks to informed consent and confidentiality.

This example demonstrates several important lessons related to sampling, access, and representation, which we will explore further in this chapter.

First, sampling methodology is important because it affects the representivity of the sample and the generalizability of the results. Generally speaking, the results from random samples – like the one in this example – can be generalized to the population from which the sample is drawn. However, even in random sampling, there is always a self-selection bias because of the requirement of voluntary, informed consent. Even if someone is randomly selected for a study, they cannot be forced to participate, thereby undermining the representivity of the sample. The risk of self-selection bias is increased when working on sensitive topics, as in this example.

Second, sampling methods are determined by one's research question and the available information about the population. While random sampling is often privileged, especially within positivist research, it is not always possible nor desirable.

Third, in research across borders, researchers often encounter challenges of access to both information about the population in the study and access to the people, institutions, or documents they want to include their research. In this example, access issues included legal precarity, language, time constraints, and lack of familiarity with research.

Fourth, sampling poses ethical issues in terms of private information and representation. These issues are exacerbated when outside researchers with little knowledge of power relationships are involved and/or when participants are involved in sampling, as in this example.

WHY IS SAMPLING METHODOLOGY IMPORTANT? PRINCIPLES OF REPRESENTIVITY AND GENERALIZABILITY

Sampling methodology – *how* a researcher selects a sample – is important because it determines what one can say about the sample and its relationship to the population. In sampling, there are two key principles:

- **Representivity** is the degree to which the sample represents the diversity of the population. It is usually a good idea to think about who or what may be excluded from the sample.
- **Generalizability** is the ability to extrapolate findings from the sample and apply them to the whole population.

In random sampling, every element of the population has a known and non-negligible chance – which can be calculated statistically – of being selected for the sample. Therefore, a random sample is *statistically representative* of the population, so results from the study can be generalized to the population from which the sample is drawn.

Random sampling is also known as **probability sampling** because one can measure the probability that a unit in a population will be selected for the sample. It is also possible to measure the probability that the results obtained from the sample are statistically representative. The **confidence interval**, sometimes called the margin of error, is a quantitative indicator of the certainty of the results. It is expressed as a number with the sign "+/-". This means that the results are believed to be accurate within this range.

The **confidence level**, expressed as a fraction or a percentage, measures the probability that the results are valid. In social sciences, normally a minimum of 95 per cent is required, while a minimum confidence level of 99 per cent is more generally accepted in medicine and natural sciences.

In **non-random sampling**, the relationship between the sample and the population is unknown. Therefore, representativity cannot be proven, and generalizations cannot be made from the sample. However, results from a non-random sample can still be used to disprove a generalization.

Let us return to the example in the first section of public school access for non-citizens. If the researcher randomly samples from the list of public schools, then results from the sample can be generalized to the whole population of public schools.

However, if the researcher uses a non-random sampling methodology – such as selecting schools which are known to have pro-active recruitment of non-citizen children – the results of the study cannot be generalized to all public schools. That being said, findings could be used to disprove a generalization. For example, imagine that there is a general consensus that public schools all require proof of residence for school registration. If the researcher finds even one example of a school that does not require proof of residence in their non-random sample, then they can use this finding to disprove the generalization that all schools require proof of residence.

Activity 7.1: Sampling Methodology and Terminology

Consider the following excerpt from the newspaper story "Poll: Most Americans Support a Path to Citizenship for Undocumented Immigrants" by Nicole Narea:

> With the White House and Congress now under their control, Democrats are hoping to legalize at least some of the estimated 10.5 million undocumented immigrants living in the US – a long-sought goal that Americans largely support.

A new poll conducted January 29 to February 1 by Vox and Data for Progress (DFP) found that a majority of 1,124 likely voters and an overwhelming proportion of Democrats "strongly" or "somewhat" supported offering a path to citizenship for undocumented immigrants broadly (69 percent and 86 percent, respectively). That support jumps to 72 percent of likely voters and 87 percent of Democrats if you ask them specifically about "DREAMers" who were brought to the US as children. Those findings are consistent with other recent surveys on legalization, including one conducted by Pew in June 2020.[4]

The poll referenced is from Data for Progress:

From January 29 to February 1, 2021, Data for Progress conducted a survey of 1,124 likely voters nationally using web panel respondents. The sample was weighted to be representative of likely voters by age, gender, education, race, and voting history. The survey was conducted in English. The margin of error is ±2.9 percentage points.[5]

In this example:

1. Identify the sample.
2. Identify the population.
3. Identify the sampling frame.
4. Identify the confidence interval.
5. To what degree is the sample representative of the population?
6. Is the title of this newspaper article accurate? Why or why not?

TYPES OF RANDOM AND NON-RANDOM SAMPLING

Because random samples are statistically representative and can be generalized, researchers generally prefer random sampling. However, not all methods of random sampling produce equally reliable samples; biases can be introduced in all sampling methods, and there could be methodological or ethical reasons why random sampling is not the preferred method for some research questions or populations.

In this section, we will discuss the main methods of sampling as well as the methodological challenges that may arise in cross-border, cross-cultural contexts.

The most basic form of random sampling is called **simple random sampling**. In this method, the researcher starts with a sampling frame and assigns a number to each unit in the sampling frame. They then use computer software – or, less technically, a hat – to randomly select numbers to identify the units that will be in their sample.

For simple random sampling, one requires **access** to a reliable sampling frame. This poses particular challenges for research across borders.

First, traditional sampling frames – such as telephone directories, electoral rolls, and census data – may be biased or incomplete. For example, mobile populations, homeless people, and non-citizens are often excluded from these formal sampling frames. When thinking about the sampling frame, it is important to consider who is excluded from these lists.

Second, as alluded to in chapter 5, in some countries, national statistic-collecting bodies lack capacity, do not have access to all areas, or are politicized. This results in incomplete or inaccurate sampling frames.

For example, administrative barriers to birth registration of Syrian children in Jordan results in under-reporting of young populations and statelessness. Under Syrian law, nationality is claimed through the father. This poses a problem for female-headed households. In Jordan, parents must present a marriage certificate in order to register the birth of their child. The Jordanian state does not recognize informal Sheikh marriages, resulting in both an under-reporting of marriages and births. This means that many Syrian children born in Jordan will not appear on lists.*

* "Syrian Refugees in Jordan."

Third, as demonstrated in the meta-example above, no sampling frames exist for certain populations who are undocumented or engaged in activities that are criminalized.

When no sampling frame exists, researchers sometimes rely on other random sampling methods, including respondent-driven sampling, as in the meta-example above. Another option is **cluster or area random sampling** that involves identifying clusters of geographic or social groups. These clusters can be randomly sampled, and then units within these clusters can be randomly sampled.

In their article "Comparison of Two Cluster Sampling Methods for Health Surveys in Developing Countries," the authors note that the World Health Organization's Expanded Program on Immunization (EPI) is used to estimate vaccine coverage in low-income communities where there is no reliable sampling frame. In this program, "30 communities (clusters) are selected with probability proportional to the most recent census estimate of the community population size, by systematic selection from a list of cumulative population sizes. In each selected cluster, the interview team starts at a central point, selects a random direction from that point, and chooses a dwelling at random among those along the line from the centre to the edge of the community. All children in the household in the age range 12–23 months are selected and the mother or caregiver interviewed (all households are visited in a multi-household dwelling). Starting from this household, the next nearest household is visited in turn until at least seven children have been found." This is a random sampling method because "clusters are selected with probability proportional to estimated size (ppes), households are selected with approximately equal (but unknown) probability, and all eligible children in a household are selected." Therefore "the overall probability of any child being selected is roughly equal, and the design is approximately self-weighting (no weighting is needed in the analysis). The sample size allows vaccine coverage to be estimated with a 95 per cent CI of ±10 percentage points, on the assumption of a design effect (increase in variance due to clustering) of 2."*

* Milligan, Njie, and Bennett, "Comparison of Two Cluster Sampling Methods for Health Surveys in Developing Countries."

In other cases, a researcher may decide to use non-random (also called purposive) sampling, even if this means they cannot generalize the results. There are many reasons why non-random sampling may be more appropriate methodologically.

First, researchers may not have enough time or resources to conduct research for the number of units required for a random sample. For example, many students must complete their thesis projects within a set timeframe, and they may have limited research funding.

Second, researchers may not have enough information about a population to determine what a statistically representative sample would be. For example, research on cross-border smuggling is complicated by differential definitions and laws on what is considered "legal" versus "illegal," and by the informal and deliberately disguised ways in which goods are transported across borders.[6]

Third, if a research topic is on a sensitive subject or with a population that is undocumented or criminalized, people who are randomly selected may not agree to participate in the research. In these contexts, researchers need to build trust and may choose snowball or respondent-driven sampling.

Fourth, if the research question is not attempting to establish causality, or if the researcher is not attempting to generalize, random sampling is not necessary. In participatory action research, for example, the purpose is to build relationships and centre the experiences of research participants. In these cases, non-random sampling is not required nor desirable.

As with random sampling, many different types of non-random sampling exist. Here, I explain the kinds you are likely to encounter in cross-border research, but this list is not exhaustive.

Convenience sampling is identifying the sample through contact with those who happen to be available at a particular place. This happens frequently in media interviews, where a reporter may stand at a busy intersection and ask pedestrians about their opinion on a topical issue. The problem with convenience sampling is that it privileges people who are visible and easily accessible. Generally speaking, it is not considered methodologically sound in academic research. However, in reality, there is always an element of convenience in all samples because of issues of consent and access (see below).

One accepted non-random sampling technique is **quota sampling**. In this sampling method, the researcher attempts to approximate the results of a random sample by purposively identifying subpopulations – for example, based on age group, sex, racialized identity, or religion – to be represented in the final sample. This method requires information about the overall population in order to purposively select people with these characteristics in the final sample. The research attempts to approximate the representivity of a random sample, but because this representivity cannot be calculated, the results cannot be generalized. Indeed, there is often a bias towards those units in a sample that are most readily available.

For example, Alice Bloch used quota sampling to identify interviewees from hard-to-access refugee communities in the UK. Because there was no sampling frame, "quotas were set for each of the communities reflecting the key explanatory variables including country of origin, gender, age, region, and length of residence."[7] These quotas were based on the previous literature as well as previous interviews with refugee-serving organizations. While not all of the quotas were met exactly as planned, "using quotas did ensure that the survey interviewers had targets to work towards and that helped to ensure better representation among key variables."[8]

Snowball sampling, sometimes called chain sampling, is a technique where a researcher starts off with a certain number of participants and then asks those participants to identify others. While respondent-driven sampling relies on the research participants themselves to contact other potential participants, with snowball sampling, the researcher contacts prospective participants identified by the original participants. There is a risk with snowball sampling that participants share similar characteristics because they are part of the same network. Therefore, it is important to have multiple, diverse entry points to try to reach different kinds of participants.

For example, Sadler et al. describe how they use snowball sampling to recruit participants who are under-represented in healthcare intervention or research studies due to language barriers, low literacy levels, cultural resistance to external medicine, or historical abuse and discrimination within healthcare systems.[9]

It is possible to combine different sampling methods. In the example to illustrate quota sampling above, Bloch also used snowball sampling through gatekeepers to identify potential participants.[10]

Activity 7.2: Analysing the Controversy over "Conflict-Related Deaths" in the Democratic Republic of Congo

Epidemiologists working with the International Rescue Committee and the Burnet Institute conducted a study of "conflict-related deaths" by undertaking five mortality surveys over seven years in eastern Democratic Republic of Congo (DRC). Due to years of conflict that undermined infrastructure and government access to areas held by rebel groups, no reliable census existed, so the researchers had no sampling frame. They therefore used cluster sampling to identify households in eastern DRC. Over the seven years, 14,000–19,500 households participated in a survey that asked for reported conflict-related deaths, both direct (i.e., due to wounds and sexual violence) and indirect (i.e., caused by lack of access to healthcare, water, and sanitation). The researchers then extrapolated the results from these households in eastern DRC to the whole country (including the west, which was controlled by the government). They compared the total number of deaths to those that would have occurred if there were no war, proxied using the average crude mortality rate for sub-Saharan Africa at the time. They concluded that there had been 5.4 million conflict-related deaths, a figure that was widely cited for aid, peacekeeping, and diplomacy purposes.

However, researchers for the Human Security Report Project at Simon Fraser University critiqued the estimated death toll as an exaggerated number for two sampling-related reasons. First, they argued that the cluster sampling over-represented eastern DRC, the area experiencing the most intense conflict. They argued, "extrapolating from a small convenience sample of five non-randomly selected populations to the region's entire population is a serious violation of basic statistical principles."[11] Second, they suggested that using the sub-Saharan African mortality rate as the baseline underestimates the "normal" death rate without war because DRC is less developed than many other African countries.

1. Identify the kind of sampling used by IRC-Burnet. Is this random or non-random? To what population, if any, could they generalize?
2. Identify the critiques from the Human Security group at Simon Fraser. In your view, are they justified? How do these critiques relate to representivity and generalizability?

3. What other sampling methods could the researchers have used given the conflict and access issues?

ACCESS ISSUES

Just because an element in a population has been selected for a sample does not necessarily mean that the researcher has access to that person, document, or place. In other words, there is a difference between the desired sample and the actual sample. As a result, researchers tend to over-sample, to allow for the possibility that they will not have access to all those chosen for the sample.

For inanimate objects – like documents – there are fewer restrictions, but there are still sometimes barriers, such as permissions, privacy, and security considerations. These will be discussed further in chapter 11. For example, if a researcher is interested in measures the Australian government has taken to mitigate the possibility of terrorist attacks against government buildings, it is unlikely that they will get access to classified government documents on this issue.

For human populations, access issues are complicated by several factors in research across borders.

First, there may be gatekeepers who formally or informally control access to populations. Examples of gatekeepers include government officials, community leaders, or organization representatives. In the example above on registration of non-citizen children in schools, the researcher would need permission from school boards and principals to access documents, staff, and students in schools.

Second, there are ethical constraints. As discussed in chapter 3, in most countries a researcher must have procedural ethics approval before collecting primary data with human populations. For some topics and groups of people, who are deemed vulnerable, ethics permission is difficult, if not impossible, to obtain. For example, one of my students was denied ethics permission to conduct research with unaccompanied minors because it was impossible to get consent from parents, and no responsible adult had been designated as their guardian. Similarly, Witham, Beddow, and Haigh describe institutional barriers to accessing health care study participants who are deemed "too vulnerable to research."[12]

Moreover, researchers require the voluntary, informed consent of each person who participates in their study. This means that even if someone is randomly selected for a study, they have the right to choose not to participate. As a result, even non-random samples have an element of self-selection, making them less random and, therefore, less statistically representative and less accurately generalizable. The risks of non-participation increase with the opportunity costs – the time, discomfort, and inconvenience – of participation in the study. Indeed, what constitutes a "sensitive" topic is context-specific and culturally constructed, thereby resulting in variability in willingness to consent to participate.[13] For example, Wayne Coetzee describes the challenges he encountered in gaining access to, and consent from, participants for his study on the arms trade between Sweden and South Africa.[14]

Third, there may be physical barriers to accessing populations. Weather and climate impact access. In some developing countries with poor infrastructure, whole areas become inaccessible during the rainy season. Armed conflict can also create physical barriers when infrastructure has been destroyed or violence makes it impossible to travel. Some institutions have risk management offices that prohibit researchers from travelling during high-risk weather, medical, or conflict events. These weather and/or insecure conditions may also cause people to move within or across borders, making it more difficult to locate them. For example, during the COVID-19 pandemic, most non-essential, in-person research was not permitted.

Fourth, political events can impact access to populations and their willingness to participate in research. Political violence that causes insecurity not only creates population movements, but also means that people may be fearful about talking to researchers about particular topics. Similarly, there may be reticence for people to participate in research during particularly politicized periods, such as election campaigns. For example, Carla Suarez describes how she adapted her research with armed groups in eastern DRC to periods of security and insecurity.[15]

Fifth, language issues need to be taken into account. In international contexts, researchers do not always speak the language of the research participants. Translation and interpretation can introduce more layers of interpersonal power dynamics with consequent access issues. There are also ethical issues with using local interpreters and translators, who will remain in the field once the researcher has gone. They could face reprisals if research findings are perceived to be critical of authorities or unflattering to their fellow community members.

Activity 7.3: Identifying Access Issues and Gatekeeping

Imagine that you plan to do research in relation to one of the donor-funded projects described in this video: "Improving the Lives of Western Colombia's Indigenous Emberra Communities" (https://www.youtube.com/watch?v=rnlEukiGBZA).

1. Identify some access issues that may affect your ability to conduct research with Indigenous people in this community.
2. Identify at least two gatekeepers. How may these gatekeepers affect sampling and access? Think of both positive and negative impacts.

CONCLUSIONS AND KEY TAKEAWAYS

In this chapter, we discussed the importance of identifying and accessing samples – subsets of a larger population of documents, organizations, communities, or people. The method a researcher uses to select a sample depends on the research question, their epistemological approach, the information they have about the population, and the access they have to the population. In cross-border research, access issues are exacerbated due to administrative permissions, violence, weather, language, and the presence of gatekeepers. When reading secondary literature, including newspaper reports and policy studies, it is important to understand how researchers selected their population. If they did not use random sampling, or if their random sampling is flawed, they cannot generalize their findings to the population. However, results from non-random sampling can still be used to disprove a generalization.

QUESTIONS FOR REFLECTION AND DISCUSSION

1. What are some of the specific issues that might prevent random sampling on topics related to your research interests? Is random sampling desirable and necessary?

2. How can one identify gatekeepers and leaders? What are the opportunities and risks involved in cross-cultural contexts?
3. What are some of the advantages and disadvantages of translation and interpretation?

FURTHER READINGS

Bernard, Josef, Hana Daňková, and Petr Vašát. "Ties, Sites and Irregularities: Pitfalls and Benefits in Using Respondent-Driven Sampling for Surveying a Homeless Population." *International Journal of Social Research Methodology* 21, no. 5 (2018): 603–18. https://doi.org/10.1080/13645579.2018.1454640.

Brigden, Noelle K., and Anita R. Gohdes. "The Politics of Data Access in Studying Violence across Methodological Boundaries: What We Can Learn from Each Other?" *International Studies Review* 22, no. 2 (2020): 250–67. https://doi.org/10.1093/isr/viaa017.

Cernat, Vasile. "Roma Undercount and the Issue of Undeclared Ethnicity in the 2011 Romanian Census." *International Journal of Social Research Methodology* 24, no. 6 (2020): 761–6. https://doi.org/10.1080/13645579.2020.1818416.

Górny, Agata, and Joanna Napierała. "Comparing the Effectiveness of Respondent-Driven Sampling and Quota Sampling in Migration Research." *International Journal of Social Research Methodology* 19, no. 6 (2016): 645–61. https://doi.org/10.1080/13645579.2015.1077614.

Lata, Lutfun Nahar. "Negotiating Gatekeepers and Positionality in Building Trust for Accessing the Urban Poor in the Global South." *Qualitative Research Journal* 21, no. 1 (2021): 76–86. https://doi.org/10.1108/QRJ-03-2020-0017.

Peticca-Harris, Amanda, Nadia deGama, and Sara R.S.T.A. Elias. "A Dynamic Process Model for Finding Informants and Gaining Access in Qualitative Research." *Organizational Research Methods* 19, no. 3 (2016): 376–401. https://doi.org/10.1177/1094428116629218.

Van Dyke, Ruth. "Investigating Human Trafficking from the Andean Community to Europe: The Role of Goodwill in the Researcher–Gatekeeper Relationship and in Negotiating Access to Data." *International Journal of Social Research Methodology* 16, no. 6 (2013): 515–23. https://doi.org/10.1080/13645579.2013.823280.

Wilson, Ian, Sharon R.A. Huttly, and Bridget Fenn. "A Case Study of Sample Design for Longitudinal Research: Young Lives." *International Journal of Social Research Methodology* 9, no. 5 (2006): 351–65. https://doi.org/10.1080/13645570600658716.

Web Resource

Types of Random Sampling: https://www.youtube.com/watch?v=Rok2pHB8ft4.

Interviewing across Borders

LEARNING OBJECTIVES

By the end of this chapter you will be able to:

- Identify different types of interviewing;
- Understand the interviewing techniques in international, cross-cultural contexts;
- Identify ways to ask questions in a culturally sensitive and methodologically appropriate way;
- Analyse how the ways in which researchers interact with respondents can affect the quality of the information they receive; and,
- Identify tools and methods for recording information from interviews.

KEY TERMS

Focus groups
Interviewing
   Elite interviewing
   Peer interviewing
   Semi-structured interviewing
   Structured interviewing
   Unstructured interviewing

Key informant
Probing techniques
Questions
   Close-ended (or fixed choice)
   Open-ended
Survey

INTRODUCTION

Interviewing is one of the most common ways of gathering information – both within and outside of academia. While the methods we discuss in this chapter are primarily intended for conducting and evaluating research, they may also be useful for you in other personal and professional contexts. In fact, most of us will have already had some experience with interviews, whether as a survey respondent or through watching media interviews on the news. This chapter will focus on the methodological tools for conducting interviews in research projects across cultural contexts.

Interviews are useful methods for generating information about people's views, beliefs, motivations, and reported behaviour. They can take many formats, from informal conversations to structured surveys with closed questions. While interviews are sometimes described as "qualitative" methods, they can actually generate both qualitative and quantitative data. This chapter will introduce each of these methods and their opportunities and challenges in cross-border research.

META-EXAMPLE: USING INTERVIEW METHODS TO UNDERSTAND CLIMATE CHANGE ADAPTATION

Climate change is one of the most important global issues of our time. Numerous studies have examined not only the impact of climate change on livelihoods, but also the ways in which individuals adapt to climate change. This meta-example focuses on a research project that combined surveys, interviews, and focus group discussions to understand how Indigenous knowledge (IK) was used by the Yao people in Bac Kan Province, Vietnam, to adapt to climate change.[1] Examples of other research projects will be used throughout this chapter to highlight different interviewing techniques.

In the Bac Kan study, data were "collected through surveys, interviews, and focus group discussions to gather Indigenous knowledge on native crop varieties and animal breeds, weather forecasting, and the timing and location of cultivation practices."[2] The objective of the study was to use IK and insights from the Yao people to inform "climate change adaptation plans and strategies on the local, regional, national, and international levels."[3]

The researchers used several different interviewing methods in this study. First, they conducted ten in-depth **semi-structured interviews** with "local representatives of varying social and economic groups in order to obtain initial impressions of their experiences with natural disasters, weather extremes, climate change, and the attributed adaptation strategies. It also provided base information on social, economic, educational, and environmental conditions of the intended study areas."[4] The researchers used the information gathered in these initial interviews to develop "a more complex interview schedule" that was tested and refined, particularly in relation to language.

A household **survey** was then carried out in two villages. Questions focused on the household's economy and on "how households and communities have been able to adapt to climate events through, for example, food sharing, (in-)formal networks, and the support of local institutions."[5]

The researchers then conducted a variety of **focus groups** of "5 discussants, ranging in age from 35 to 60 years old" to both collect more data and to also "cross-check and clarify information" generated through the individual interviews and surveys.[6] The first set of focus group discussions (FGDs) were "segregated by gender to address cultural norms where women may have found it difficult to express themselves in the presence of their husbands or elderly male villagers. The second set of FGDs reintegrated respondents to illicit their observations on similar themes, such as impacts of climate change on the Yao people, the use of IK by the community, and how IK was being combined with scientific knowledge."[7]

Finally, the researchers undertook forty-two **key informant** interviews with "experienced farmers knowledgeable of the area" and government staff members of the Department of Agriculture: "Key respondents included an IK scientist, district and commune agricultural extension and development officers, village head, women's union head, and selected elderly with standing peerage. Interview questions focused on assessing the impacts of climate change on the Yao people, the use of IK by the community, how IK was being combined with scientific knowledge, and the identification of entry points for IK promotion."[8]

This meta-example demonstrates three key points that will be discussed in this chapter. First, there is a spectrum of interviewing. Interviews, surveys, and focus groups all involve asking people questions and are sometimes used in the same study, as in this example. The difference is in the format and the control the interviewer has over the questions and the process. This chapter will explain these different methods, and the kinds of information and research they are best suited to address. As shown in this example, different interview methods generate different kinds of information.

Second, the way a researcher asks questions is important. We will talk about the art and science of question formulation and word choice, especially in cross-border contexts. In this example, initial interviews were important in deciding how to ask questions and to address linguistic issues.

Third, how a researcher interacts with respondents can affect the quality and kind of information they receive. In this example, all data collection took place in person, but we will also discuss other methods, including telephone and web-based methods.

A SPECTRUM OF INTERVIEWING

Interviewing is a method for collecting data on reported behaviour, emotions, opinions, perceptions, reactions, and rationale for behaviour. It is important to note that reported behaviour should not be conflated with actual behaviour. People will tend to under-report "negative" behaviour and over-report "positive" behaviour. They may also forget details or the sequencing of specific events.

This report from CNN demonstrates different accounts of the same incident by different eye witnesses: "The Unreliability of Eyewitness Testimony" (https://www.youtube.com/watch?v=TJK4pvmbkBo)/).

The way in which a researcher asks questions also has an impact on the type of information we receive. The way interviews are structured is as important as, and can influence, the formulation of questions. In this section, we will discuss the different kinds of interviewing, which lie on a spectrum from informal to structured surveys.

In **unstructured interviewing,** the interviewer has minimum control over the interview and allows respondents to express themselves in their own terms and at their own pace. The interviewer will have a topic for discussion and some prompts, but no set interview questions. Unstructured interviewing is useful in preliminary and exploratory stages of research to help narrow down a research topic, to understand context, or to find out how people are talking about a particular issue. In cross-border research, it can be particularly useful for researchers from outside the context to get a sense of the "lay of the land," cultural cues, power relations, and the words people use to describe their experiences and the topic under study. It can also be used if the researcher is interested in having the respondent direct the subject of the research, such as in life stories or with participatory research. The data cannot be compared across interviews because each interview is so different.

For example, researchers undertook informal interviews in villages in rural Nepal to explore localized understandings of food insecurity and vulnerability in relation to climate change adaptation. The researchers chose informal interviewing to gain insight into "people's perceptions of key factors causing vulnerability and how their concerns were taken into account in decision-making processes."* Because the dialogue had been dominated by external, formal voices, such as the World Food Programme, it was important for the researchers to allow interviewees to express their opinions in their own words and in their own way.

* Nagoda and Nightingale, "Participation and Power in Climate Change Adaptation Policies."

In semi-structured interviewing, the interviewer has an interview guide or map with a list of topics and questions to be covered. However, the exact wording of questions will vary, and researchers can change the order of questions in response to what the respondent says or to follow the natural "flow" of the conversation. This can be particularly useful in cross-border or multilingual research when researchers can use the flexibility to adapt wording to the context. Semi-structured interviewing results in comparable data that can be analysed qualitatively or quantitatively.

> For example, Singh did semi-structured interviews with female heads of households in informal urban spaces in Mumbai, India, to try to understand the lived experiences of gender relations and urban flooding. She used semi-structured interviews to provide respondents with "flexibility [. . .] so that they could talk at length on topics of interest and describe things on their own."*
>
> * Singh, "Gender Relations, Urban Flooding, and the Lived Experiences of Women in Informal Urban Spaces."

Structured interviewing is based on preset questions that need to be asked in the exact same way and order to each respondent. Because researchers cannot alter the way questions are posed, it is important that the questions be pretested for understanding, especially in cross-cultural and multilingual contexts. This is the kind of interviewing found in surveys and questionnaires. Data are comparable and can be analysed for statistical correlations.

> For example, researchers undertook surveys with citizens in China, the United States, and Germany to understand the degree to which there was public acceptance of "national and international adaptation and mitigation efforts" in the three countries.* In total, 1,430 Chinese, 1,005 German, and 1,010 US respondents completed the thirty-minute questionnaire that asked the same questions, translated into the national languages.
>
> * Schwirplies, "Citizens' Acceptance of Climate Change Adaptation and Mitigation."

The format of interviews also varies depending on the number of, and type of, participants. Focus group discussions are defined as "any group-based research activity that is grounded in regular interaction among the participants such that it becomes a social and political forum in its own right."[9] Essentially, focus group discussions are unstructured or semi-structured interviews in groups. The group interaction may produce different kinds of data. In cross-cultural contexts, it is important for the researcher to be aware of power relations when deciding on the composition of groups and the topics of discussion. In the meta-example above, initial focus groups were segregated by gender because researchers were concerned that women would not speak up in the presence of men. In multilingual contexts, focus groups organized by language is often a good idea to reduce logistical challenges of interpretation.

In focus groups, researchers have to bear in mind both the interviewer-respondent relationship and the interpersonal relationships among the respondents. These relationships are both individual and embedded in social structures and power relations. A researcher should take the time to understand this broader context before running focus groups, especially in cross-cultural contexts and in areas where there is explicit or latent conflict. This is an ethical imperative because of the lack of confidentiality within focus groups and thus the level of trust that is required. It is also a methodological consideration: respondents may be hesitant to advance their opinions – especially those that contradict dominant norms and authorities – in contexts of power imbalances. Recognizing social hierarchies based on gender, age, social class, leadership, ability, race, ethnicity, and many other intersectional markers of "difference," it is sometimes a good idea to separate out groups based on key characteristics.

For example, in Sigrid Nagoda and Andrea Nightingale's research on climate adaptation in Nepal (also cited above in relation to informal interviewing), focus groups were explicitly used to have conversations with individuals whose positionality was marginalized, in relation to caste, gender, age, and class.* These focus group discussions were intended to gather information on the ways in which social processes and marginalization operated within committees created by the World Food Programme. The data demonstrated how climate

> change adaptation policies "contribute to reinforc-
> ing, rather than transforming, the underlying causes of
> vulnerability" (85).
>
> * Nagoda and Nightingale, "Participation and Power."

In focus groups, the researcher is also the moderator or facilitator. They lead and stimulate the discussion and manage participation to try to ensure everyone has an opportunity to contribute. At times, a facilitator may need to manage conflict within the group or facilitate the exchange of opposing ideas. Ideally, it is helpful to have two researchers: one to facilitate and the other to take notes.

> For example, researchers undertook interviews with
> national and municipal government officials and non-
> governmental organization leaders in Dhaka, Bangladesh,
> to understand decision-making around climate change
> adaptation planning.* These individuals were explicitly
> selected for their expertise, and the interviews focused on
> decision-making, which relied on their inside knowledge
> of their organizations.
>
> * Araos et al., "Climate Change Adaptation Planning for Global South Mega-
> cities: The Case of Dhaka."

Key informant interviewing has its origins in anthropology and involves sustained interviews with individuals who have in-depth knowledge about a topic or community. A key informant is different than a regular interviewee in the sense that this individual is expected to have information and opinions that extend beyond their own individual experiences. In the meta-example above, key informants had insights into Indigenous knowledge based on their long-term experience with farming in the area.

Elite interviewing involves individuals who have social, economic, or political power in a society. Although this technique emerged in political science to describe interviews with powerful decision-makers, it can also apply to other contexts from arts to sports to business. While key informants have in-depth knowledge, they are not necessarily formally recognized as having leadership positions. So, key informants are sometimes also elites, but this is not always the case.

> For example, Rebecca Williams used reciprocal peer interviewing with young people who experienced violence in Honduras as a way to make the research more participatory and to enrich the data.* Similarly, Anna Oda et al. reflect on peer interviewing in a longitudinal research project documenting the integration of Syrian newcomers in Canada. While they highlight the benefits of such an approach in terms of building trust with participants and gathering rich data, they also reflect on the ethical challenges, especially to peer researchers, who struggle to maintain boundaries between personal and professional spaces.**
>
> * Williams, "Silence Is Not Always Golden."
> ** Oda et al., "Ethical Challenges of Conducting Longitudinal Community-Based Research with Refugees."

Peer interviews involve individuals, who have direct experience with the topic under study, conducting interviews with their peers – that is, others with similar experiences or sharing similar characteristics.

It is, of course, possible to combine different interviewing techniques, as in the meta-example above. If an international researcher is new to a context, they may conduct some unstructured interviews to better understand the power dynamics and to test out localized understandings of particular vocabulary. The researcher could then use this information to inform the formulation of questions that would be asked in a questionnaire.

Activity 8.1: Choosing Interviewing Methods

1. For each of the research scenarios below, identify the interview method (i.e., informal, semi-structured, or structured/survey/ questionnaire) that is best suited to the kind of data you need.
   a) From a random sample of 2,500 people, analyse the relationship between climate change adaptation and migration towards urban areas.
   b) Explore different local terms and vocabulary for "climate change adaptation."
   c) Understand how individuals and households have adapted their daily routine in response to climate change.
2. For each of the scenarios, could focus group, elite, key informant, or peer interviewing be used?

THE ART AND SCIENCE OF ASKING QUESTIONS

How a researcher asks questions will determine the quality of the data as well as how that data can be analysed. In this section, we will discuss factors to take into account when asking questions in interview contexts.

Before we get into the way we pose questions, we need to distinguish between open and closed questions.

Closed-ended (or fixed-choice) questions are questions to which a limited number of options are given as possible responses. These include multiple choice, ranking, true-false, and so on. These types of questions are easier and faster to analyse and can produce comparable statistical results across respondents. However, because the wording of the question and the fixed-choice answers are so important (see next section), they are much more complicated and time-consuming to formulate. This is particularly the case in cross-cultural and multilingual contexts where words have different meanings.

SUMMARY OF KINDS OF FIXED-CHOICE QUESTIONS

Multiple choice questions provide a set of answers to a question. These may include options for "all of the above," or "none of the above," or "select all that apply."

Rating scales or ordinal questions provide a range of options from 0 or 1 up to as high as 100. In cross-cultural contexts, it is important to define whether the lower end of the scale is the least or the highest ranking.

Likert scales are like rating scales, but are specifically intended to rank respondents' feelings or opinions. Again, it is important to define what the researcher means by the different ends of the scale.

Ranking scales require respondents to order their answers according to their preference. In these questions, respondents need to compare across different choices, so it takes longer to complete each question. They also need enough information about each choice. As with rating and Likert scales, the researcher needs to define the scale – that is, is 1 the first choice or the least favourite choice?

Open-ended questions are questions to which respondents can give their own answer. This allows respondents to provide richer responses, including answers that were not anticipated by the researcher. However, there is more limited comparability than close-ended questions because of this diversity of responses. Moreover, because they are more time-consuming for the respondent to answer, in some cases, respondents will skip these questions, especially in surveys.

For example, in an HIV intervention study in Zimbabwe, Daniel Hruschka and colleagues compared "responses of women to two questions (one open-ended and one fixed-choice) about male condom negotiation strategies used with their partners."* They found that the responses to the two kinds of questions varied significantly, with condom use reported much more frequently in response to open-ended questions. The researchers concluded that "asking key study questions in both open-ended and fixed-choice formats may provide a valuable form of perspective for social and behavioral data" (184).

* Hruschka et al., "Fixed-Choice and Open-Ended Response Formats," 184.

Table 8.1. Advantages and disadvantages of open vs. closed questions

	Open-ended questions	Fixed-choice questions
Advantages	• Allows respondents to interpret the questions in their own way, especially in cross-cultural and multilingual environments • Researcher can rephrase if respondents don't understand the question • Allows for answers that the researcher did not anticipate • Can elicit more information on sensitive topics	• Easier to analyse data • Answers are easily comparable • Faster for respondents to complete
Disadvantages	• More time-consuming to analyse data • Answers are not easily comparable • More time-consuming for respondents to answer; in self-administered surveys, there is a greater chance that they will skip these questions or provide few details	• Question formulation has to be especially clear, so it can take more time to compose the questions and the fixed-choice answers • Researcher has to anticipate a range of answers, so that respondents can "find" the most appropriate answer; this can be more challenging in cross-cultural, multilingual environments • Respondents may select "any" answer in order to complete the interview as quickly as possible

When formulating questions, it is important to bear in mind the following key principles:

• Be as clear as possible.
• Try to anticipate ambiguities in the interpretation of the question, especially in cross-cultural contexts where words may have different meanings.

- It is a good idea to pretest closed-ended questions to ensure that the fixed-choice answers are clear and adequately distinct from one another.
- Avoid technical terms, jargon, and acronyms.

For example, researchers conducting a study among injured workers in Malaysia noted that their sample included multi-ethnic, multicultural, and multilingual participants with varying income and education levels. In order to ensure that their questions were clearly understood by the diverse group of respondents, the researchers developed a "4-step Interview Protocol Refinement (IPR) framework," including "(1) ensuring alignment between interview questions and research questions, (2) constructing an inquiry-based conversation, (3) receiving feedback on interview protocols and (4) pilot testing of the interview questions."*

* Yeong et al., "Interview Protocol Refinement."

Related to the first point about clarity, researchers should use vocabulary that is appropriate to the audience and be aware of any language and translation issues. If you are translating questions, ensure that they are back-translated into the original language to ensure there has been no misunderstanding.

For example, the Health Literacy Questionnaire (HLQ) was initially developed in Australia in English, but is now being used in different countries and languages. German researchers translated and "culturally adapted to German context" forty-four items in the HLQ.* This cross-border adaptation allowed for collection of similar data, so that there is comparability across contexts, but in a way that ensured that

> the data collection tool made sense to German-speaking respondents in Germany.
>
> * Nolte et al., "German Translation, Cultural Adaptation, and Validation of the Health Literacy Questionnaire (HLQ)."

When formulating a question, one also needs to ensure that respondents will have enough information or context to answer the questions. For example, it is unreasonable to expect the average person to understand complex scientific information about climate change. Therefore, interview questions on adaptation should focus on how households react to specific climate change–related events, such as flooding or severe weather.

Researchers should avoid leading questions that prejudice the response. It is important to acknowledge the acquiescence problem, where people tend to agree with statements, even when they are posed in a disagree/agree format.

For example, the Pew Research Center asked the same respondents the following questions:[10]

Agree/disagree format
"The best way to ensure peace is through military strength."
   54% agree
Forced choice format
"Diplomacy is the best way to ensure peace."
OR "The best way to ensure peace is through military strength."
   33% for military intervention; 53% for diplomacy

The responses demonstrate the acquiescence bias. Even in open-ended questions, one needs to be aware of the way a positive adjective or framing can affect results.

Sensitive/threatening questions should be preceded by a preamble, but the question itself should be short. For example:

- We are trying to understand the different ways in which people attempt to feel secure and to protect themselves. Do you own a gun?

Similarly, researchers collecting data about tourism and terrorism in Nigeria acknowledge that "participants may find discussing terrorism distressing due to its complex interaction with religion, politics, and ethnicity as well as personal experiences."[11] They suggest that such interviews should centre researcher and participant well-being, giving them time and space to answer difficult questions and also respecting silence.[12]

Researchers should avoid double-barrelled questions, which contain assumptions that two phenomena are related, even though they are not. They should also avoid asking more than one question at the same time.

For example, Ping-Chun Hsiung provides the following example of a double-barrelled question:

"Interviewer: *At the time of marriage would you expect your child (male vs. female) to be able to talk about private things and to be experienced or knowledgeable about sex?*

Diane: He does. He's very open. Once his firend [*sic*] wanted to set him up with a girl and I said and I was against it because, "you're not an Indian, where people set their children up." I want him to choose his own mate. Like Marcus Garvey says, you have to be a leader. You choose your own person and it's fine with me. (Caribbean Interview #2)"

Hsiung recommends that the question be "replaced by a series of open-ended questions, which should be asked one at a time:

• At the time of marriage, what kinds of personal things would you expect your son to be able to talk to you about?
• How knowledgeable about sex would you expect him to be?
• How experienced about sex would you expect him to be?
• How would your answers differ for your daughter?"*

* Hsiung, "Avoid 'Multiple-choice' and Double-barreled Questions."

Finally, when formulating interview questions, it is important to provide alternatives, if possible. Avoid "either/or" scenarios when reality can be much more complex. In fixed-choice questions with a limited number of answers, try to ensure that there are enough answers to cover different scenarios, and/or add a "none of the above" option.

It is usually a good idea to end an interview with an open-ended question like, "Do you have anything to add?"

Activity 8.2: Analysing a Survey

1. Consider the following potential survey questions to evaluate student experience in a course:
   a) Please indicate your reaction to this sentence: The course is structured in a logical way.
      O Strongly disagree
      O Disagree
      O Neutral
      O Agree
      O Strongly agree
   b) Please comment on the balance between course lectures, guest speakers, discussions, and activities. Would you like more or less of one kind of teaching method?
   c) Please choose the statement below that best describes the material covered in the course.
      O The material is too basic for an undergraduate university course.
      O The material is basic, but includes some material appropriate for an undergraduate university course.
      O The material is pitched at the right level for an undergraduate university course.
      O The material is advanced, but includes some material appropriate for an undergraduate university course.
      O The material is too advanced for an undergraduate university course.
   d) Please comment on the explanation of assignment requirements. How easy or difficult are they to understand and follow?
   e) How likely is it that you would recommend this course to a student in your program?

Not at all likely   Extremely likely

0	1	2	3	4	5	6	7	8	9	10

2. Identify a fixed-choice question and an open-ended question. As a respondent, which kind do you prefer? From a data-gathering perspective, what are the opportunities and challenges of open versus closed questions in this example?
3. Considering the key principles on formulating questions covered above, are there any questions that are problematic? Which ones? Why?
4. Reformulate one of the open-ended questions into a potential fixed-choice question. What was challenging about this? Would the question benefit from more than one kind of fixed-choice question?

INTERACTING WITH RESPONDENTS

The quality of the data from interviews depends not only on the way one poses questions, but also on how one interacts with respondents.

Self-Administered Surveys and Questionnaires. In the case of structured interviews such as surveys and questionnaires, respondents may self-administer them. In the past, this was done primarily by regular postal service delivery, but now it is more common for respondents to be asked to complete surveys online. There are several considerations to keep in mind when using self-administered surveys.

First, there is an assumption that respondents are literate in the language of the survey. In parts of the world where illiteracy rates are high, or where "national" languages are not the first language of the people you are working with, you need to think carefully about whether self-administration is the best approach.

Second, access to and literacy in internet technologies cannot be assumed. This may disproportionately affect particular individuals – for example, poor people and the elderly – resulting in biased sampling and results.

Third, as mentioned in chapter 3, electronic communications can be intercepted and subject to surveillance. For example, under the USA Patriot Act, the US government can access records of survey companies, such as SurveyMonkey, which store data in the US. This means that information that research participants share through these online survey companies could be accessed by the US government.

In consent forms, research respondents must be made aware of this. In some cases, the risks that this poses to the privacy of research respondents may mean that the researcher should choose an alternative survey method.

Fourth, the formulation of questions and fixed-choice answers is very important because respondents do not have the opportunity to ask for clarification.

Finally, with self-administered surveys, there are increased challenges of non-response or incomplete responses, resulting in biases in your sample.

Interviewing by Telephone or Internet Technologies. Telephone or videoconferencing technologies are sometimes good ways of accessing respondents who are geographically distant, especially when you have limited time and financial resources. These techniques have also increased in popularity due to the global COVID-19 pandemic, which resulted in restrictions to in-person interviews. Telephone and internet technologies allow for some interaction between the interviewer and interviewee and thus can be used for all types of interviewing. Research across borders sometimes requires these kinds of long distance interactions, which can approximate an in-person interview. However, it is more difficult to establish rapport, and the researcher cannot always (fully) see the body language of the respondent. Moreover, the connection can be poor, making it more difficult to hear respondents.

> For example, researchers conducted telephone interviews with 136 HIV-positive individuals in Uganda to ascertain the impact of COVID-19 measures on their health outcomes. Trained interviewers asked fixed-choice and open-ended questions in English and Luganda, with interviews lasting twenty to thirty minutes. While there were some challenges in "building rapport and responding to visual cues," the researchers concluded that telephone interviews were effective in "enhancing access to geographically dispersed participants, increasing interviewee privacy, reducing cost, and enriching data collection

as interviewees must be explicit in explaining their points of view, not relying on visual cues."*

* Linnemayr et al., "HIV Care Experiences during the COVID-19 Pandemic," 28.

In Person. All kinds of interviews can be done in person. It is important to reflexively think about the way power relations and personal dynamics may affect the interviewing process. When there are multiple interviewers, it is a good idea to decide in advance how each will respond to particular scenarios to maintain some kind of coherence across the interviews. This is particularly important in unstructured and semi-structured interviews, as well as focus group discussions, where respondents have more control over the interviewing process, and where personal interactions are important.

In-person interviewing often requires establishing rapport. The researcher should allow time at the beginning to exchange greetings, which in some cultures can last a long time. In some cases, respondents will also want to know more about the interviewer – their personal background and research trajectory. While some researchers find these questions invasive or irrelevant, it is important to recognize reciprocity: researchers ask questions of respondents, so they should also be prepared to answer some questions. Before delving into the questions, it is also a good idea to provide context to the study.

Probing Techniques. During unstructured, semi-structured, and group interviews, the researcher may use several **probing techniques** to encourage the respondent to provide more information. Probing is an art; the researcher needs to strike a fine balance between encouraging more information and leading the interviewee and/or injecting too much of themselves into the interview process. Probing is also context-specific. Some techniques will work better with some respondents and in some cultures more than others.

- Silent probe: This is when the researcher pauses to allow time for the respondent to add more. It is sometimes tempting for an interviewer to rush through questions in order to make sure they "cover" all the areas. But, this can sometimes result in a series of surface answers. Interjecting silence into the interview can provide space for a respondent to collect their thoughts or add information. But, too much silence can also be awkward. Researchers need to manage this.
- Repetition or echo probe: In this technique, the interviewer paraphrases the respondent's response and then asks them to continue. The echo probe not only allows the interviewer to confirm that they adequately understood the respondent's answer, but also establishes rapport by demonstrating that the researcher is actively listening. That being said, it should not be used after every question; otherwise, the interview can become too long and tedious.
- Follow-up probe: This probing method involves asking the respondent to provide more details or examples based on what they have already said. Researchers can ask, "Can you give me an example of __?" Or "When you say ___, what do you mean?" Or simply, "Can you tell me more?" The follow-up probe signals to the respondent that the researcher is interested in what they have to say and would like more details.

Activity 8.3: Analysing Interviews

1. Watch the examples of interviews in this video: "How to Do a Research Interview" (https://www.youtube.com /watch?v=9t-_hYjAKww).
2. What are some probes that were used?
3. How did the interviewer establish (or not) rapport?
4. What are the strengths and weaknesses of the interview techniques in this video?

RECORDING INTERVIEW DATA

Researchers need a reliable way to record information that they gather during the interview process. In the case of structured interviews whether online or on paper, the data will already be recorded. However, for all other interviews, a researcher needs to decide how to document the interview.

Voice and/or Video Recorders. Using voice or video recorders means that the researcher has a permanent record of the interview. This can be useful for fact-checking, especially when there is a dispute about what was said. Visual recordings can also be helpful for observing body language and other non-verbal cues.

Always ask for permission first. A researcher needs explicit informed consent for recording, and this should be indicated in the consent form, with the possibility of respondents opting out of recording. Another ethical consideration is the fact that the recording can raise confidentiality issues, since a person's voice and/or image can be identified.

In some cultures, recording may be regarded with suspicion as a way to capture a person's soul. It can also inhibit interviewees, or make them talk in a much more formal way.

From a technical perspective, it is important to ensure that you master the recording technology before using it. It is also a good idea to take some notes in case there is a technical problem with the recording and it is unusable. You will then, at least, have some written data from the interview. Also, if using only voice recording, researchers should take observational and methodological notes to complement the audio recordings (see next section).

Finally, a researcher needs to decide what they will do with the recordings. Transcribing verbatim generally takes five to six times the recording time. This means that for each hour of interview, a researcher must set aside five to six hours to transcribe the recordings. In other cases, a researcher uses the recordings simply as a reference to complement written notes, fact-check, and/or to pull out specific quotes.

Taking Notes. Taking written notes during an interview is an important practice. Even when one is recording an interview, written notes are important to set the context, record any observations (e.g., the interviewee was visibly upset), and any methodological issues (e.g., the respondent didn't seem to understand the question).

Taking notes can inhibit the flow of the interview if the researcher does not make occasional eye contact. It is therefore a good idea for researchers to practise taking notes quickly, with regular breaks from looking at the page.

That being said, at times, the act of taking notes underscores the importance of what the respondent is saying. They may specifically ask a researcher to "write this down."

Interview Notes. Whether a researcher uses voice/video recording or notes, they will have to compile the data into structured interview notes, unless they are using a transcription service. These notes are important as data, as well as a preliminary analysis tool. Researchers should write up these notes as soon as they are able – ideally at the end of each research day. Sometimes these interview notes are part of longer **fieldnotes**, as discussed in chapter 9.

Activity 8.4: Analysing Interview Notes

These notes were collected from a study of non-governmental organization members from a national network on refugee rights.

Date	13 November 2019
Time	3:01–3:25 p.m.
Location	*Over the phone*

Q: BEFORE WE START, DO YOU HAVE ANY QUESTIONS IN REGARDS TO THE CONSENT FORM?

R: No.

Q: YOU HAVE FULLY READ, UNDERSTOOD, AND SIGNED THE CONSENT FORM PRIOR TO THIS INTERVIEW?

R: Yes.

Q: WHAT ARE YOUR EXPECTATIONS OF [ORGANIZATION'S NAME IS REDACTED IN THIS EXCERPT]?

R: That [redacted] continues to advocate for refugees globally as a primary goal of the organization.
For [redacted] to connect the different organizations working towards the resettlement of refugees.

Q: Any other expectations?

R: "I appreciate the level of knowledge of [redacted] on refugee resettlement and the variety of issues concerning refugees, even if they are not active in those specific spheres."

Q: Please comment on the ways in which you and your colleagues participate in the following activities:

a. Working groups;

[The participant did not address this point.]

b. Consultations;

- Connects oversees refugee protection to local resettlement programs.
- They attend when possible.
- They experience challenges when it comes to attending due to the travel and distance connecting various places in Canada.

c. Webinars and virtual meetings;

- Useful to overcome barriers restricting attendance to other larger meetings like the consultations.
- "Useful to keep up to date and be well-rounded on all sorts of issues pertaining to refugees."

Q: Do you face any internal or external barriers to participation in [redacted] activities?

[This question was asked as a follow-up to point C of the question above.]
R: "Basically, time commitment and the ability to attend where most of the consultations are organized."

Q: Do you have any needs which are not currently served by [redacted]?
[Needs to be reformulated – it was later asked again and paired with What are your suggestions for themes and resources that [redacted] could propose to members (for example, Frequently Asked Questions, monthly bulletin, or practical tools)?]

R: No. Overall, [redacted] addresses our main needs, we know it has a broad spectrum of members implicated in various types of issues concerning refugees, mostly resettlement, and it cannot realistically provide resources for all.

[Content uncertain, the participant mumbled: the underlined words were clear enough to be written as is.]

Q: Do you have any other comments or suggestions?

R: It is an important organization that provided "an outstanding helpful voice" in our field and to others organization like ours.
It is important to figure how to work at making sure they can connect with people in refugee resettlement and other organizations [signal malfunction at 3:21; a comment about OPR? was missed]
They need to find ways to do so – face to face meetings are crucial, but connecting virtually increasingly becomes a useful tool and needs to be exploited by [organization name], especially in our position when time or money can be an issue.

We thanked the interviewee for their time.

The interview was very brief, and the participant did not have many points to contribute to the questions.

1. Can you identify observations and methodological notes in the example above?
2. Can you identify any probes?
3. Do you think this is a semi-structured or structured interview? Explain your response.
4. The interview took place by phone. What are some of the opportunities and challenges of this method of interviewing?
5. The interview was not recorded. How has the interviewer distinguished between paraphrase and exact wording in these notes?
6. What are some ethical issues in this example?

CONCLUSIONS AND KEY TAKEAWAYS

Interviews are one of the most commonly used data collection methods – both in research and in everyday life. The art of good interviewing is not only asking clear and concise questions, but also managing interpersonal relationships and power dynamics between the researcher and respondent, as well as among respondents. In cross-cultural research across borders, building these relationships and understanding power relations may take some time. Question formulation will also vary depending on language and cultural context. Like all research methods, honing interview techniques requires practice.

DISCUSSION QUESTIONS

1. What are the opportunities and challenges of conducting interviews and focus groups in cross-cultural and cross-border environments?
2. What kinds of research questions and contexts lend themselves particularly to focus groups?
3. How do political, social, cultural, and economic dynamics affect survey methods?
4. What ethical issues are posed by focus group discussions?

FURTHER READINGS

Archibald, Mandy M., Rachel C. Ambagtsheer, Mavourneen G. Casey, and Michael Lawless. "Using Zoom Videoconferencing for Qualitative Data Collection: Perceptions and Experiences of Researchers and Participants." *International Journal of Qualitative Methods* 18 (2019). https://doi.org/10.1177/1609406919874596.

Brown, Courtney A., Anna C. Revette, Sarah D. de Ferranti, Holly B. Fontenot, and Holly C. Gooding. "Conducting Web-Based Focus Groups with Adolescents and Young Adults." *International Journal of Qualitative Methods* 20 (2021). https://doi.org/10.1177/1609406921996872.

Cyr, Jennifer. "The Unique Utility of Focus Groups for Mixed-Methods Research." *PS: Political Science & Politics* 50, no. 4 (2017): 1038–42. https://doi.org/10.1017/S104909651700124X.

Liu, Xu. "Interviewing Elites: Methodological Issues Confronting a Novice." *International Journal of Qualitative Methods* 17, no. 1 (2018). https://doi.org/10.1177/1609406918770323.

Lokot, Michelle. "Whose Voices? Whose Knowledge? A Feminist Analysis of the Value of Key Informant Interviews." *International Journal of Qualitative Methods* 20 (2021). https://doi.org/10.1177/1609406920948775.

MacNamara, Noirin, Danielle Mackle, Johanne Devlin Trew, Claire Pierson, and Fiona Bloomer. "Reflecting on Asynchronous Internet Mediated Focus Groups for Researching Culturally Sensitive Issues." *International Journal of Social Research Methodology* 21, no. 5 (2021): 553–65. https://doi.org/10.1080/13645579.2020.1857969.

Nyumba, Tobias O., Kerrie Wilson, Christina J. Derrick, and Nibedita Mukherjee. "The Use of Focus Group Discussion Methodology: Insights from Two Decades of Application in Conservation." *Methods in Ecology and Evolution* 9, no. 1 (2018): 20–32. https://doi.org/10.1111/2041-210X.12860.

Panter-Brick, Catherine, Rana Dajani, Dima Hamadmad, and Kristin Hadfield. "Comparing Online and In-Person Surveys: Assessing a Measure of Resilience with Syrian Refugee Youth." *International Journal of Social Research Methodology* 25, no. 5 (2022): 703–9. https://doi.org/10.1080/13645579.2021.1919789.

Stewart, David W., and Prem Shamdasani. "Online Focus Groups." *Journal of Advertising* 46, no. 1 (2017): 48–60. https://doi.org/10.1080/00913367.2016.1252288.

Williams, Rebecca J. "Silence Is Not Always Golden: Reciprocal Peer Interviews as a Method to Engage Youth in Discussion on Violence in Honduras." *International Journal of Social Research Methodology* 24, no. 4 (2021): 453–67. https://doi.org/10.1080/13645579.2020.1801601.

Windsong, Elena Ariel. "Incorporating Intersectionality into Research Design: An Example Using Qualitative Interviews." *International Journal of Social Research Methodology* 21, no. 2 (2018): 135–47. https://doi.org/10.1080/13645579.2016.1268361.

Yaylacı, Şule. "Utility of Focus Groups in Retrospective Analysis of Conflict Contexts." *International Journal of Qualitative Methods* 19 (2020). https://doi.org/10.1177/1609406920922735.

Zimbalist, Zack. "Bystanders and Response Bias in Face-to-Face Surveys in Africa." *International Journal of Social Research Methodology* 25, no. 3 (2022): 361–77. https://doi.org/10.1080/13645579.2021.1886397.

Web Resources

Eye Witness Accounts: https://www.youtube.com/watch?v=TJK4pvmbkBo.

Lives and Legacies, Asking Questions: https://www.utsc.utoronto.ca/~pchsiung/LAL/interviewing/phrasing.

UBC Learning Commons, How to Run a Focus Group: https://www.youtube.com/watch?v=Auf9pkuCc8k&t=251s.

Ethnographic Approaches across Borders: Observation, Participant Observation, Netnography, and "Hanging Out"

LEARNING OBJECTIVES

By the end of this chapter, you will be able to:

- Define ethnography;
- Understand the origins of classic ethnography and its critiques;
- Identify ethnographic methods within interdisciplinary and mixed methods research;
- Understand the evolution of ethnography, including netnography as a methodology; and,
- Critically analyse the "insider-outsider" debate in relation to ethnographic methods.

KEY TERMS

Autoethnography
Emic perspective
Ethnography
Fieldnotes
Netnography

Observation
   Direct observation
   Indirect observation
   Participant observation
Thick description

INTRODUCTION

Starting with a critical historical overview of **ethnography** within classical anthropology, this chapter demonstrates how ethnographic approaches have been used to empower, but also to co-opt and betray, "others" in international contexts. Ethnography literally means studying and writing about *ethnos* – a "people" or a culture. This chapter introduces key ethnographic techniques, including observation, participant observation, netnography, and "hanging out," and how these can be used in interdisciplinary and mixed methods contexts. At its core, ethnography is rooted in the analytical description of a particular group of people or of a particular social practice based on in-depth research and first-hand experiences. We will discuss the ethical and methodological opportunities and constraints of these methods in contemporary research in cross-cultural contexts. The chapter also explains the classic "insider-outsider" debate and challenges students to think beyond this binary in international research.

META-EXAMPLE: ETHNOGRAPHIC RESEARCH ON HISTORY EDUCATION IN SOUTH SUDAN

Merethe Skårås has undertaken video observation, "hanging out," and key informant interviews in South Sudan in order to understand how history is taught in a new country (created in 2011) and in the midst of ongoing conflict after decades of civil war in what was then a unified Sudan.[1] As Skårås points out, a primary objective of history education "is to develop a sense of nationalism, patriotism, and national unity among students," but there is little information on how history is actually taught in the classroom and on the role of the teacher as "the main medium through which the curriculum speaks to the students."[2]

Research on schools in South Sudan is challenging given the "restricted access, psychological stress, complexity, positionality of the researcher, and unpredictability" in uncertain security contexts. To respond to these challenges, Skårås and her research assistants engaged in "focused ethnographic fieldwork."[3] They shortened the length of time spent in the classroom by adapting classic ethnographic methods, such as using video observation instead of in-person observation.

However, they still engaged in classic ethnographic methods like "hanging out," and collecting relevant documents, such as curriculum and teaching materials and conducting key informant interviews (see chapter 9 and below). Skårås argues that such focused ethnography in conflict zones allows "for an in-depth analysis and triangulation of data both in the field and after leaving the field, and specifically under the conditions of psychological stress that such conflict settings can put the researcher in."[4]

This meta-example highlights several points that will be addressed in this chapter. First, ethnography has traditionally been undertaken by "outsiders" to better understand the "inside" culture and knowledge of a particular society or social practice. In this example, an international researcher used ethnographic methods to understand the everyday teaching of history in classrooms in South Sudan.

Second, ethnography is a research approach that uses a collection of methods. In this chapter, we will discuss the key components of ethnography as well as some of the methods that are used.

Third, ethnography has evolved, especially through the use of online technologies and in response to conflict, migration, and other contexts that make "traditional" ethnography difficult. In this example, "focused ethnography" shortened the period of fieldwork and also introduced innovative methods of video observation.

Fourth, ethnographic methods pose particular ethical opportunities and challenges, because of the long-term nature of research relationships. We will also discuss the specific ethical considerations when conducting online observation, including the use of social media data.

ORIGINS OF ETHNOGRAPHY IN CROSS-CULTURAL CONTEXTS

Ethnography is a methodological approach first developed in the discipline of anthropology. While some argue that there are earlier examples, many trace it back to the work of Bronisław Malinowski, who undertook in-depth fieldwork with Trobiand Islanders in the South Pacific and published the ethnography *Argonauts of the Western Pacific* in 1922. Early ethnographic research in classic anthropology was based on long-term, in-depth immersion in a particular place and on a corresponding **"thick description"** (see below) of the everyday practices and social structures of the people and cultures under study.

Early ethnography was thus inherently cross-cultural, but it was not necessarily culturally sensitive. There are several critiques of this traditional approach to ethnography. First, it was couched in "othering" practices. Indeed, only the "exotic" or "different" were deemed worthy of ethnographic study. While anthropologists tended to focus on international "others," sociologists used ethnography to study "deviant," counter- or sub-cultures within Western contexts.

Second, it was at best an extractive research process and at worst appropriation of other people's lives, stories, and experiences. Through the publication of a definitive ethnography of a particular group of people, the researcher became the "expert" on that culture.

Third, partially in response to these extractive processes, some groups deliberately misled researchers, resulting in inaccurate or biased information. In some cases, this has resulted in "Indigenous revisions of ethnography."[5]

Fourth, in some cases, ethnography has been used against the people who opened their communities and homes to researchers. Historically, anthropologists were sometimes used by colonizing powers to gather information on the groups they sought to repress. Militaries have recruited anthropologists to help them understand the cultural contexts in which they are working, so that they are more effective at fighting against these groups.

HUMAN TERRAIN SYSTEM

In 2006, the US military launched the Human Terrain System project, which embedded anthropologists and other social scientists in US military teams in Iraq and Afghanistan. The objective of the project was to make US military personnel more culturally aware so as better to implement counter-insurgency. Researchers conducted ethnographic-type studies and reported these findings to the US military. On 31 October 2007, the Executive Board of the American Anthropological Association (AAA) issued a statement that

outlined the ways in which the Human Terrain System project violated the AAA Code of Ethics, including the provision
that anthropologists do no harm to their research subjects.*
The project was closed in 2015.

* American Anthropological Association, "American Anthropological Association's Executive Board Statement on the Human Terrain System Project."

Activity 9.1: Imagining an Ethnography

1. Think about a social group that you belong to. For example, this
   could be a community of faith; a club at your college or university;
   an organization you volunteer at; a friend group you have been
   part of for many years; your college or university dorm floor; or
   any other group of people you belong to.
2. Imagine that a researcher who is not part of this group wanted to
   study the social practices and customs within your group. How
   would you feel? Are there any activities that are too sacred or
   personal for an outsider?
3. In order to understand the social practices and culture of your
   group, who would the researcher need to speak with? What kinds
   of activities should they observe? What documents or written
   materials (including websites, social media, and so on) would
   they want to consult?
4. If the researcher wrote a book about your group, how would you
   feel? Would you want to be listed as a co-author or contributor
   to the book or in the acknowledgements? How do you think you
   would feel if the book became a bestseller and lots of people read
   it? What about if the researcher made money or gained professional promotion from the book?

THE CONTEMPORARY ETHNOGRAPHIC TURN

Despite these controversies, ethnography is still a core anthropological
method, and ethnographic techniques have become popular in other
disciplines and in interdisciplinary studies. Indeed, in the context of

this "ethnographic turn" within globally focused research, it is important to identify the key elements of ethnographic methods, as some researchers may claim that their research is "ethnographic" without having invested the necessary time and relational approach.

First, ethnographic approaches require sustained, long-term interaction with individuals and communities. While it is difficult to specify a precise timeframe, there is consensus that ethnography requires weeks and months of interaction, not just a few hours or days of "field research." In the case of netnography, this means online, rather than physical, presence and interaction. In conflict zones or in areas of restricted mobility and access – such as prisons or refugee camps – researchers may not be able to live continuously in the areas over the length of the fieldwork, but there has to be a sustained interaction over time. As shown in the meta-example above, this sometimes means the use of creative methods and technology to "fill in the gaps" when physical presence in the field is not possible.

Second, this interaction should be embedded in the everyday lives, events, and practices of the organization or community in the study. In classic ethnography, the researcher would "participate" in this daily life and their observations would become key data. Because of logistical and security constraints, it is not always possible for the researcher to become an active member of the communities in which they are conducting ethnographic research. However, they should be actively "hanging out"[6] with people in everyday spaces, such as community centres, religious institutions, shops, businesses, and so on, and recording their conversations and observations in detailed fieldnotes (see below). Ethnography centres on the lived experiences of people and social practices in their ordinary contexts.

Third, the researcher, over time, needs to demonstrate basic cultural and linguistic competence. Ethnographic methods do not lend themselves to interpretation and translation. This means that a researcher needs to have a deep understanding not only of the language, but also of the socio-linguistic context in which they are researching.

Fourth, ethnographies provide rich and contextualized details. Anthropologist Clifford Geertz famously referred to this as "thick description."[7] While there are variations on what this means in practice, Joseph Ponterotto summarizes it as follows: "thick description involves much more than amassing great detail: It speaks to context and meaning as well as interpreting participant intentions in their behaviors and actions."[8]

Fifth, ethnography requires sustained relationships with individuals in the field of study. It cannot be based solely on one-off interviews. In classic ethnography, researchers identify one or more "key informant(s)." These are individuals who have deep knowledge and connections to their communities, which they can share with the researcher. Consequently, ethnographic approaches privilege an **emic perspective** – that is, an insider's view of cultural processes and practices.

KEY METHODS OF ETHNOGRAPHY

As demonstrated in the meta-example above, ethnography is a methodology that relies on multiple mixed methods. Not all of these need to be present, but ethnographers generally use a combination of some of the following methods. Moreover, these methods are not necessarily exclusive to ethnography. They can be used and adapted in other studies and methodological approaches.

Observation. Observation involves the act of monitoring and documenting details related to events, contexts, or individuals. Observation generates data on behaviour, occurrences, and environments. While it is often under-utilized in mainstream social sciences, it is an effective and relatively low-cost way of generating information. **Direct observation** occurs when researchers witness the event or behaviour themselves. They are bystanders; they are not normally directly involved in the activities as they unfold. Their purpose is to document what happens. **Indirect observation** happens when the researcher is not present, but has access to the information generated, such as by closed-circuit television or the results of a test.

For example, in the meta-example above, the researcher used indirect video observation in the classroom to observe how history was taught. The researcher contends, "This unstructured observation enables unforeseen issues to be included, which is of specific value in a chaotic, stressful environment in the midst of conflict."*

* Skårås, "Focused Ethnographic Research," 224.

Participant observation is the observation of social structures from the perspective of a researcher who is also participating in the daily life of the people, institution, or culture under study. In the meta-example above, participant observation would have occurred if the researcher had taught in the school or lived long-term in the community. Participant observation is a key method in classic ethnography because insights and knowledge are gained from observing while participating in the events or behaviour under study.

> *Pro Tip*: Participant observation is *not* a participatory methodology (see chapter 11). It is the researcher who is participating in the lives of the respondents in order to understand the "insider" perspective. The respondents are not participating in research design or methods.

Alpa Shah identifies "four core aspects of participant observation [. . .] *long duration* (long-term engagement), *revealing social relations of a group of people* (understanding a group of people and their social processes), *holism* (studying all aspects of social life, marking its fundamental democracy), and the dialectical relationship between *intimacy and estrangement* (befriending strangers)."[9]

"Hanging Out" or Immersion. Sometimes considered to be part of participant observation, but less structured and formal, is "hanging out" or immersion: the researcher should have sustained presence and interaction in everyday spaces and places. These can include religious buildings, markets, public squares, cafés, restaurants, and other places that people regularly gather. The idea is that hanging out and "being there" help to immerse the researcher in the cultural practices and world views of the group they are studying. As Turid Hagene argues, "Along with the fieldwork 'immersion' goes an 'ethnographic sensibility,' useful for gleaning the subjects' understanding of their

experience, the meanings that people attribute to their actions in the social world."[10]

For example, Hagene describes the multiple ways in which he informally interacted with people during ethnographic fieldwork in Mexico, "When I first arrived in the village, I noticed that socio-religious practices mobilized large numbers of villagers on a continuous and highly visible scale. I started participating in these activities, which also made me a well-known figure among large numbers of villagers. I took two long morning walks, which turned out to be a pleasant way to get acquainted with other morning-walkers, to have informal conversations, and get updates on the latest gossip. I could also observe a variety of housing conditions, spot calls for meetings at the village *zócalo* (central square), and experience the mass of stray dogs that caused many women to bring broomsticks along on their walks. These walks furthermore allowed me to witness the numerous religious *ermitas* (shrines) at different points in the village, and women queuing up with their buckets for water distributed from *pipas* (transportable water-tanks) in the dry season."*

* Hagene, "The Power of Ethnography," 309.

Interviews, Including with Key Informants. Ethnography may also include interviews, especially with individuals who are designated as key informants. As discussed in chapter 8, key informants are people with in-depth knowledge and experience of the phenomenon or social relationships that are the focus of the research. These interviews can also include formal or informal focus group discussions.

For example, Hagene conducted a series of informal and semi-structured interviews with key informants in a village in Mexico to understand the ways in which clientelist

> networks operated in influencing local elections. One of
> these key informants ended up becoming the "new Delega-
> tion Chief (a delegation is similar to a municipality in Mex-
> ico outside the Federal District), thereby providing impor-
> tant insights into the inner political workings."*
>
> * Hagene, "The Power of Ethnography," 309.

Collection of Key Documents and Records. Ethnography may include the collection of key archival materials that are specific to the group or phenomenon under study. These include maps, photographs, demographic records, surveys, police reports, newspaper articles, posters, and so on. In some cases, these documents may also be digital, such as social media posts, text messages, websites, or emails.[11] For example, in the study referenced in the meta-example above, Skårås took copies of curriculum documents and teaching materials.

Netnography. Combining "ethnography" and "internet," **netnography** is the study of cultural interaction through computer-mediated spaces, such as social media and web conferencing platforms. As with all ethnography, netnography requires a sustained presence in and interaction with these spaces. In some cases, netnography is combined with in-person ethnographic methods. In other studies, the researcher exclusively engages with participants in digital spaces. As Leesa Costello and colleagues argue, "despite netnography often being explicitly described and understood as online ethnography, it is not synonymous with this term nor is it suitable for use as a generic term applicable to any study of material generated in online environments."[12]

Netnography involves everyday interaction, immersion, and analysis of online communities and interactions within these communities.[13] Because online users can be anonymous, netnography "is particularly well suited to dealing with personally or politically sensitive topics or illegal acts."[14] It is also particularly well suited to cross-border research because online communities often defy geopolitical borders, although caution here must be paid to governments that prohibit or infiltrate online spaces.

For example, researchers undertook a netnography to analyse YouTube as a community of online users interested in the "democratization" of news. They were interested in YouTube's "distinctive features as a global news style and culture."* They analysed, as a case study, the YouTube video "Flotilla News Event," during which "Israeli forces raided a group of ships attempting to deliver humanitarian aid to Gaza on 31 May 2010 and killed nine Turkish activists aboard the *M/V Mavi Marmara*. Videos of the raid quickly spread to YouTube as both the activists and the Israeli Army circulated visual material related to the events" (Sumiala and Tikka, 318). During their netnographic study of the YouTube news on this event, the authors spent several hours each day on YouTube navigating content, tracking specific categories, keywords, and users, and taking detailed notes of their observations and the content (see below).

* Sumiala and Tikka, "Broadcast Yourself – Global News! A Netnography of the 'Flotilla' News on YouTube," 318.

Activity 9.2: Identifying Methods in a Potential Ethnography

1. Return to the analysis of the social group that you started in Activity 9.1.
2. For this social group, identify at least three of the methods outlined in the above section that could be used to engage in ethnographic research with this group. What are the strengths and weaknesses of each method for the group?
3. Does your group have a social media presence? If so, to what extent do you believe that the social media materials represent the culture and inner workings of your group? Would there be sufficient material to do a netnography? What permissions would an outside researcher require to access these social media posts? What are the ethical implications?

FIELDNOTES OR RESEARCH DIARY

One of the key elements of ethnography is recording observations and information in **fieldnotes** or a research diary. These notes then form part of your data, but they can also help to articulate reflections on your methodology as well as your preliminary analysis. Regularly writing fieldnotes and/or a research diary also helps researchers get into the habit of writing and analysing. While many people are daunted by the "writing up" stage (see chapter 12), good fieldnotes help to get past the "blank page" stage of writing.

As with interview notes (see chapter 8), quality fieldnotes are the basis of data in ethnographic research. In these fieldnotes, you need to record different kinds of information:

Administrative notes provide important the date, place, time, and other aspects that would need to be included in references, for example.

Methodological notes document how the information was collected as well as any factors that may have affected the quality and quantity of the information. This could include information on interruptions, technical problems, the fact that someone didn't understand a question, and so on. These should also include reflexive analysis of your positionality within the research site and research relationships.

Observational notes record data from observations, as discussed above.

Interview notes record key data and context from interviews (see chapter 8).

Analytical notes allow the researcher to begin making connections among data and identifying themes that could be useful for coding later (see chapter 11). They can also help the researcher to identify new lines of enquiry or emerging issues that were not anticipated in the original research question.

Some researchers also keep a research diary to complement more formal fieldnotes. Marion Engin suggests that research diaries can assist with "scaffolding" the "process of learning about research, and learning how to be a researcher."[15] Sarah Li used longitudinal research diaries during her doctoral research to "locate critical moments of reflexivity" that were "practical, theoretical, analytical, and personal."[16] Research diaries can thus serve both a pedagogical and a methodological purpose.

Activity 9.3: Writing Fieldnotes from Observations in a Public Space

This activity will provide a preliminary introduction to writing fieldnotes based on direct observation in a *public space*.

First, some *caveats:*

Generally, procedural ethics approval is not required for non-participant observation where the researcher does not interact with people they are observing; where those in the space have no reasonable expectation of privacy; and where the notes do not personally identify any specific individual.[17] However, before you do this activity, double check with your instructor about the specific rules in your institution and country. Also, make sure you are doing this activity in a public place where you do not require permission from a gatekeeper. Finally, do not engage in any direct interaction with other people while you are doing this activity.

For the purposes of this exercise, imagine that you are collecting information to answer the following research question: "What are the physical barriers that people in wheelchairs face?"

To provide you with some context and barriers you may not be aware of, please watch this video: "A Day in a Wheelchair – a First-Person Perspective" (https://www.youtube.com/watch?v=V6TW0jDLPyA).

Now, devote thirty minutes to direct observation during the course of a regular, everyday activity, such as walking to the grocery store, commuting to work or school, or sitting in a public park or square.

During these thirty minutes, take notes of your observations with a pen and paper, or by typing on your cell phone, tablet, laptop, or other device. *Do not take any video or voice recordings.*

In your notes, you must record:

- Administrative notes, including time, place, date, and so on
- Methodological notes, including how you collected the information and your own positionality within the space

- Observational notes, including the context, the number of people present, what they did, barriers to access, and so on
- Analytical notes that reflect on what this data means for the research question

Now, reflect on your experiences of observation and note-taking. What went well? What would you do differently next time? How detailed are your notes? Would they be useful in helping to answer the research question?

ETHICS, POSITIONALITY, AND OWNERSHIP: ETHNOGRAPHY IN CONTEXTS OF GLOBAL INEQUALITIES

In the first section of this chapter after the meta-example, we discussed how ethnographies were historically situated within unequal power relations. It is important to think about researchers' positionality within the ethnographic production of knowledge, as well as the specific ethical issues that may arise from the methods used.

Participant observation and interviewing do generally require formal ethics approval. As mentioned in the activity above, from a procedural ethics point of view, direct observation and "hanging out" in public spaces generally do not require ethics board approval. This is because there is no research interaction with human beings. Researchers are simply observing and experiencing life in a public space where people do not have a reasonable expectation of privacy.

Research in semi-public spaces is trickier. Gatekeepers may control access to these places and researchers may need ethics clearance. A good example of these are social media sites. While they may seem "public," users have signed specific user licences with different terms and conditions on the use of their data by third parties, including researchers.[18] From a research across borders perspective, these companies may be based in countries other than the country in which the research is taking place and/or the users are contributing content. In addition, research ethics boards do not yet have standardized approaches to the use of social media across different institutions. All this being said, generally speaking, the public-private question can be summarized as follows: "Questions of whether online postings are public or private are determined to some extent by the online setting itself, and whether there is a reasonable expectation of privacy on behalf of the social media user (British Psychological Society 2013) – for example a password protected 'private' Facebook group can be considered private, whereas an open discussion on Twitter in which people broadcast their opinions using a hashtag (in order to associate their thoughts on a subject with others' thoughts on the same subject) can be considered public."[19]

When accessing social media data, researchers need to "respect the privacy restrictions, user settings, and legal requirements of the particular social media platform they intend to use."[20] Each platform has different policies, which can also change over time. There are also risks involved in using data that may not actually belong to the person posting the information on social media or a website.

From a relational ethics perspective, ethnographic methods can pose ethical questions about voluntary, informed consent and privacy because the lines between the researcher and their roles in the community are blurred. While participants may consent to the overall research project, they may not want their every action and interaction with the researcher to be recorded as "data." Consent should therefore be a continuous process, rather than a one-off event of signing a consent form.

Consent is further complicated in ethnographic research because researchers often have to negotiate access to the community or group through gatekeepers. If a powerful gatekeeper has allowed access to the community and "vetted" the researcher, individuals may feel pressured to participate. On the other hand, in some cases gatekeepers prevent access to groups that want to share their experiences, especially if they are being oppressed or do not have a platform to share their story.

Ethnographic research can also pose ethical issues in relation to anonymization of data. The more "thick description" one does, the more likely people and places will be identified. This is particularly the case where gatekeepers only allow access to certain people or places. In small communities or social groups, all members may be affected by the information presented in an ethnography. In some cases, researchers choose to anonymize the place, group, or organization. We will return to some of these questions in the last chapter.

For example, Arlene Stein did ethnographic research in a "small town divided by a local ballot initiative against gay/lesbian civil rights."* To preserve confidentiality, the researcher used pseudonyms for respondents and changed the name of the town when publishing findings in a book. But, the author used her real name and positioned herself reflexively within the research. The book was reviewed by a statewide newspaper, who identified the name of the town based on the author's identity. As a result, the individuals in the book, including a self-defined lesbian, were identified and "outed," causing anger and personal harm. One prominent anti–gay rights leader in the community, who was easily identified because of her position as well as the "thick description" of her social context, publicly accused the researcher of deception and having a hidden "gay agenda" and "an axe to grind."

* Stein, "Sex, Truths, and Audiotape: Anonymity and the Ethics of Exposure in Public Ethnography."

This example also raises questions about ownership in ethnography. By privileging long-term relationships and emic perspectives, ethnographic methods have the potential to bridge insider-outsider dichotomies. This is particularly important in international, cross-cultural research, where external researchers – often from the global north – sometimes adopt an extractive approach to research in poor and marginalized communities.

Ethical ethnography, which privileges co-creation of knowledge, can instead draw on the deep-seated knowledge of communities' own lived experiences and external researchers' privileged access to resources and decision-makers. In this way, it can use the relative strengths of both insider and outsider perspectives to improve the lives of people in situations of conflict, poverty, migration, or marginalization.

For example, in a study of HIV/AIDS in rural South Africa, "'insider' community members work[ed] with 'outsider' investigators as participant observers to document every-day conversations taking place in public settings in their communities."* The researchers raised some ethical challenges, such as ensuring data remain confidential and navigating positionality within power relations, but also showed how such a project cannot only diversify ethnography methodologically, but also be based on relational ethics.

* Angotti and Sennott, "Implementing 'Insider' Ethnography: Lessons from the Public Conversations about HIV/AIDS Project in Rural South Africa," 437.

However, outside researchers still usually hold the authorship and copyright of ethnographies, along with the corresponding material and professional benefits. This has led to some calls for decolonizing ethnography, including through the use of Indigenous methods.[21] There is also a growing move towards **autoethnography**, where members of a community or social group document their own customs, social structures, and relationships.

CONCLUSIONS AND KEY TAKEAWAYS

Despite its colonial roots and the dangers of othering and appropriation, ethnographic methods are increasingly popular in international, cross-cultural research. By privileging long-term research into the everyday lives of people, ethnography can result in rich, contextualized accounts of complex phenomena like conflict, displacement, and development. Ethnographic studies vary, but most include at least some of the key methods of observation, participant observation, interviews, immersion, and/or collection of documents and archival materials, including digital records.

DISCUSSION QUESTIONS

1. How do personal and professional relationships become intertwined in ethnographic methods? Is it possible to separate them? How are these research relationships related to positionality and reflexivity across borders?
2. Who "owns" ethnographic data? Are cross-border ethnographies inherently extractive?
3. How have social media and technology opened up new ways of doing ethnography across borders? What are the opportunities and challenges?

FURTHER READINGS

Airoldi, Massimo. "Ethnography and the Digital Fields of Social Media." *International Journal of Social Research Methodology* 21, no. 6 (2018): 661–73. https://doi.org/10.1080/13645579.2018.1465622.

Brigden, Noelle, and Miranda Hallett. "Fieldwork as Social Transformation: Place, Time, and Power in a Violent Moment." *Geopolitics* 26, no. 1 (2021): 1–17. https://doi.org/10.1080/14650045.2020.1717068.

Costello, Leesa, Marie-Louise McDermott, and Ruth Wallace. "Netnography: Range of Practices, Misperceptions, and Missed Opportunities." *International Journal of Qualitative Methods* 16, no. 1 (2017). https://doi.org/10.1177/1609406917700647.

Hagene, Turid. "The Power of Ethnography: A Useful Approach to Researching Politics." *Forum for Development Studies* 45, no. 2 (2018): 305–25. https://doi.org/10.1080/08039410.2017.1366360.

Henne-Ochoa, Richard. "Sustaining and Revitalizing Traditional Indigenous Ways of Speaking: An Ethnography-of-Speaking Approach." *Language & Communication* 62 (2018): 66–82. https://doi.org/10.1016/j.langcom.2018.07.002.

Hordge-Freeman, Elizabeth. "'Bringing Your Whole Self to Research': The Power of the Researcher's Body, Emotions, and Identities in Ethnography." *International Journal of Qualitative Methods* 17, no. 1 (2018). https://doi.org/10.1177/1609406918808862.

Lavorgna, Anita, and Lisa Sugiura. "Direct Contacts with Potential Interviewees when Carrying Out Online Ethnography on Controversial and Polarized Topics: A Loophole in Ethics Guidelines." *International Journal of Social Research Methodology* 25, no. 2 (2022): 261–7. https://doi.org/10.1080/13645579.2020.1855719.

Phillippi, Julia, and Jana Lauderdale. "A Guide to Field Notes for Qualitative Research: Context and Conversation." *Qualitative Health Research* 28, no. 3 (2018): 381–8. https://doi.org/10.1177/1049732317697102.

Rankin, Janet. "Conducting Analysis in Institutional Ethnography: Guidance and Cautions." *International Journal of Qualitative Methods* 16, no. 1 (2017). https://doi.org/10.1177/1609406917734472.

Storm-Mathisen, Ardis. "Visual Methods in Ethnographic Fieldwork – On Learning from Participants through Their Video-Accounts." *Forum for Development Studies* 45, no. 2 (2018): 261–86. https://doi.org/10.1080/08039410.2018.1450287.

Sumiala, Johanna Maaria, and Minttu Tikka. "Broadcast Yourself – Global News! A Netnography of the 'Flotilla' News on YouTube." *Communication, Culture & Critique* 6, no. 2 (2013): 318–35. https://doi.org/10.1111/cccr.12008.

Thaler, Gregory M. "Ethnography of Environmental Governance: Towards an Organizational Approach." *Geoforum* 120 (2021): 122–31. https://doi.org/10.1016/j.geoforum.2021.01.026.

10

Participatory Research in International, Cross-Cultural Contexts

LEARNING OBJECTIVES

By the end of this chapter, you will be able to:

- Critically analyse participatory research approaches and methods and place them on a spectrum of participation;
- Identify participatory methods and assess the degree to which they incorporate participation;
- Understand the epistemological and methodological orientations of participatory action research; and,
- Discuss the opportunities and challenges of participatory methodologies in international, cross-cultural contexts.

KEY TERMS

Participatory action research
Participatory mapping
Participatory methods
Participatory research design

Participatory ranking and scoring
Photovoice
Sound postcards
World Café

INTRODUCTION

Claims to participatory methodologies are common in many international, cross-cultural research contexts. However, "participation" means different things to different people, and methods lie across a spectrum of participatory approaches. Epistemologically, participatory methods are linked to critical and Indigenous approaches because they privilege the knowledge of those with direct experiences of global inequalities and colonization. Robert Chambers, who has worked with participatory methodologies in development contexts since the 1970s, summarizes three key elements of participatory research: (1) "people are creative and capable, and can and should do much of their own investigation, analysis, and planning"; (2) "outsiders have roles as convenors, catalysts and facilitators"; and (3) "the weak and marginalized should be empowered."[1] But, participatory methods can be used in any research project. Conversely, it is possible to use "participatory" methods in non-participatory ways.

META-EXAMPLE: PARTICIPATORY ACTION RESEARCH PROJECTS IN AGROECONOMY IN CENTRAL AMERICA

A team of researchers undertook a series of **participatory action research (PAR)** projects focused on agroeconomy – a transdisciplinary approach to sustainable agricultural production – in Central America.[2]

In one PAR project, the researchers worked with small-scale coffee farmers and cooperatives in El Salvador to "develop/maintain strategies that supported both biodiversity conservation (more specifically, native trees) and household livelihood strategies."[3] Initially, the lead researcher, who was doing his PhD at the time, set the objective of the project. However, as he developed relationships and gained a better understanding of the context, shared research interests emerged, and the farmers were able to choose the research theme. Despite an initial distrust of outside researchers and scepticism in the power of the research project, farmers became more engaged when they "were

able to attain tangible benefits from the process, such as organic cer-
tification and learning about the factors affecting food security levels
in the different households."[4] The authors contend that humility and
trust were central to the PAR in order to "valu[e] the different types
of knowledge held by different actors." However, it was not possible
to avoid conflict all together, especially as the research and initiatives
challenged dominant power structures. For example, "The farmers
were able to legalize their union of cooperatives – the Association of
Organic Coffee Producers of Western El Salvador (ACOES) – but in
the process the largest of the organizations decided to pull out, leaving the union with a relatively small number of farmers and coffee
volume."[5]

A second PAR project undertaken by the researchers involved
young people and women as leaders in livelihood initiatives "to alleviate food insecurity and seasonal hunger" in coffee-growing communities in Nicaragua.[6] These included, for example, "the integration
of vegetable-focused homegardens into crop production systems to
improve household dietary diversity and diversify women's income,
and the development of AgroEco® Coffee's Women's Unpaid Labor
Fund, which recognizes women's reproductive and productive labor
in coffee production."[7] In this project, the initiatives were proposed by
community partners, with researchers supporting the research agendas identified locally through methodological guidance and "development of evidence-based actionable results."[8] In contrast to the first
example, the Nicaraguan project was initiated by the community, with
research partners joining to support the agenda and initiatives identified by those most affected by food insecurity. However, the initiative
did challenge localized power structures and knowledge hierarchies
based on gender and age.

This meta-example highlights several points that we will explore
in this chapter.

First, there is a spectrum of participation, and there are different
interpretations of what participation means in research practice.
In this meta-example, the researchers highlight five key principles
that they believe are central to participation: shared interest in
research; collective power; commitment to participation; humility;
and trust and accountability. However, they acknowledge that different partners had different interpretations and priorities amongst

these principles. In this chapter, we will discuss other approaches to participation, too.

Second, participatory research design is rooted in critical and Indigenous epistemologies that centre relationships within the research process. It involves meaningful engagement throughout the research with those who are most affected by the research, as well as the recognition of power relations in the production of knowledge. Moreover, participatory approaches explicitly value other ways of knowing beyond traditional academic "expertise."

Third, participatory research design usually includes participatory methods, but the use of participatory methods does not necessarily mean that the research design is participatory. Even in the meta-example above, the authors acknowledge where the research process could have been more participatory. Conversely, even non-participatory projects can benefit from participatory methods. Indeed, the first project started off as a fairly standard research project, then integrated participatory methods, and was eventually transformed into a PAR. However, this transformation and deep commitment to participatory approaches cannot be assumed in every project involving participatory methods.

Fourth, while there are many advantages to participatory approaches and methods, they do pose some challenges in cross-border research in relation to co-authorship, research funding, and timing.

WHAT IS PARTICIPATION?

Before we delve into methodological discussions about participatory research, it is helpful to first consider what we mean by participation. As demonstrated in the meta-example above, even when researchers agree on key elements of participation, their interpretation and implementation can vary, especially in cross-cultural, cross-border and multilingual contexts.

At its core, participation means that people have meaningful opportunities to take part in decision-making that affects their lives.[9] Since research both intrudes on people's lives (see chapter 3) and has the potential to have practical and policy impacts (see chapter 1), this means that a participatory approach to research would involve those who are most affected by the research.

Early theories of participation drew on a ladder analogy.[10] (See figure 10.1.) This perspective saw participation as a step-by-step process where decision-makers could move from lower levels of non-participation to the ideal end point of citizen control over decisions. As work on participation in many different contexts has evolved over the past decades, many researchers and practitioners now think of participation as a spectrum. Figure 10.2 shows one such conceptualization of participation.

Whether or not viewed as a hierarchy or a spectrum, it is clear that most research projects lie at the non-participatory end of the spectrum. At best, communities most affected by the research are asked for permission to conduct the research, but they usually have very little input into the research question, design, data collection, or analysis. Power relations within communities also present barriers to meaningful participation from diverse perspectives.

So, how can participation be practically implemented? Drawing on the work of Robert Chambers, the participation research team at the University of Sussex's Institute of Development Studies (IDS) has

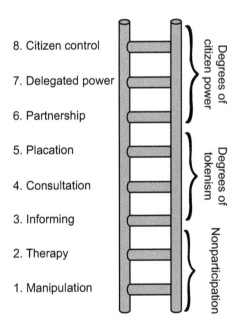

Figure 10.1. Ladder of participation. Adapted from Sherry R. Arnstein, "A Ladder of Citizen Participation," *Journal of the American Institute of Planners* **35, no. 4 (1969): 216–24.**

IAP2 Spectrum of Public Participation

IAP2's Spectrum of Public Participation was designed to assist with the selection of the level of participation that defines the public's role in any public participation process. The Spectrum is used internationally, and it is found in public participation plans around the world.

INCREASING IMPACT ON THE DECISION →

	INFORM	CONSULT	INVOLVE	COLLABORATE	EMPOWER
PUBLIC PARTICIPATION GOAL	To provide the public with balanced and objective information to assist them in understanding the problem, alternatives, opportunities, and/or solutions.	To obtain public feedback on analysis, alternatives, and/or decisions.	To work directly with the public throughout the process to ensure that public concerns and aspirations are consistently understood and considered.	To partner with the public in each aspect of the decision including the development of alternatives and the identification of the preferred solution.	To place final decision making in the hands of the public.
PROMISE TO THE PUBLIC	We will keep you informed.	We will keep you informed, listen to and acknowledge concerns and aspirations, and provide feedback on how public input influenced the decision.	We will work with you to ensure that your concerns and aspirations are directly reflected in the alternatives developed and provide feedback on how public input influenced the decision.	We will look to you for advice and innovation in formulating solutions and incorporate your advice and recommendations into the decisions to the maximum extent possible.	We will implement what you decide.

Figure 10.2. Spectrum of participation. "IAP2 Spectrum of Public Participation," IAP2, accessed 10 November 2022, https://cdn.ymaws.com/www.iap2.org/resource/resmgr/pillars /Spectrum_8.5x11_Print.pdf.

developed the following "Key Principles of Participatory Learning and Action":

1. The right to participate: "All people have a right to play a part in shaping the decisions that affect their lives." This right is codified in international law, including the Convention on the Rights of the Child, the most widely ratified treaty globally.
2. "Seeking out unheard voices and creating the safe spaces to allow them to be heard." In cross-border and cross-cultural contexts, it may take some time for researchers to understand local power structures and the ways in which certain individuals and groups are marginalized within these processes. As demonstrated in the meta-example above, in some cases, participatory research will explicitly focus on gender, or age, or other power inequalities.
3. "Seeking local knowledge and diversity": Participatory approaches explicitly seek out other ways of knowing and centre on the experiences and knowledge of those who are most affected by the phenomenon under study. The diversity element recognizes that people will have differential experiences, knowledge, realities, and truths, even if they live in the same place.
4. "Reversing learning" or "letting go of preconceptions in order to learn from the wisdom of community members. This means being prepared to unlearn what has already been learned." In other words, in participatory approaches, researchers recognize the limitations of their own knowledge, similar to the principle of humility raised by Méndez et al. in the meta-example above.
5. "Handing over the stick (or pen or chalk)": This expression came out of the early work on participatory research by Robert Chambers and his colleagues in South Asia and Africa. It involves reflexively thinking about the researchers' and participants' positionalities in relation to decision-making, knowledge, and expertise. Implementing participatory approaches often requires "those considered 'expert' – or powerful, or of higher status – sitting back, keeping quiet, and allowing space for others to participate."
6. Attitude and behaviour change: Ultimately, participatory approaches require researchers to share power, control, and decision-making. They become enablers, facilitators, and allies, rather than the leaders of a research project.[11]

Activity 10.1: Identifying the Spectrum and Principles of Participation

1. For each fictious scenario below, rate it on the spectrum of participation.
2. Now, think about how a participation principle – either from the meta-example or the IDS work – could be implemented to make this project more participatory.

    Scenario A: An instructor decides to experiment with the layout of her classroom to see if it has an impact on student learning. She divides the class into five groups and asks each group to propose different seating arrangements. The instructor then selects one of the proposals to try out.

    Scenario B: On an informal mid-term course evaluation, several students identified the classroom layout as a challenge to learning. Based on this feedback, the instructor held a focus group to better understand what the key problems were in the current layout. A committee, made up of the instructor and four student representatives from different backgrounds, was created to propose solutions.

    Scenario C: A group of students comes to the instructor to propose a different classroom layout that they think will better enable their learning. The instructor changes the classroom set-up based on the students' plan, but some students who were not consulted, including a student in a wheelchair, complain to the instructor because they feel that the new layout is detrimental to their learning.

PARTICIPATORY RESEARCH DESIGN

Participatory research design is an approach in which the researcher hands over to research participants control of the research agenda, process, and results. Participatory research is driven by the epistemological belief that those most affected by an issue are the real experts who should determine the research agenda and (co-)create knowledge. It is thus rooted in critical and Indigenous epistemologies.

As mentioned in the previous section, there are different perspectives on participation, but participatory research design tends to coalesce around these key principles:

- There is a strong partnership between the researcher and the community most affected by the research. This partnership is based on mutual trust, open communication, and humility.
- People who are most affected by the research and its outcomes are involved in key decision-making processes about the research design, including the research question, objectives, ethical considerations, methodological approach, and methods.
- In addition to respecting procedural ethics procedures, all who are involved in the research project are committed to relational ethics.
- People who are most affected by the research project are involved in the (co-)production of knowledge, including data collection, analysis, and dissemination.
- Participants own the research, including the data and any benefits from the research outputs.

Implementing these principles requires fundamental changes in the ways in which research is conceived, knowledge is generated, and findings are disseminated and used. For example, Cindy Peltier explains how a Mi'kmaw Two-Eyed Seeing approach to participatory research uses "Indigenous voices and ways of knowing as a means to shift existing qualitative research paradigms."[12] Indeed, some researchers believe that participatory design is fundamental to the decolonization and/or Indigenization of knowledge.[13] Others describe it as a "counterhegemonic approach to knowledge production."[14]

Because participatory research design involves both epistemological and "attitude and behavior change,"[15] it requires conscious reflections and proactive use of participatory principles throughout the whole project. It cannot be added retroactively as an "add participation and mix" approach. This poses some challenges to its implementation in cross-border research, as will be discussed in the last section.

PARTICIPATORY ACTION RESEARCH

Participatory action research is a specific kind of participatory research design. It combines the principles of participatory research, outlined above, with an explicit focus on practical action and change as a result of the research project. It is "a collaborative process of research, education, and action (Hall 1981) explicitly oriented towards social transformation (McTaggart 1997)."[16]

The meta-example above highlighted two projects with a PAR approach. Drawing on these experiences, Méndez et al. have adapted the work of Bacon et al. to visually represent the PAR process, as shown in figure 10.3.[17] It shows how research, action, and reflection are intertwined at all stages of the research project.

Generally speaking, a PAR project has a practical end goal as well as research objectives, all of which are defined by the community or individuals who are most affected by the project. The ultimate purpose is to effect social change and transformation through participation in both research and action.

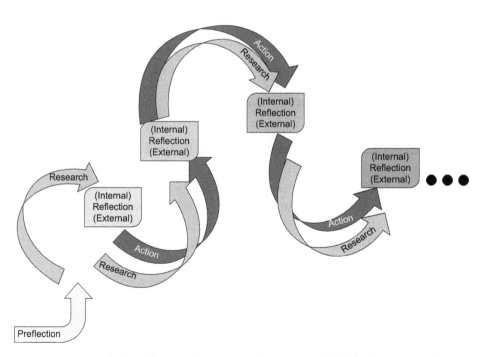

Figure 10.3. Iterative participatory action research (PAR). Méndez et al., "Integrating Agroecology," 711.

For example, Cindy Peltier combined Indigenous methodologies with PAR to understand cancer needs and priorities within the seven First Nations communities on Manitoulin Island. She stresses the importance of "considering relevance of the topic to the communities prior to the development of a research proposal," including through seeking wisdom from Elders. Peltier reflects on negotiating power relations as an Indigenous scholar who grew up on Manitoulin Island: "as researchers-in-relation, we are often held at a greater level of accountability than a researcher who may not be a member of the community." In addition to obtaining procedural ethics approval from her university and hospital research ethics boards, there was also a community ethics process based on the locally developed Guidelines for Ethical Aboriginal Research in the Manitoulin Area. A community advisory committee was created to provide "guidance in all aspects of research: planning, implementation, production of knowledge, and action." Through this PAR, "a collective story was produced as a wellness teaching tool to foster the transfer of knowledge in a meaningful way."*

* Peltier, "An Application of Two-Eyed Seeing."

Activity 10.2: Conceptualizing a PAR Project

1. Think about the social group you identified in Activities 9.1 and 9.2. As a member of that group, identify a specific need you have in terms of information (research) and action.
2. Given the information you need, which kinds of researchers would you want to work with? Think about (inter-)disciplinary and methodological training, as well as the specialized knowledge that would be most useful from external researchers.
3. Now, think about the action that you would want to undertake based on the information gathered in step one of this exercise. Do you think a researcher would be interested in participating in these activities?
4. What would be some of the opportunities and challenges of collaborating with external researcher(s) to address a practical issue identified by you and your group?

PARTICIPATORY METHODS

There are epistemological, practical, and institutional barriers to the implementation of participatory research design, as will be discussed later in the next section. Therefore, some projects adopt **participatory methods** without necessarily adopting a participatory research design. Similarly, not all research that takes a critical or Indigenous epistemological approach is necessarily participatory. It is important to be able to distinguish between research that has a participatory design and research that incorporates some participatory methods or approaches without fundamentally re-orienting in line with participatory principles.

Participatory methods are growing in popularity across different academic programs and can even be used in positivist or interpretivist studies. In many cases, they are combined with more traditional methods, such as interviews or observation. In this section, I will summarize some key participatory methods, but these are not exhaustive. Generally speaking, a participatory method is one in which participants have an active role in creating, generating, and interpreting data.

Photovoice is a participatory photography method in which participants produce photographic data that represents their experiences and perspectives. Photovoice has become a popular research tool across different disciplines and contexts since its inception in the mid-1990s.[18] One of the co-founders of Photovoice, Caroline Wang, summarizes the method as the use of photography to "to enable people (1) to record and reflect their community's strengths and concerns, (2) to promote critical dialogue and knowledge about personal and community issues through large and small group discussion of their photographs, and (3) to reach policymakers."[19] While there are variations in the way Photovoice is applied in practice, it generally involves some photographic training of participants, who are then provided with cameras to document their experiences and views. Participants are then invited to interpret the visual data by explaining why they took certain photos and what the images demonstrate about their experiences and knowledge on the topic. Photovoice projects culminate in an exhibition or presentation, where participants are involved in disseminating knowledge and results from the research, with a view to effecting change.[20] Leibenberg summarizes the Photovoice process in figure 10.4 below.[21]

Participatory mapping involves participants representing key geographic areas (e.g., a town or school), resources, social groups,

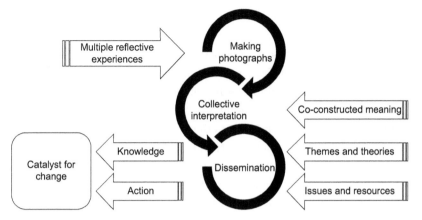

Figure 10.4. Leibenberg's representation of Photovoice. Liebenberg, "Thinking Critically."

An example of Photovoice in cross-border research is the initial use of the method by Wang and Burris with sixty-two women in two rural counties in Yunnan, China. The women used photography to document health issues of greatest concern to them by taking pictures of the "home place, village, or environment in which they work, play, worry, and love."* These photos contributed to their individual and collective knowledge about health issues and also served as public education and advocacy tools at the village, county, and national levels. Because many of the women could not read or write, photography allowed them to participate in a different way and to produce and communicate their own experiences and knowledge.

* Wang and Burris, "Empowerment through Photo Novella: Portraits of Participation."

health issues, mobility routes, and so on in visual form. People have, of course, been making maps since the beginning of time. However, map-making has often been part of colonial projects and hegemonic meaning making.[22] Participatory mapping therefore shifts the focus to ordinary people and everyday practices. It allows them to describe their own reality and to emphasize what is important to them.

Participatory mapping methods emerged in the 1980s, primarily using hand-drawn techniques to visually represent geographical areas and socially significant markers. They were usually done on the ground before being transferred to paper. Now, information technologies, including Geographic Information System (GIS) mapping, allow for the use of digital maps, although there are barriers to participation in relation to training and resources.[23]

For example, Shashini Gamage and Danesh Jayatilaka used a variety of participatory mappings to understand experiences of people in Colombo, Sri Lanka, who had been displaced by poverty and violence.* They used GIS to trace daily and weekly routines; to create movement maps that showed where people identified home; and resource maps within communities. Participants also drew hand-drawn maps of their memories of displacement. These maps were then combined with other methods to develop mobility videos, using digital story-telling methods, where narratives are supplemented with images, audio, text, graphics, and animations. You can see images of these participatory mapping methods and find out more about the project on The Unknown City: The (In)visibility of Urban Displacement website (http://www.cmrd.lk/en/projects/unknown.php).

* Gamage and Jayatilaka, "Life-story Narratives, Memory Maps, and Video Stories."

Participatory ranking and scoring involves participants determining categories of importance, which they then rank – individually and/or collectively – in terms of importance.

For example, participatory ranking and scoring was used to inform land-use policies around El Yurique National Park in Puerto Rico.* First, participants living in the area were asked to list (a) the ecosystem services provided by El Yurique and (b) the factors driving ecosystem change in the park and surrounding area. Participants explained their lists to other participants, and collectively the group came up with a list for "A" and "B" that incorporated all of the ideas. Then, participants were asked to rank their top three choices from list A – the ecosystem services – from 1 (most important) to 3 (least important). Finally, participants were asked to score each item on list B – the factors driving change – on a scale of 1 (least change) to 5 (most change).

* López-Marrero and Hermansen-Báez, *Participatory Listing, Ranking, and Scoring of Ecosystem Services and Drivers of Change.*

World Café is a group-based participatory method that is used to foster dialogue and brainstorming, build relationships, and facilitate collaborative learning and knowledge production.[24] It is often used to promote "conversations that matter"[25] to address complex, controversial, and/or emerging topics with a heterogenous group of people,[26] so this method is especially relevant to cross-border research. The World Café method is based on a conversational, iterative, and collaborative process "through evolving rounds of information exchange and the use of a café-style social context."[27] While the exact implementation of the World Café method depends on the topic, the number of participants, and the power relations amongst participants and ethical considerations, the following elements are usually present:

- A welcoming, comfortable, café-like space that sets the tone for collaboration and conversations. Clusters of tables are set up with five to seven seats at each table.
- Participants start off at one table and discuss a set of questions for twenty to thirty minutes. There is usually a designated "host" at each table to encourage participation and respectful dialogue.
- After the initial period, participants move to a different table with a new set of interlocutors to continue the discussion of the questions. Usually, there are three to five rotations, depending on the size of the group and the number of questions.

- As ideas are generated at each table, participants draw out key points and write them on boards or papers taped around the walls of the room. This allows all participants to engage with themes from different groups.
- Participants can begin to analyse the information generated by grouping themes and identifying patterns and/or points of divergence. This step is facilitated if the information is written on moveable boards, paper, or sticky notes.
- Depending on the size of the group, at the end of the session, a larger discussion can be facilitated.

For example, Emee Estacio and Toni Karic used the World Café method in a research project on internationalization of education at their university.* To create a welcoming environment even before the event started, they created posters about the event in several languages that were spoken by international students. They also decorated the room, played background music, and provided lunch and coffee breaks in a "café-like" setting. Each table had a different theme question: personal concepts of internationalization; issues and challenges to internationalization; recommendations to promote internationalization; and an open topic option, where participants could raise any question or issue related to internationalization. A topics "menu" was placed at each table to summarize the key points and questions of each theme. At each table, a volunteer facilitated the discussion, which was audio-recorded, while paper tablecloths could be used by participants to write down their key ideas and contributions to the discussion. A central wall allowed participants to post sticky notes of their main ideas. The café was operated as a drop-in event over a period of four hours, so no facilitated discussion with the whole group was held.

* Estacio and Karic, "The World Café: An Innovative Method to Facilitate Reflections on Internationalization in Higher Education."

Sound postcards are an emerging participatory method, originally created by Ciutat Sonora (Sound City), a Barcelona-based action-research collective, which allows researchers to capture the affective nature of sound and music.[28] Participants take part in music workshops and then record "postcards" to capture memories, experiences, or significant events in audio form.

> For example, Andrea Rodríguez-Sánchez collaborated with the Batuta Foundation to implement a participatory research project with young people affected by violence in Colombia. The project involved a music training program for young people, as well as data collection through sound postcards. They asked each participant, "If you had to send a sound to someone you know, who had never been to the place of the research, what sound or sounds would you choose which would be representative of the space in question?" The result is a rich and diverse set of participatory audio recordings, which you can hear on the Sound Postcards website (https:// musicsocialfabric.wixsite.com/sound-postcards).

Participatory Arts-Based Methods. There are also a growing number of participatory arts-based methods, where participants create art as a way of expressing their feelings, beliefs, experiences, and stories. A full exploration of these methods is beyond the scope of this chapter. However, like Photovoice and sound postcard methods, they provide participants with creative ways of producing knowledge that goes beyond the written word, so they are especially well suited to groups who have little or no formal literacy skills.

Activity 10.3: Identifying a Participatory Method

1. Return to the hypothetical Scenario C in Activity 10.1 above.
2. Select two of the methods above and explain how they could be used in this scenario to better include diverse perspectives of the whole class.
3. What are the advantages and disadvantages of each method? Could they be combined?

BARRIERS AND RISKS TO PARTICIPATORY DESIGN AND METHODS

This chapter has focused primarily on the opportunities that participatory approaches and methods bring to research across borders, including centring the knowledge and priorities of those who are most affected by the research and challenging unequal power relations. However, there are several barriers to the implementation of participatory design and methods, particularly in formal academic contexts, and there are also ethical challenges and risks.

First, degree programs often explicitly require that the research project be the sole work of the person who is obtaining the degree. This means that aspects of participatory research – such as co-producing knowledge and co-authoring results – may not be possible. For example, Yuriko Cowper-Smith outlines the disconnect between her doctoral research using participatory, community-action methodologies and the writing up and defence stages, when she was expected by her university to be the sole author.[29]

Second, when researchers turn over control of the project to participants, they lose the ability to clearly articulate the aims and methods of the study, since these are subject to negotiation by the participants. This poses problems both in terms of ethics approval and funding applications, which require detailed information on research questions, methodology, and timelines.

Third, because participatory projects work mostly on consensus, it takes more time to come to an agreement. This means that these projects may take more time and resources than more traditional projects.

Fourth, while participatory approaches attempt to address power inequalities between the researcher and the participants, they can exacerbate these power dynamics *within* participants' communities. Moreover, participatory research in and of itself will not change deep-rooted structural inequalities, which often surpass the community context where the research is being conducted.

Fifth, because participatory methods rely on co-production of data, ethical issues sometimes arise about who owns the information that is produced and how they are permitted to use it. For example, who owns the copyright of the photos that are taken in a Photovoice project?

Sixth, many participatory methods generate audio or visual data that subsequently needs to be "interpreted" and analysed to be presented to academic, practitioner, and policy audiences. Unless those who generated the data are involved in this process, their knowledge can be misinterpreted or appropriated.

Seventh, participatory methods usually need to be combined with other methods to generate the quality and quantity of data needed to respond to research questions in cross-border research.

Finally, it should be noted that some researchers misuse "participatory" methods in non-participatory ways.

Activity 10.4: Analysing Proposals

Read the two hypothetical research proposals below, then answer the following questions:

1. Which one is a participatory research design? How do you know? Does it use participatory methods?
2. Which one uses participatory methods, but does not have a participatory research design? How would the research have been different if the researcher had adopted a participatory design?

Research proposal 1: This project aims to understand the ways in which informal traders avoid customs officials on the India-Bangladesh border. One hundred traders will be invited to participate, with attention to gender, caste, and age distribution. These participants will then be invited to a two-hour information-gathering session in which they will map out their daily route, and also take part in participatory scoring and mapping exercises. They will be paid the equivalent of US$5 for their time.

Research proposal 2: The Alliance of West Bengal Truckers has partnered with the University of Calcutta to understand the impact of COVID-19 restrictions on the livelihoods of truck drivers who carry goods across the India-Bangladesh border. One hundred truck drivers have volunteered to participate in semi-structured interviews, so that researchers better understand their lived experiences of work during COVID-19. With the data generated from the research project, they propose to advocate for better protections and working conditions for truckers during COVID-19.

CONCLUSIONS AND KEY TAKEAWAYS

Participatory research design requires a fundamental shift in the way knowledge is valued and generated. While there are growing examples of participatory approaches, especially within Indigenous and critical epistemologies, they are still fairly rare in academia in general, although they are gaining popularity in cross-border research. In some cases, participatory approaches are combined with action research with the dual purpose of knowledge co-production and social change. Given practical, epistemological, and academic constraints, it may not always be possible to implement participatory research design in all circumstances. However, participatory methods can still be used even within more traditional research projects. The data that are co-generated through these methods can complement other information gathered through other methods.

DISCUSSION QUESTIONS

1. In participatory research projects, who owns the data?
2. What are the opportunities and challenges to participatory methods in your institution?
3. Some argue that democracy is a prerequisite for participatory methodology. Do you agree?
4. Why is participant observation not considered a participatory method? Could it be made more participatory? Could it be part of a participatory research design?

FURTHER READINGS

Akesson, Bree, Miranda D'Amico, Myriam Denov, Fatima Khan, Warren Linds, and Claudia A. Mitchell. "'Stepping Back' as Researchers: Addressing Ethics in Arts-Based Approaches to Working with War-Affected Children in School and Community Settings." *Educational Research for Social Change (ERSC)* 3, no. 1 (2014): 75–89.

Angeles, Leonora C. "Feminist Demands, Dilemmas, and Dreams in Introducing Participatory Action Research in a Canada-Vietnam Capacity-Building Project." In *Feminist Community Research: Case Studies and Methodologies*, edited by Gillian Creese and Wendy Frisby, 37–57. Vancouver: UBC Press, 2011.

Greene, Stuart, Kevin J. Burke, and Maria K. McKenna. "A Review of Research Connecting Digital Storytelling, Photovoice, and Civic Engagement." *Review of Educational Research* 88, no. 6 (2018): 844–78. https://doi.org/10.3102/0034654318794134.

Jull, Janet, Audrey Giles, and Ian D. Graham. "Community-Based Participatory Research and Integrated Knowledge Translation: Advancing the Co-creation of Knowledge." *Implementation Science* 12, no. 1 (2017): 1–9. https://doi.org/10.1186/s13012-017-0696-3.

Liebenberg, Linda. "Thinking Critically about Photovoice: Achieving Empowerment and Social Change." *International Journal of Qualitative Methods* 17, no. 1 (2018). https://doi.org/10.1177/1609406918757631.

Mayoux, Linda, and Robert Chambers. "Reversing the Paradigm: Quantification, Participatory Methods and Pro-Poor Impact Assessment." *Journal of International Development* 17, no. 2 (2005): 271–98. https://doi.org/10.1002/jid.1214.

Shamrova, Daria P., and Cristy E. Cummings. "Participatory Action Research (PAR) with Children and Youth: An Integrative Review of Methodology and PAR Outcomes for Participants, Organizations, and Communities." *Children and Youth Services Review* 81 (2017): 400–12. https://doi.org/10.1016/j.childyouth.2017.08.022.

Wilson, Elena, Amanda Kenny, and Virginia Dickson-Swift. "Ethical Challenges in Community-Based Participatory Research: A Scoping Review." *Qualitative Health Research* 28, no. 2 (2018): 189–99. https://doi.org/10.1177/1049732317690721.

Web Resources

Database of Resources on Participatory Methods: https://www.participatorymethods.org/resources/language/english-5426.

Food and Agricultural Organization. Training on Participatory Approaches, Tools and Methods: http://www.fao.org/3/ad424e/ad424e03.htm.

Oxfam International. 2004. "Community-Based Human Rights Impact Assessment: The Getting It Right Tool – Training Manual": https://s3.amazonaws.com/oxfam-us/www/static/media/files/COBHRA_Training_Manual_-_English.pdf.

Participatory Methods: http://participatesdgs.org/methods/.

University of Sussex, Institute of Development Studies. About Participatory Methods: https://www.participatorymethods.org/page/about-participatory-methods.

11

Analysing Text and Images in Cross-Border Research

LEARNING OBJECTIVES

By the end of this chapter, you will be able to:

- Identify how to find and access texts as data;
- Explain different methodological approaches to textual and image analysis;
- Understand coding mechanisms; and,
- Critically analyse issues of cultural interpretation and appropriation.

KEY TERMS

Codes
   Administrative codes
   Topical codes
Connotative
Content analysis

Critical discourse analysis
Denotative
Grounded theory
Intra-coder reliability
Text

INTRODUCTION

Students in internationally focused programs regularly encounter **texts** such as international legal conventions, government policy documents, media reports, social media messages, and promotional materials from non-governmental organizations. We may not realize it, but all of these texts are data. Indeed, one way that researchers who have limited time and funding can make original empirical contributions to their fields of study is to analyse seminal texts in their field as data. This chapter introduces key methodological tools for accessing and analysing these textual data.

The methods discussed in this chapter can be used for primary data that the researcher has collected themselves – for example, field-notes (see chapter 9) or interview transcripts (see chapter 8). They can also be used with any kind of oral, written, or visual data that the researcher obtains from other sources. These include letters, diaries, speeches, public debates in government or inter-governmental forums, media reports, social media posts, government documents, resolutions, religious texts, international conventions, laws, policies, non-governmental reports, and so on. The list is long and diverse. The point is that textual data is all around us. In order to have a methodologically sound approach to analysing and interpreting this data, we need a systematic way of approaching it.

META-EXAMPLE: TEXTUAL ANALYSIS OF REPORTS AND APPEALS FROM THE UN REFUGEE AGENCY (UNHCR)

Researchers analysed the UN High Commissioner for Refugees' (UNHCR) reports and appeals over a ten-year period to understand the ways in which different age categories were represented in these fundraising and programing documents. Through quantitative and qualitative "age-specific visual and textual references in UNHCR documents," the research project aimed to answer two questions: "Are children disproportionately represented in UNHCR discourses in comparison to their demographic presence in refugee populations? What are the socially constructed meanings and roles ascribed to different stages of the life cycle in refugee situations?"[1]

To answer the first question, quantitative visual and textual analysis was undertaken. Photographs were coded based on the absolute presence or absence of physical age categories – baby, child, young person, adult, and elders – for "principal subjects – those engaging in the primary activity or in the central frame of the photograph – or secondary subjects – those in the background and/or not engaging in the primary activity in the photograph."[2] **Content analysis** was used to identify and count age-specific textual references in all the documents. This quantitative analysis of photographs and text revealed that "adults are present in the greatest number of photographs across the time period studied. However, children, particularly girls, are mentioned much more frequently than adults in the texts."[3]

To understand the social age meaning and roles, researchers combined qualitative and quantitative analysis of images and text in the documents. For the photographs, a verbatim transcript of the caption and any text within photographs (for example, on banners or t-shirts) was recorded. Connotative and denotative meanings of the photograph were recorded. They were then grouped into ten themes, which were used to code the depiction of the principal subject (see above) in each photograph, allowing for a qualitative and quantitative analysis of themes across age categories, documents, and the ten-year timeframe. Similarly, the age-specific textual references were analysed qualitatively using grounded theory and then coded to allow quantitative comparison. This analysis demonstrated that children were primarily represented – both visually and textually – in relation to "'vulnerability' and protection, education and health."[4] There were also some contradictions between the text and photos. For example, while in the text child labour was portrayed in a negative way as something to be avoided, there were several photos of children engaging in work.

This meta-example reveals several points that will be explored in more detail in this chapter.

First, there are different quantitative and qualitative methods for analysing textual and visual data. The method(s) a researcher selects depends on the research question(s) and data available. Different methods can be combined in the same study, as in this example.

Second, this example illustrates the importance of codes, coding, and coders. The codes a researcher chooses, the textual analysis methods they use, and consistency across coders are all important. In this meta-example, the coding of age categories in photos by physical appearance could vary across cultures, but it could also vary depending on how individual coders perceived age. It is thus important to have an explicit coding guide or glossary so that those assessing the research can evaluate the validity of codes and that multiple coders have a reference point.

This example also demonstrates the importance of images. Whether or not these images are gathered as primary data (for example, through some of the participatory methods discussed in chapter 10) or are a part of secondary sources, as in this example, they provide important sources of information on meaning and representation. While social sciences have historically under-used images as data, this chapter provides some strategies for analysing them.

Finally, this meta-example highlights the importance of texts and images in cross-border contexts as sources of representation and discourse. How a particular topic is framed and discussed both reflects and influences programing and policy in relation to that issue. Policy and legal documents also contain important guidelines and laws that affect people's lives. Textual analysis can help identify biases in the way groups are represented.

ACCESSING DOCUMENTS

Before we delve into the analysis of documents, this section discusses how to access them. With the advent of internet technologies, many key documents are freely available to download. However, researchers should not limit themselves to these easy-to-find texts. In some cases, the texts that are most relevant for a research question may require a combination of access strategies.

LIBRARIES

Both public and private libraries contain primary documents that may not be available online. In some cases, these resources can only be consulted on site. Visiting a library may also allow the researcher to browse other related documents that are located in physical proximity to the document in question. Sometimes this "browsing" function is important to getting a different perspective on the research.

ARCHIVES

Governments, international organizations, museums, and private organizations host repositories of documents, artifacts, and audiovisual materials. These archives can be digital and/or physical. Access is often restricted, so researchers need to check these restrictions and, in many cases, apply for access. When attempting to access archives across borders, it can be confusing to navigate the myriad permission structures. In some cases, information has been centralized into a hub or portal for a country or regions. Some examples of these are in the resource section at the end of this chapter. However, a note of caution is in order, as these centralized sources of information on archives do not always include "community archives and charity/ third sector collections."[5] Moreover, some institutions' websites do not mention their collections or only provide online access to some objects or archives.[6] It should also be remembered that archives and museums are often part of colonialization and nation-building projects, so they may present only a partial representation of events in their archives.[7]

ACCESS TO INFORMATION OR FREEDOM OF INFORMATION REQUESTS

Some government documents are only available through access to information (also called freedom of information) requests as part of transparency initiatives, particularly in democracies or democratizing states.[8] In other words, these documents are available, but only if requested through particular processes and/or for particular reasons and usually after paying a fee.[9] Different governments have different processes, and sometimes the documents are restricted to their own citizens. In some cases, parts of the documents will be redacted if they contain sensitive or confidential information, and the quality of the information varies across topic and jurisdiction.[10] In all cases, these requests take time to process, so researchers need to factor this into their research design.

PERSONAL COPIES

In addition to formal archives and processes, researchers may be able to secure personal documents – such as maps, letters, diaries, meeting minutes – in their research. Access to these documents often requires personal connections to the individuals and organizations who own them and can be part of the interview process (see chapter 8) or ethnographic methods (see chapter 9).

SOCIAL MEDIA

As discussed in chapter 9, some social media data are public, while some are semi-public or private. Once you have established the nature of the information, the ethics approval, and the consent required, social media information can provide rich sources of textual and visual information at little to no financial cost. However, the volume of data can be difficult to manage, and the quality varies significantly.

LANGUAGE ISSUES

Another access issue in relation to textual data is language. In general, it is best for researchers to access texts in their original language, as translation can introduce errors of interpretation and fact. Application processes for accessing archives and freedom of information requests are also usually only available in the official language(s) of the country holding the documents.

Activity 11.1: Accessing Texts

1. Identify at least three texts that you could use for a research project in your program.
2. How would you access them? Are there any restrictions?
3. Now think of an alternative text that would require permission to access. What additional insights would this document provide?

CODES AND CODING

In essence, analysing text, including images, involves identifying meanings within the text, categorizing these meanings into themes, and assigning codes to these themes. It is important to distinguish between **denotative** – the literal, explicit, or direct – meanings and **connotative** meanings, which can be inferred or implied.

In order to get at these denotative and connotative meanings and adequately represent them in their analysis, researchers need to devise a system of coding. The next sections will walk you through different textual analysis methods that have different approaches to coding, but we first need to understand the basic terminology and principles.

- Codes can be encryption devices to protect information.
  For example, as discussed in chapters 8 and 9, interview and field-notes may include code names for respondents to protect their identity.
- **Administrative codes** can also be used to organize and categorize types of information.
  For example, in coding field or interview notes the administrative code "METH" indicates information related to methodology.
- **Topical codes** are indexing devices that help to analyse data.
  These are the subject of this chapter.
  For example, in the meta-example above, vulnerability was identified as a topical code.

Some topical codes have been standardized. For example, the Outline of Cultural Materials (OCM) provides numerical codes that assist with standardized topical coding of ethnographic data (https://hraf .yale.edu/wp-content/uploads/2018/05/Subjects-in-eHRAF.pdf). These standardized topical codes are useful for comparability across different case studies and contexts.

However, some researchers choose to develop their own mnemonic codes for specific topics. For example, in the meta-example above, "DOCU" was used as a mnemonic code to signify textual references to documentation. If a researcher develops their own coding system, they need to develop a code book, especially if there are multiple people in a cross-cultural, cross-border team. Indeed, when more than one person is using the same code, it is common practice to periodically calibrate findings by having everyone code the same piece of text to ensure there are no discrepancies in meaning. This ensures **intra-coder reliability**, that is, the standardization of coding across different researchers.

In developing codes, it is important to ensure that categories are both exhaustive and mutually exclusive. This means that researchers need to anticipate all possible categories. If categories become too large, they can be split into sub-categories. For example, in the OCM, there is a code for education (870), and then separate codes for educational system (871) and teachers (875). Categories also need to be mutually exclusive so that coders are clear how to code potentially ambiguous themes. In the meta-example above, elders are technically also adults, but the codebook clearly indicated that they should be categorized as elders and *not* as adults for the purposes of the age analysis.

Coding can be done by hand or using a textual analysis software. Computer-assisted coding allows researchers to code larger amounts of text. It can be used in both qualitative and quantitative analysis. There are a number of different computer-assisted coding software packages. We will not delve into the details of any particular program. However, it is important to recognize three different kinds of textual analysis software. The dictionary method involves the researcher(s) providing a list of words or phrases for which the computer "searches" in textual data.[11] Dictionary methods are simple and fairly low-tech, as they can be performed using regular search techniques in widely available computer software. Supervised machine learning (SML) programs require researchers to hand-code a set of "learning documents," which are then turned into an algorithm to "train" the computer to code in a similar way.[12] Unsupervised machine learning methods are fully automated, inductive computer techniques that "simultaneously generate categories and classify text into those categories."[13]

In cross-cultural and multilingual environments, it is usually better to analyse text and develop codes in the source language of the document. In many cases, researchers compare across countries with different national languages, or within countries that have more than one official language. Coding, including computer coding, can be done in multiple languages at the same time, with variations to incorporate different vocabulary, meanings, and linguistic characters. In some cases, it is more efficient to first translate all texts into one language and then adapt coding to these translations.[14]

For example, Didier Ruedin compared party manifestos of the thirteen parties in the 2011 election in Switzerland. These manifestos were originally written in German or

French and then translated into the other language as a line-by-line translation. By comparing coding results for the manifestos in the two languages, he found that "language differences can indeed affect the results of automatic approaches" unless provisions are made to coding.*

* Ruedin, "The Role of Language in the Automatic Coding of Political Texts."

Activity 11.2: Coding Fieldnotes

1. Using the fieldnotes you created from your observation in Activity 9.3, hand code them with:
   a. The administrative code "METH" to indicate a methodological comment.
   b. The following topical codes to categorize your data:
      i. PHYS: to indicate physical barriers
      ii. WEATH: to indicate any weather-related challenges
      iii. DESIGN: to indicate design features of buildings and spaces that are not wheelchair accessible
2. Are there any other topical codes you would add?
3. Do any of the codes need sub-categories?
4. Identify the codes above that are *not* mutually exclusive. How would you suggest changing the descriptions in a code book to avoid ambiguity in the case of multiple coders?
5. Compare your coding and notes with others in your class. Did you get similar or different results? Why? Is it because of the data or the coding?

METHODS FOR ANALYSING TEXTS

Once a researcher has gathered textual data, they need a systematic way of analysing and interpreting it. In this chapter, we will consider three key methods for analysing texts. This is intended as an introductory starting point and not an exhaustive list of all methods.

CONTENT ANALYSIS

Content analysis is a deductive approach to analysing text. A researcher starts with a pre-established question or hypothesis and applies previously developed codes to textual analysis. While there may be some adaptation of the coding throughout the research process, the approach to the textual analysis is based on pre-existing theoretical and empirical knowledge. The analysis can be both quantitative and qualitative.

Generally speaking, in content analysis, the following steps are taken:

1. The researcher formulates a hypothesis or research question.
   In the meta-example above, this was: "There are more visual and textual references to children than adults in UNHCR annual reports and appeals."
2. They then create a set of topical codes to represent the key variables in the hypothesis or research question.
   In the meta-example, children and adults were coded based on specific references in the text (including gendered language, such as boy or girl; or wom*n or m*n).
3. These codes are applied to the text.
   a. A quantitative analysis would involve counting and comparing statistically the frequency of the occurrence of particular codes.
      In the meta-example, multiple coders counted the number of times the age categories appeared.
   b. A qualitative analysis would involve searching the data for examples to support or refute the hypothesis.
4. The hypothesis or research question is reformulated or refined, depending on the quantitative and/or qualitative findings.
   In the meta-example, the research findings support the following new hypothesis: Children are proportionately represented in visual representations of refugees, but are over-represented in textual references in UNHCR appeals and reports.

For example, in a report by Pulker and colleagues, the researchers undertook content analysis to answer the following question: "What public health related CSR [corporate social responsibility] commitments have been made by supermarket chains globally?" Thirty-one supermarkets operating in up to fifty countries were selected based on the largest retailers in the 2018 *Global Powers of Retailing* report. Researchers then searched their websites to locate CSR or sustainability reports in English. The researchers used the software NVivo11 to undertake content analysis of these reports for seventy-nine themes related to the fourteen pre-identified attributes: "general governance, influencing policy, setting supplier rules, influencing livelihoods, influencing communities, accessibility, availability, food cost and affordability, food preferences and choices, food safety and quality, nutritional quality, animal welfare, food and packaging waste, and other sustainability issues." This content analysis revealed that "most (57/79) themes related to public health nutrition, followed by food governance (10/79), and then food system (12/79) themes."[*]

[*] Pulker et al., "Global Supermarkets' Corporate Social Responsibility Commitments to Public Health."

GROUNDED THEORY

Grounded theory is a method to analyse text from an inductive approach. While researchers start with a research question, they do not have pre-established themes or codes. Rather, they engage with the text to allow for themes to emerge.

The following steps are undertaken in a grounded theory approach:

1. The researcher reads through the text several times to get a sense of the themes that emerge.
2. They then develop codes based on these themes.
   In the meta-example above, one theme that emerged from reading the texts was labour – how different age groups were constructed in relation to work.

3. The researcher brings in data from the same categories to compare them and to see how they are linked.

   For example, children were portrayed visually in productive and reproductive labour, but in the text "child labour" was constructed as something to be eliminated, as a barrier to education, and so on.

4. They then use these linkages to build theory (thereby explaining why the methodology is called grounded *theory*).

   For example, in the article cited in the meta-example, the author used the concept of social age to compare localized realities of childhood (as represented in the photos of child work) to idealized international norms of childhood free from labour.

5. They identify examples of texts and quotes to support this theory.

   For example, they compared a picture of a child working to a quote from the text about the negative impacts of child labour.

For example, researchers used Indigenous methodologies and grounded theory to understand Maori women's self-protection strategies in contexts of unsafe relationships. The research project generated a large amount of data through mixed methods, including interviews, focus groups, narratives, media stories, genealogies, traditional stories, proverbs, and messages from spiritual ancestors. When analysing the transcripts and texts, the researchers used "a collective Indigenous approach, Mahi a Roopū (collaborative group work), to guide the process of constructing the grounded theory. [. . .] Gathering together enabled researchers to engage in critical discussions to reach a consensus decision about what was arising from the data and the emerging codes, categories, and properties."*

* D. Wilson et al., "Using Indigenous Kaupapa Māori Research Methodology with Constructivist Grounded Theory."

CRITICAL DISCOURSE ANALYSIS

Critical discourse analysis (CDA) is a particular method for analysing text that focuses on the ways in which power is constructed by and through discourse. Discourse is a system that "governs the way that a topic can be meaningfully talked about and reasoned about."[15] Van Djick, who was instrumental in developing CDA, describes it as "*focusing on the role of discourse in the (re)production and challenge of dominance.* [...] More specifically, critical discourse analysts want to know what structures, strategies, or other properties of text, talk, verbal interaction, or communicative events play a role in these modes of reproduction."[16]

Table 11.1 summarizes the steps in CDA, as interpreted by Cummings et al.[17]

Table 11.1. Steps in critical discourse analysis

Phase 1: Select research topic
Step 1.1: Formulate a research question that can be answered by analysing "dialectical relations between semiotic and other elements"
Step 1.2: Understand the "genealogy" of past discourses
Phase 2: Select and analyse texts
Step 2.1: Select texts related to the research question
Step 2.2: "Describe how the text was created"
Step 2.3: Analyse the texts in terms of "vision, strategy, means of implementation, goals, and targets at the level of:
• individual words and phrases
• how the words and phrases relate to each other in the text
• the priority given to different themes"
Step 2.4: "Identify discourses in the texts" based on past discourses identified in step 1.2
Phase 3: "Consider how the social order 'needs' the social question" – that is, whether changing the social order is necessary
Phase 4: Identify "possible semiotic solutions" – that is, using "discourses, narratives, and arguments" to "identify ways past the obstacles"

Source: Cummings et al., "Critical Discourse Analysis."

For example, Cummings et al. used CDA to understand knowledge production within the Sustainable Development Goals (SDGs) by analysing discourses in the UN outcome document, "Transforming Our World: The 2030 Agenda for Sustainable Development." They analysed the origins of the text, as well as the power relations that are reproduced in the document. They found that "techno-scientific-economic discourse is the dominant discourse at the level of implementation and goals, while there is some evidence of the pluralist-participatory discourse at the level of vision and strategy."* They suggest that the latter provides opportunities for change.

* Cummings et al., "Critical Discourse Analysis," 727.

Activity 11.3: Analysing a UN Security Resolution

Use the following UN Resolution 2573 (2021) as the basis for your textual analysis (https://undocs.org/en/S/RES/2573(2021):

1. Identify all mentions of "civilian" (hint: you can use the search function) and code the surrounding text in relation to the following themes:
   a. Education
   b. Health
   c. Human rights
   d. Humanitarian assistance/aid
2. Now, read through the text several times and identify at least one theme that is not listed in question 1 above.
3. Think about the way civilian protection is framed in the resolution and the power relations that this discourse supports.
4. What are the different textual analysis methods represented in questions 1–3 above?
5. If you speak another UN language, select one of the passages you coded in question 1 above and then compare it to the English version. Are they qualitatively and quantitatively the same? Would you need different codes?
6. If you do not speak another UN language, copy and paste one of the passages you coded in question 1 into Google Translate. Compare the English translation to the original. Imagine that you only had access to the translated version. How accurate would your textual analysis be?

INTERPRETING IMAGES

While in-depth training in visual analysis is beyond the scope of this book, here I provide a preliminary overview of some considerations when interpreting images. This is important given the increased popularity of arts-based participatory methods (see chapter 10) and the ways in which images are often used in cross-border contexts to represent "others."

Photographs are often included in documents, both to break up the text and to visually represent cross-border issues. In some cases, photographs are used as documentary evidence and are sometimes perceived to be an objective representation of "facts." However, many analysts point out that photographs have an ambiguous "truth value."[18] Not only can they be modified by technologies, but they also depend on the photographer's "interpretations of events and subjects which he or she chooses to place in front of the camera lens"[19] as well as on the subsequent decisions of editors, who "select [photographs] out from their original ordering and narrative context, [and . . .] place [them] alongside textual information and reports in a publication."[20] Where photographs are part of texts, it is therefore important to interpret them within this textual context and also to record the caption and other text specifically associated with the photo.

When analysing images, it is also important to acknowledge the positionality of researchers interpreting them, especially in cross-border research involving different world views. As Nandita Dogra argues, "The 'reading' or the process of decoding any given image(s) is done by people in divergent ways often based on their identity and life experiences. While there may be a 'preferred,' or 'dominant,' or 'hegemonic' reading, which is intended by the author or reinforces a prevailing ideology, 'oppositional readings' can be made of the same text which contest the dominant meanings of the image."[21] This is why participants involved in generating visual data through participatory methods (see chapter 10) should be given an opportunity to explain and contextualize the information.

For example, Godin and Dona reflect on Displaces,[22] a participatory photography project with people in transit through the "Calais Jungle." Participants were provided with training on photographic methods, as well as cameras. They owned the copyright to their images, made editing decisions, and decided on how the photographs would be interpreted and presented, including the captions of the photos, which were translated from the participants' language of choice.

Activity 11.4: Analysing the Displaces Project

1. View some of the photographs from the Displaces project on the Displaces – Calais and Beyond website (https://educatingwith outborders.wordpress.com/displaces-a-project-by-gideon-mendel -and-calais-jungle-residents/).
2. Without reading the caption, what do you notice in the photo? Write down two to three key words from each photo.
3. Now, look at the caption. How does it compare to the themes you identified?
4. How did your positionality affect the way you viewed, analysed, and reacted to the photos?

TEXTUAL AND VISUAL REPRESENTATION ACROSS BORDERS

Textual and visual analysis involves categorizing and analysing nuanced, complex data and attempting to draw conclusions in relation to a research question. The researcher – through the generation of data and/or its analysis – is involved in meaning making and representation. In international programs focused on global inequalities, this often involves what Susan Sontag has described as "regarding the pain of others."[23] Researchers have a responsibility to reflexively consider our own positionalities in the (re)production and consumption of these representations. As Machiel Lamers argues, a "discursive approach provides us not only with insights on 'how' the 'other' is represented but also 'by whom' and for 'what reasons.'"[24]

Indeed, one of the powerful contributions of textual and visual analysis is exposing biases in dominant discourses and documents about a phenomenon or group of people. Evi Chatzipanagiotidou and Fiona Murphy suggest that researchers need to engage in methodological "dubiety" in their "responsibility (not) to document loss."[25] In other words, phenomena like conflict, displacement, and poverty are multi-faceted, and people have a range of lived experiences in these contexts, so it is important that visual and textual representations reflect this complexity.

Activity 11.5: Representation of University Students in a Study on Instagram Posts

Read the following methodology section, from a textual analysis of 600 Instagram posts, written by Stefanie E. Davis:

> A total of 600 Instagram posts from Four Year Party and College Nationwide were analyzed during this textual analysis. A total of 300 posts from each site were collected through screenshots. The number of likes and top comments were included in the screenshot. The two sites were chosen based on number of followers, frequency of posts, and dedication to showcasing the collegiate lifestyle. Four Year Party has over 81,500 followers and posts videos or photos several times a day. College Nationwide has 57,600 followers and posts daily. Using the previous research detailed above as a guide, a textual analysis was conducted to tease out common themes among the 600 posts. These themes are as follows: objectification of female college students, submissiveness of female college students, and emphasis on a young, white collegiate experience.[26]

1. To what extent does the title of the article – "Objectification, Sexualization, and Misrepresentation: Social Media and the College Experience" – represent the methods used in the article?
2. How do the themes that emerge from the textual analysis make you feel? Reflect on your own positionality as a student, and also in relation to social constructions of gender and racialization.
3. Given your reflections in relation to question 2, what lessons do you draw about researching "other" people's realities?

CONCLUSIONS AND KEY TAKEAWAYS

Words and images matter. Representation is important in cross-border, cross-cultural research. These representations merit greater critical analysis by researchers working in interdisciplinary, international programs. Documents are rich sources of textual and visual data. With the advent of communication technologies, many texts are easily accessible to researchers and can be a way of contributing to knowledge even with limited time and resources. Other documents require more effort to find and access, but they can potentially make a greater contribution to knowledge, or provide insights into policies that are publicly accessible but not easily available.

DISCUSSION QUESTIONS

1. What are the opportunities and challenges of analysing texts in multiple languages?
2. Discuss specific issues that may arise with intra-coder reliability in cross-border and cross-cultural contexts.
3. How do epistemological and world view differences affect textual and visual analysis?

FURTHER READINGS

Ahmed, Wasim. "Using Twitter as a Data Source: An Overview of Social Media Research Tools (2021)." *LSE Impact Blog*, 18 May 2021. https://blogs.lse.ac.uk/impactofsocialsciences/2021/05/18/using-twitter-as-a-data-source-an-overview-of-social-media-research-tools-2021/.

Balcells, Laia, and Christopher M. Sullivan. "New Findings from Conflict Archives: An Introduction and Methodological Framework." *Journal of Peace Research* 55, no. 2 (2018): 137–46. https://doi.org/10.1177/0022343317750217.

Bouvier, Gwen, and David Machin. "Critical Discourse Analysis and the Challenges and Opportunities of Social Media." *Review of Communication* 18, no. 3 (2018): 178–92. https://doi.org/10.1080/15358593.2018.1479881.

Champagne-Poirier, Olivier, Marie-Ève Carignan, Marc D. David, and Tracey O'Sullivan. "Understanding and Quantifying: A Mixed-Method Study on the Journalistic Coverage of Canadian Disasters." *International Journal of Qualitative Methods* 20 (2021). https://doi.org/10.1177/1609406921990492.

Cummings, Sarah, Barbara Regeer, Leah de Haan, Marjolein Zweekhorst, and Joske Bunders. "Critical Discourse Analysis of Perspectives on Knowledge and the Knowledge Society within the Sustainable Development Goals." *Development Policy Review* 36, no. 6 (2018): 727–42. https://doi.org/10.1111/dpr.12296.

Kapoor, Kawaljeet Kaur, Kuttimani Tamilmani, Nripendra P. Rana, Pushp Patil, Yogesh K. Dwivedi, and Sridhar Nerur. "Advances in Social Media Research: Past, Present and Future." *Information Systems Frontiers* 20, no. 3 (2018): 531–58. https://doi.org/10.1007/s10796-017-9810-y.

Khan, Mohsin Hassan, Hamedi Mohd Adnan, Surinderpal Kaur, Rashid Ali Khuhro, Rohail Asghar, and Sahira Jabeen. "'Muslims' Representation in Donald Trump's Anti-Muslim-Islam Statement: A Critical Discourse Analysis." *Religions* 10, no. 2 (2019): 115. https://doi.org/10.3390/rel10020115.

Nasheeda, Aishath, Haslinda Binti Abdullah, Steven Eric Krauss, and Nobaya Binti Ahmed. "Transforming Transcripts into Stories: A Multimethod Approach to Narrative Analysis." *International Journal of Qualitative Methods* 18 (2019). https://doi.org/10.1177/1609406919856797.

Williams, Matthew L., Pete Burnap, Luke Sloan, Curtis Jessop, and Hayley Lepps. "Users' Views of Ethics in Social Media Research: Informed Consent, Anonymity, and Harm." In *The Ethics of Online Research*, edited by Kandy Woodfield, 27–52. Bingley, UK: Emerald Publishing, 2018.

Wilson, Denise, Alayne Mikahere-Hall, and Juanita Sherwood. "Using Indigenous Kaupapa Māori Research Methodology with Constructivist Grounded Theory: Generating a Theoretical Explanation of Indigenous Womens Realities." *International Journal of Social Research Methodology* 25, no. 2 (2022): 375–90. https://doi.org/10.1080/13645579.2021.1897756.

Web Resources

Archives Hub, UK: https://archiveshub.jisc.ac.uk.

Archives Portal Europe: https://www.archivesportaleurope.net.

Outline of Cultural Materials (OCM): https://hraf.yale.edu/wp-content/uploads/2018/05/Subjects-in-eHRAF.pdf.

Social Media Research: A Guide to Ethics: https://www.gla.ac.uk/media/Media_487729_smxx.pdf.

12

Presenting Research Findings across Borders: Reach, Responsibility, and Representation

LEARNING OBJECTIVES

By the end of this chapter, you will be able to:

- Identify tools and resources to disseminate research within and beyond academia;
- Explain open access and identify copyright licences that indicate variations of open access;
- Discuss opportunities and challenges of copyright ownership in international contexts;
- Understand ethical issues related to sharing other people's stories and experiences across borders;
- Critically reflect on issues of representation in international, cross-border research; and,
- Identify methods of, and limitations to, evaluating impact.

KEY TERMS

Copyright
Creative Commons licence
Infographics
Knowledge mobilization

Open access
Plain language summaries
Policy briefs

INTRODUCTION

So far in this book, we have focused primarily on how to find and access information related to international issues. In this final chapter, we will discuss practical tools and ethical considerations in sharing research findings across borders. As discussed in chapter 1, most researchers in our fields hope that their findings will bring about practical change. But, how can we translate our academic work into easily accessible communication pieces that reach across borders? And, how do we know that we are having the impact we intended? In this chapter, we will also reflect on our positionality in representing other people's experiences and stories, especially in the context of global inequalities.

META-EXAMPLE: PUBLIC HEALTH DECISIONS DURING THE COVID-19 PANDEMIC

COVID-19 is a disease caused by a new strain of coronavirus. On 30 January 2020, the World Health Organization declared the COVID-19 outbreak as a "Public Health Emergency of International Concern" and, on 11 March 2020, a pandemic.[1]

As the pandemic spread globally, researchers around the world worked to discover information on transmission and prevention, as well as to develop vaccines. This science evolved as more data became available in both clinical research and real-world contexts. There was also the spread of misinformation and rumours about the virus through social media. As a result, ordinary people and government decision-makers received a lot of information that was conflicting, overwhelming, and usually beyond their own area of expertise. In this context, how could they make informed personal and policy decisions?

Researchers conducted an online experiment as part of a longitudinal study in Italy, Spain, and the United Kingdom to understand the role of expert endorsement in the perceived legitimacy of public policy on COVID-19.[2] They found that democratic governments who justified public policy on the basis of advice and research of experts and who communicated effectively acquired public legitimacy.[3] Another study showed that academics were the second most frequently quoted in media reports on the H1N1 pandemic after ministers of health.[4]

This meta-example demonstrates several key issues that will be explored in this chapter. First, for research to have any impact – whether in academia or beyond – it needs to be communicated effectively.

Second, technical expertise needs to be "translated" into an accessible format in order for it to reach a wider audience. This is especially important in the context of the popular spread of misinformation.

Third, academic research has the potential to have important impacts on real world problems, but it is sometimes difficult to measure this impact or attribute it to any one research team or project.

Finally, with this potential impact comes responsibility. Researchers need to think carefully about the veracity and validity of their findings, as well as the impact, both negative and positive, of their work on people's lives. In the COVID-19 context, this meant revising information as more data became available, even if this could potentially undermine credibility.

WRITING AN ACADEMIC PAPER TO PRESENT FINDINGS

Before turning to dissemination of research outside of academia, we discuss here standard ways of "writing up" research results in a scholarly paper. You will likely have some specific requirements from your program and your instructor. However, generally speaking, all academic papers – whether they are written for a course or in a scholarly journal – have the following key components:

- Research question/hypothesis and puzzle: The paper should clearly articulate the specific research question or hypothesis the research is trying to answer or test. This question should be situated within the research puzzle. The researcher should show why this question is important.
- Literature review: The researcher should show what other research is already available on the topic. This should not simply be a list of other studies. Rather, it should summarize the key findings and debates about the topic and situate the author's research question within this literature. Key questions to address in the literature review are What do we know already? Where are the gaps? What

are the points of convergence and divergence? How will this paper help to (partially) address these?

- Analytical framework: In this section, the paper should provide conceptual and operational definitions of key terms. It should also clearly articulate the theoretical approach adopted in the paper.
- Methodology: The researcher needs to communicate to the reader how they conducted the research for the paper. If the paper makes an empirical contribution, the methodology section should include details on research design, sampling, methods, ethics, and so on. If the paper is based on secondary literature or data or makes a conceptual or theoretical contribution, this section can explain the search techniques used to find the resources. The researcher's positionality can also be included in this section.
- Findings and analysis: This is the core of the paper. It is often organized into several sub-sections based on themes from coding.
- Conclusion: A good conclusion not only summarizes the key arguments, but also proposes ideas for future research and recommendations.
- Bibliography: This includes a list of all the references used in the paper.

The best way to write a paper is to start! Students often get paralyzed starting at a blank paper or computer screen. You don't have to write the paper in the order presented above. Rather, like doing a puzzle, you can start with a section and then fit it into other sections as you go along. However, it is generally a good idea to have a clear outline of the paper, so that you can ensure that the pieces fit together and that there is a coherent structure.

Another helpful strategy is to keep a notebook or an open page to jot down key thoughts and ideas as they come to you. This allows you to retain information, while still working on another section.

Some other resources and tips are included at the end of this chapter.

Activity 12.1: Writing a Paper for a Course

1. Think about a paper that you need to write for this or another course.

2. Write an outline for the paper using the information provided in the syllabus, the points in the section above, and the resources at the end of this chapter.
3. Will you write the paper in the sequence of the outline or by section? Why?
4. Many academic institutions have writing centres or student support services to help students write. What tools and resources are available at your college or university?

BARRIERS TO ACCESSING ACADEMIC RESEARCH

Academic research has historically privileged published, scholarly literature – such as books and academic journal articles – as the key mechanisms for dissemination of research findings. As we saw in chapter 4, scholarly, published literature is the "gold standard" in scientific research. But, these outlets are limiting because of access issues, which are exacerbated in cross-border, cross-cultural research.

First, resource constraints mean that many individuals and institutions may not be able to afford to buy books or subscribe to journals. While academic libraries may allow registered users to borrow these publications, they are generally limited to students and instructors at these institutions. In the context of global inequalities, it is also important to recognize that academic institutions based in the global south have fewer financial resources than those in the global north. Moreover, participants who shared their experiences and whose lives are affected by our research may not be able to access these resources. To partially address this access issue, there is a growing movement within academia to publish **open access** materials, discussed in the section below.

Second, there are language issues. English is still the dominant language of academic literature, even though the global issues we study affect many different language groups. Indeed, many academics who work and study in languages other than English still publish and present in English.[5] To respond to this, researchers are encouraged to translate their findings into the local language of the communities impacted by their research.

Third, there are linguistic issues. Academic research tends to be full of technical terms, jargon, and long theoretical explanations. In response, there is a growing trend towards knowledge mobilization – the explicit process of presenting findings in a way that is understandable to a broad range of audiences, including those outside of academia. We will discuss some of these **knowledge mobilization** tools in this chapter.

OPEN ACCESS, COPYRIGHT, AND OWNERSHIP

To partially address some of these access issues, there is a growing move towards open access publication and resources. Indeed, some research funders now require that all research findings be made available as open access as a condition of their funding.

What is open access? At its core, it means "free, immediate, online availability."[6] Generally speaking, open access data, education resources, and documents have three characteristics:

1. "Is freely available on the internet";
2. "Permits any user to download, copy, analyse, re-process, pass to software, or use for any other purpose"; and,
3. "Is without financial, legal, or technical barriers other than those inseparable from gaining access to the internet itself."[7]

Open access is intimately related to **copyright**. Generally speaking, in traditional publishing, when an author signs a publication agreement, they transfer their copyright to the publisher. This allows the publisher to subsequently sell books and journals. While the author usually receives royalties, it is the publisher who owns and controls the copyright. This means that, under most traditional publication agreements, an author needs to get permission – and often pay – to reuse or reproduce their own publications! As Peter Suber argues, "The deeper problem is that we donate time, labour, and public money to create new knowledge and then hand control over the results to businesses that believe, correctly or incorrectly, that their revenue and survival depend on limiting access to that knowledge."[8]

In most open access publishing, the author retains the copyright and makes it open access through one of the **Creative Commons licences** shown in figure 12.1.[9]

As both producers and consumers of knowledge, it is important that researchers understand their rights and obligations under copyright law. In cross-border research, this is complicated by different legislation

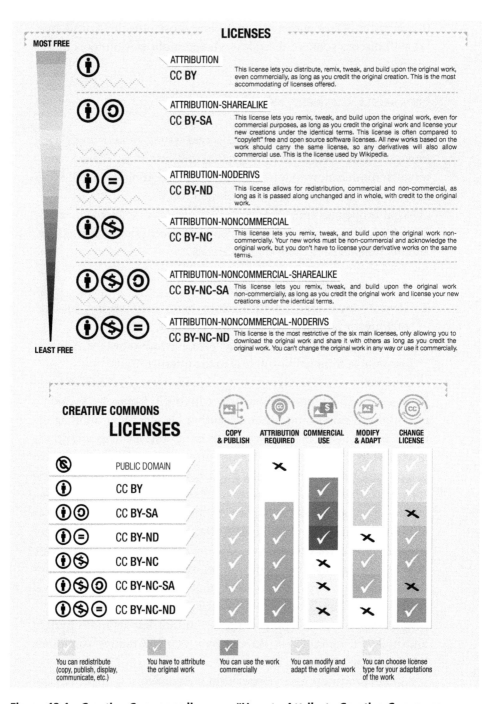

Figure 12.1   Creative Commons licences. "How to Attribute Creative Commons Photos," *foter* (blog), 4 March 2015, https://foter.com/blog/how-to-attribute-creative -commons-photos/.

in different jurisdictions. It is therefore a good idea to check with your institution's copyright librarian or copyright office, if you have one, to ensure you understand the specific legal context in your country. When knowledge is co-produced and co-authored, these copyright issues must also be negotiated with your research partners and participants, who may live in different countries or have different world views. As mentioned in chapter 10, copyright and ownership questions need to be explicitly addressed in participatory methods, where participants produce art, photographs, or other creative works that also serve as data.

Activity 12.2: Finding Open Access Images

We frequently use images in our personal, professional, and academic lives to illustrate posters, put on a title page, or jazz up a presentation. But, do you know how to identify the licence of the images you use and whether you are allowed to use them? In this activity, you will apply the information on copyright above.

1. First, think of a research question or puzzle. This can be the same one that you used in Activity 12.1, chapter 4, or a totally new topic.
2. Now, search for three open access images that you could use on a poster advertising a free public event about the research question you identified above. (Hint: If you search on Google, you can filter them by "Creative Commons" under the "Usage Rights" tool; or you could search in the Creative Commons database: https://search.creativecommons.org/.)
3. What licence do these images have?
4. Would you be able to use these same images if you wanted to sell the posters?

KNOWLEDGE MOBILIZATION ACROSS BORDERS

While open access addresses some of the technical, financial, and legal barriers to access, there is still often the problem of communicating results in a way and in a language that resonates with a non-academic audience. In this section, we explore some of the ways in which researchers can undertake knowledge mobilization activities that translate academic findings into formats that are more easily accessible to a diverse, general public.

Plain language summaries are short pieces that communicate the key findings of the research in layperson's terms. "A communication is in plain language if its wording, structure, and design are so clear that the intended audience can easily find what they need, understand what they find, and use that information."[10] The Plain Language Association International (PLAIN) recommends that a writer starts by thinking carefully about the purpose of the document and who the audience is – that is, their background and the kind of information they need from the document.[11] PLAIN also recommends structuring the document in a way that is both logical and interesting, designing the layout to be visually attractive, and conveying the information in different ways.

Policy briefs are plain language summaries with recommendations aimed at key decision-makers in government and civil society. The key points related to plain language summaries, discussed above, also apply to policy briefs. In addition, they include recommendations. Researchers often have difficulty writing recommendations because it requires putting oneself in the position of the decision-maker and focusing on the practical steps that need to be taken towards change. Generally speaking, recommendations should:

- Clearly specify the key actor(s) who is expected to implement the recommendation. Avoid passive voice.
- Be realistic in terms of the mandate, capacity, and resources of the actor(s) involved.
- Be practical – that is, the recommendation should specify what steps need to be undertaken and in what sequence.
- Be actionable within a specified timeframe.

Infographics display research findings in a visual format. Infographics can be an effective tool for communicating findings in a different way and can be added to other knowledge mobilization strategies. The *Journal of Marketing Management* has a detailed reference on how to turn research into an infographic.[12] They recommend starting with a storyboard that summarizes the research question, context, and key findings. They encourage researchers to zero in on "the big idea" and to prioritize other key points in a hierarchical way. There are a number of web-based programs (see the resource section at the end of this chapter) to help you design and display your information in a visually attractive way, but you need to first identify the main substantive points of the research story you want to tell.

Posters also display information visually, but are more common in academic formats. Similar to infographics, when designing an academic poster, a researcher needs to think first and foremost about the central idea they wish to communicate.[13] One of the main challenges is to distil a complicated research project into a few key messages. Think about how you can display some of the information visually – such as in graphs or tables as well as one central image – to summarize the main focus of the research.

Oral presentations are the main way of disseminating information to both academic and non-academic audiences. Formats and lengths vary, but you should be able to summarize your key points in three minutes or less – the so-called elevator pitch. Similar to other methods of knowledge mobilization, your presentation should have one central argument with a few key supporting points. Practice these points and make sure you can fit your ideas within the time allocated to you. Visual supports – such as slides – can help support the oral presentation, but these should be complementary to the oral presentation. Oral presentations are often followed by a question and answer period. Anticipate some of these questions and have specific data and examples on hand to answer them.

Activity 12.3: Creating an Infographic

1. Read the following short introductions for creating an infographic:

   "How to Turn Your Journal Article into an Infographic," *Journal of Marketing Management* (https://www.jmmnews.com/how-to-turn-journal-article-into-infographic/); "Presenting Research in Infographics," *Research Retold* (https://www.researchretold.com/presenting-research-in-infographics/).
2. Now, use the information in the following abstract[14] to create an infographic:

   "The outbreak of COVID-19 affected the lives of all sections of society as people were asked to self-quarantine in their homes to prevent the spread of the virus. The lockdown had serious implications on mental health, resulting in psychological problems including frustration, stress, and depression. In order to explore the impacts of this pandemic on the lives of students, we conducted a survey of a total of 1182 individuals of different age groups from various educational institutes in Delhi–National Capital Region (NCR), India. The article identified the following as the impact of COVID-19 on the students of different age groups: time spent on online classes and self-study, medium used for learning, sleeping habits, daily fitness routine, and the subsequent effects on weight, social life, and mental health. Moreover, our research found that in order to deal with stress and anxiety, participants adopted different coping mechanisms and also sought help from their near ones. Further, the research examined the student's engagement on social media platforms among different age categories. This study suggests that public authorities should take all the necessary measures to enhance the learning experience by mitigating the negative impacts caused due to the COVID-19 outbreak."*

* Chaturvedi, Vishwakarma, and Singh, "COVID-19."

3. Compare your product to other students. What did you learn?

MEASURING RESEARCH IMPACT

Just as knowledge mobilization strategies have changed, so too have metrics to measure research impact. In the past, academics were primarily concerned with citations in other academic literature. Publications in prestigious academic journals and with well-known academic presses were also valued more highly than "lower-impact" publishing outlets.

While this is still true, especially within established disciplines, there is a growing recognition of other impact measures, especially in applied, inter-disciplinary fields. As Bornmann argues, "the scope of research evaluations becomes broader as the societal products (outputs), societal use (societal references), and societal benefits (changes in society) of research come into scope."[15] In these contexts, impact on policy or legislative changes may "count" as much as academic publications. Similarly, many universities now have awards to recognize scholars who contribute to public debate through media interventions.

However, as with any causal mechanism (see chapter 4), it is difficult, and sometimes impossible, to isolate the impact of research on any specific policy or program. There are many other factors that can contribute to change, and it would be presumptuous to attribute them solely to a research project.

ETHICS AND REPRESENTATION ACROSS BORDERS

As discussed throughout this book, global inequalities are often (re)produced through research. I would like to end by recounting a cautionary tale and the lessons we can draw for research across borders.

In 2002, the Norwegian journalist Åsne Seierstad published a book entitled *The Bookseller of Kabul*, based on her interactions with a bookseller and his family in Kabul, Afghanistan. The book became a bestseller in Norway and was translated into English in 2002 and then into many other languages.

Although aspects of the book were fictionalized and Seierstad used a pseudonym for the bookseller, because he was the only bookstore owner in Kabul who sold international books, he was easily identified and sought out by journalists interested in pursuing his story further.

The real bookseller, Shah Muhammad Rais, objected to the way he and his family were portrayed in the book. He also contended that allegations of infidelity in the book put him and his family in jeopardy. His second wife Suraia Rais sued Seierstad for defamation. Shah Muhammed Rais also published his own version of his story, which was translated into English as *Once Upon a Time There Was a Bookseller in Kabul*.

What can we learn from the bookseller's experiences? First, in applied fields of study, researchers often aspire to change public opinion and policy. However, it is difficult to predict the scale and impact of research, especially in cross-border contexts. When Seierstad first published her book in Norwegian, she could not have anticipated that it would eventually be read by millions of people around the world. She also likely did not think about the negative impact the book could have on the bookseller and his family.

Second, there are fundamental questions of ownership and representation that need to be clearly addressed in any cross-border information gathering. While Seierstad maintains that the book is based on what she observed, Shah and Suraia Rais contend that she misunderstood and misrepresented their realities. Not only were they negatively impacted by the findings, but they also did not gain any of the financial benefits from the sales of the bestseller. Ownership and control over the research findings are not always clear, as demonstrated in this case.

Third, even if one tries to anonymize data, it is possible that identities will be discovered, especially if one has done detailed, long-term work with individuals and communities. This has implications not only for the individuals who are directly involved in research, but also for their family members, friends, and others in their social networks. Indeed, in some cases, as demonstrated by Arlene Stein's experiences (see chapter 9), even the identification of a researcher can breech confidentiality.

Fourth, this example shows how research that occurs outside of academic processes may not be subject to the same ethics review and scholarly norms. Seierstad is a journalist. This chapter suggested some ways to mobilize knowledge outside of academia, but this can then create overlapping relationships of power and knowledge that complicate ethics and representation.

CONCLUSIONS AND KEY TAKEAWAYS

For research to make a difference, researchers need to proactively seek out ways to make their findings known to a broad range of audiences, including decision-makers. This chapter highlighted the importance of open access mechanisms, as well as knowledge mobilization activities. With this increased potential impact, there is increased need to reflexively think about ethical issues of representation and about potential negative impacts of the findings on research participants. These ethical considerations are embedded in power relations within globalized contexts of inequalities across borders.

FURTHER READINGS

Bastow, Simon, Patrick Dunleavy, and Jane Tinkler. *The Impact of the Social Sciences: How Academics and Their Research Make a Difference*. London: Sage Publications, 2014.

Evans, Megan C., and Christopher Cvitanovic. "An Introduction to Achieving Policy Impact for Early Career Researchers." *Palgrave Communications* 4 (2018): 88. https://doi.org/10.1057/s41599-018 -0144-2.

Georgalakis, James, Nasreen Jessani, Rose Oronje, and Ben Ramalingam, eds. *The Social Realities of Knowledge for Development: Sharing Lessons of Improving Development Processes with Evidence*. Brighton, UK: Institute of Development Studies and The Impact Initiative, 2017. https://opendocs .ids.ac.uk/opendocs/handle/20.500.12413/12852.

Reed, Mark S., Rosalind Bryce, and Ruth Machen. "Pathways to Policy Impact: A New Approach for Planning and Evidencing Research Impact." *Evidence & Policy: A Journal of Research, Debate and Practice* 14, no. 3 (2018): 431–58. https://doi.org/10.1332/174426418X15326967547242.

Rojas, Lucero Ibarra. "On Conversation and Authorship: Legal Frameworks for Collaborative Methodologies." *International Journal of Qualitative Methods* 20 (2021). https://doi.org/10.1177/1609406921993289.

Sousa, Bailey J., and Alexander M. Clark. "Six Insights to Make Better Academic Conference Posters." *International Journal of Qualitative Methods* 18 (2019). https://doi.org/10.1177/1609406919862370.

Suber, Peter. *Open Access*. Cambridge, MA: MIT Press, 2012.

Wilkinson, Catherine, and Samantha Wilkinson. "Doing It Write: Representation and Responsibility in Writing Up Participatory Research Involving Young People." *Social Inclusion* 5, no. 3 (2017): 219–27. https:// doi.org/10.17645/si.v5i3.957.

Web Resources

CMI. How to Write a Policy Brief: https://www.cmi.no/guide/policy-brief.

The Copyright Office at the University of Alberta created a series of short modules on copyright: https://sites.library.ualberta.ca/copyright/. Some of the content is specific to Canada, but these modules are less country-specific:

– Asking Permission and Transactional Licences

– Finding Open and Creative Commons Content

– History of Copyright

– Images

– Including Third Party Content in Your Work

– Open Licensing and Creative Commons

– Public Domain

– Theoretical Foundations for Copyright

This overview of using copyright protected images is based on US law but it has some good advice that applies in any case of using images: https://www.pixsy.com/academy/image-user/using-copyrighted-images/.

EU. How to Write Clearly: https://op.europa.eu/en/publication-detail/-/publication/725b7eb0-d92e-11e5-8fea-01aa75ed71a1.

Ffrench-Constant, Laura. How to Plan, Write and Communicate an Effective Policy Brief: Three Steps to Success: https://www.researchtoaction.org/wp-content/uploads/2014/10/PBWeekLauraFCfinal.pdf.

Golash-Boza, Tanya. Six Tips for Giving a Fabulous Academic Presentation: https://www.wiley.com/network/researchers/promoting-your-article/6-tips-for-giving-a-fabulous-academic-presentation.

IDRC. How to Write a Policy Brief: https://www.idrc.ca/en/how-write-policy-brief?gclid=CjwKCAjwy42FBhB2EiwAJY0yQgusPkL6hZUMP04xA17-aY9Hcd-13_8D1mFfYXtgd4LOQL_WxgrIyRoC0tkQAvD_BwE.

Journal of Marketing Management. How to Turn Your Journal Article into an Infographic: https://www.jmmnews.com/how-to-turn-journal-article-into-infographic/.

Plain Language Association International. International Resources: https://plainlanguagenetwork.org/plain-language/plain-language-around-the-world/.

– What Is Plain Language?: https://plainlanguagenetwork.org/plain-language/what-is-plain-language/.

Research Retold. Presenting Research in Infographics: https://www.researchretold.com/presenting-research-in-infographics/.

SPARC Open Access Initiative: https://sparcopen.org/.

Stanford Law School. How to Write Policy Papers: https://www-cdn.law.stanford.edu/wp-content/uploads/2015/04/White-Papers-Guidelines.pdf.

USC Libraries. How to Prepare an Oral Presentation: https://libguides.usc.edu/writingguide/oralpresentation.

Glossary

Abstract A summary at the beginning of an article or book that describes the research and key findings.

Academic integrity Also known as "scholarly ethics," this refers to principles and rules that govern what is and is not acceptable in university and academic work.

Academic journals Peer-reviewed, published collections of articles based on academic research.

Academic literature Books, articles, and scholarly works that have been peer reviewed, have an analytical framework, and provide references for their sources.

Academic, published literature Documents that have been peer reviewed and published by a publishing company.

Advocacy Action that is intended to effect change.

Analytical framework A clearly defined approach to analysing data, based on a conceptual framework, plus a theoretical framework.

Analytic generalization Similar to the logic of experimentation, if two or more cases are shown to prove a hypothesis, then replication can be claimed.

Anonymity A process by which participants' identities are hidden from researchers, so that they cannot associate data with any particular individual.

Anonymized A characteristic used to describe data that have been disassociated from identifying characteristics, so that analysts are not able to connect any piece of information with any particular participant.

Antidisciplinary   Rejects disciplines all together and tries to find a new way of research and learning that goes beyond disciplinarity.

Applied (research)   Research that has a practical purpose.

Assent   Agreement provided by a research participant who is deemed not capable of consent. It must also be accompanied by consent of a person responsible for their care.

Attribution   Crediting the author of a study or a document.

Autoethnography   Ethnography where members of a community or social group document their own customs, social structures, and relationships.

Basic (research)   Research that has a scientific purpose.

Beneficence   In research ethics, the principle that the research should seek maximum benefit to the participants and society generally.

Big data   Large amounts of diverse information that are generated from everyday activities and are beyond the capacity of regular databases to capture and manage.

Borders   Socially constructed processes that categorize and divide.

Case study   An in-depth analysis of a unit of analysis.

Causality   A relationship between variables in which one (the independent variable) is causing a change in one or more dependent variable(s).

Closed-ended questions   Also known as fixed-choice, questions to which a limited number of options are given as possible responses. These include multiple choice, ranking, true-false, etc.

Cluster random sampling   Also known as area sampling, a sampling method that involves identifying clusters of geographic or social groups. These clusters can be randomly sampled, and then units within these clusters can be randomly sampled.

Codes   Indexing devices that help to analyse data.

Cognitive dissonance   A feeling of mental discomfort caused by competing beliefs, attitudes, or behaviours.

Concept   A way of framing and thinking about an idea or phenomenon.

Conceptual definitions   A meaning of a term that is abstract or theoretical.

Confidence interval   Sometimes called the margin of error, a quantitative indicator of the certainty of the results.

Confidence level   Expressed as a fraction or a percentage, measures the probability that the results are valid.

Confidentiality   In research ethics, the principle that researchers must protect the personal information of research participants.

Constructivism/Interpretivism   An epistemological approach that views knowledge as constructed. Ontologically, this means that truth is never absolute.

Content analysis   A deductive approach to analysing text. A researcher starts with a pre-established question or hypothesis and applies previously developed codes to textual analysis.

Control for   In causal analysis, the process of isolating a particular variable to remove its effect on the causality outcome.

Convenience sampling   Identifying a sample through contact with those who happen to be available at a particular place.

Copyright   The legal right to use or reproduce scholarly, literary, artistic, or musical materials.

Correlation (also called covariation)   Two variables that are related to each other.

Counterfactual   A situation that has not happened or is not true.

Creative Commons licences   A series of standardized licences that provide a range of open access copyright provisions to creative works.

Critical analysis   An approach to thinking about information that is based on asking questions to determine an evaluation of that information.

Critical discourse analysis (CDA)   A particular method for analysing text that focuses on the ways in which power is constructed by and through discourse.

Critical epistemology   An epistemological approach that maintains that power relations operate in the construction of knowledge so that information upholds dominant interests.

Cross-cultural   An approach that involves more than one world view or culture.

Data   Information (plural; singular is datum).

Decolonizing   An approach that seeks to uncover oppressive power relations.

Dependence relationship   The relationship between two variables where one is causing the other to change.

Direct observation   A data collection method in which researchers witness and document events or behaviours but are not directly involved in the activities as they unfold.

Discipline   Within a university or academic context, the structuring of knowledge into programs, methods, and associations to codify a particular way of studying and understanding a phenomenon.

Do no harm   An ethical principle that holds that research should not cause harm to participants.

Elite interviewing   Interviews with individuals who have social, economic, or political power in a society.

Emic perspective   An insider's view of cultural processes and practices.

Empirical   Based on evidence or data.

Epistemology   The study of, or approaches to, knowledge.

Ethics   Moral behaviour.

Ethics of care   Also known as "relational ethics," an approach to morality based on relationships, responsibility, connection, reciprocity, and emotions.

Ethnography   Studying and writing about *ethnos* – a "people" or a culture – through in-depth, long-term research, including observation, participant observation, netnography, or "hanging out."

Evidence-based policy-making   Decision-making in public spheres that is based on information and data.

Falsifiable   The characteristic of a hypothesis that means it is possible to disprove it.

Falsify evaluations   This is an action that is considered plagiarism in which a student or researcher deliberately attempts to change the result of an academic evaluation.

Fieldnote   A detailed recording of data, observations, and methodology based on the researcher's experience in a site of data collection.

Fields of study   A thematic area of study that may not necessarily be an academic discipline.

Fixed-choice questions   See **closed-ended questions**.

Focus group discussions   Group-based interviews that generate data from answers to questions and the interactions between participants.

Gatekeepers   People who formally or informally control access to a population.

Generalizability   In sampling, the ability to extrapolate findings from the sample and apply them to the whole population.

Grey literature   Documents that have not been published by an organization whose mandate is to publish.

Grounded theory   A method to analyse text from an inductive approach, where researchers start with a research question, but do not have pre-established themes or codes. Rather, they engage with the text to allow for these themes to emerge.

Heisenberg principle   Named after the physicist Werner Heisenberg, this is the principle that the act of observing changes the nature of the person or thing under observation.

Hypothesis   A predicted answer to a research question.

Indicator   A quantitative or qualitative measure of a concept.

Indigenous epistemologies   Ways of knowing and being based on connections to the land, ancestors, and spirits; emphasis on relationships, responsibility, reciprocity, respect, and relevance.

Indirect observation   A data collection method in which a researcher is not present but has access to the information generated, such as a closed-circuit television or the results of a test.

Infographics   Display of research findings in a visual format.

Institutional Research Board (IRB)   See **Research Ethics Board**.

Interdisciplinary   An approach to research that combines more than one discipline.

Intra-coder reliability   The standardization of coding across different researchers.

Key informant   An individual with in-depth knowledge about a topic or community.

Knowledge mobilization   Activities that translate academic findings into formats that are more easily accessible to a diverse, general public.

Knowledge production   The ways and systems in which information is created, valued, and disseminated.

Life history An in-depth, chronological account of an individual's life that is solicited and recorded by a researcher.

Life story or narrative An account of an individual's lived experiences that is not necessarily in chronological order and is not as complete or detailed as a life history.

Literature An accumulated body of specialized knowledge and research.

Literature review A systematic and comprehensive analysis of scholarly, published literature on a particular topic.

Lived experiences The knowledge a person gains from having lived through and personally experienced a particular event or phenomenon.

Longitudinal An approach to research in which data are collected on more than one occasion, usually over a long period of time.

Maximizing benefits An ethical principle that means that researchers must seek to ensure the greatest number of people gain from the research process.

Measurability A criterion applied to variables to ensure that they can be observed and evaluated – qualitatively or quantitatively.

Meta- In the context of methodology, overarching or a combination of multiple studies. For example, a meta-analysis includes an analysis of several research findings. In this book, a meta-example is found at the beginning of each chapter to highlight overarching trends of issues related to the topic of that chapter.

Methodology How one does research.

Methods The research tools used to gather data.

Mind map A visual representation of information, organized hierarchically.

Minimizing harm The ethical principle that researchers should attempt to reduce negative emotional, physical, psychological, and other impacts of the research on participants.

Multidisciplinary An approach that combines more than one discipline.

Netnography Combining "ethnography" and "internet," the study of cultural interaction through computer-mediated spaces, such as social media and web conferencing platforms.

Non-random sampling A sampling method in which the relationship between the sample and the population is unknown; also known as purposive sampling.

Observation   A method of monitoring and documenting details related to events, contexts, or individuals. Observation generates data on behaviour, occurrences, and environments.

Ontology   The nature of reality and existence.

Open access   The characteristic of documents, resources, data, images, or music that is free, online, and immediately available.

Open-ended questions   Questions to which respondents can give their own answer.

Operational definition   A definition that provides a clear indication of the data that will be required to measure a concept.

Over-research   A situation in which research participants feel that there are too many requests to participate in research projects, often on the same or similar topics.

Participant observation   The observation of social structures from the perspective of a researcher who is also participating in the daily life of the people, institution, or culture under study.

Participatory action research   A specific kind of participatory research design that combines the principles of participatory research with an explicit focus on practical action and change as a result of the research project.

Participatory mapping   A method in which participants represent key geographic areas (e.g., a town or school), resources, social groups, health issues, mobility routes, and so on in visual form.

Participatory methods   Methods that involve the research participants in the generation of data.

Participatory ranking and scoring   A method in which participants determine categories that are significant to them, and then they rank these – individually and/or collectively – in terms of importance.

Participatory research design   An approach in which the researcher gives research participants control over the research agenda, process, and results. Participatory research is driven by the epistemological belief that those most affected by an issue are the real experts who should determine the research agenda and (co-) create knowledge.

Pedagogical   Related to teaching.

Peer interviews   Individuals, who have direct experience with the topic under study, conducting interviews with their peers – that is, others with similar experiences or sharing similar characteristics.

Peer review   A process by which professionals with relevant expertise evaluate the quality of a research study.

Photovoice   A participatory photography method in which participants produce photographic data that represents their experiences and perspectives.

Plagiarism   Also known as "academic fraud," this entails passing off another person's work or ideas as one's own, falsifying evaluations, or falsifying data.

Plain language summaries   Short pieces that communicate the key findings of the research in lay-person's terms.

Policy briefs   Plain language summaries with recommendations aimed at key decision-makers in government and civil society.

Population   In sampling, the totality of the elements representing the topic under study.

Positionality   The process by which a researcher reflexively considers their role and position within power relations in the research process and context.

Positivism   An epistemological approach that views knowledge production as an objective and neutral process of discovering truth and facts.

Primary research   Research that involves generating new data.

Privacy   The ethical principle that participants have a right to protection of their personal information.

Probability sampling   See **random sampling**.

Probing techniques   Methods that interviewers use to encourage the respondent to provide more information.

Procedural ethics   The process by which moral questions are assessed through institutional ethics boards or structures.

Professional ethics   Codes of conduct that set guidelines for moral behaviour within particular professions, like medicine or journalism.

Pseudonyms   A fictitious name given to a research participant in order to protect their privacy.

Published literature   Documents that are produced by an organization who has a mandate to publish.

Published, scholarly literature   Documents that are produced by a publishing company and subject to scholarly peer review and norms.

Qualitative Expressed in words, images, and non-numerical symbols.

Quantitative Expressed in numbers and statistics.

Questionnaire See **structured interviewing**.

Quota sampling A non-random sampling method in which the researcher purposively identifies subpopulations – for example, based on age group, sex, racialized identity, religion – to be represented in the final sample.

Random sampling Also known as probability sampling, a sampling method where every element of the population has a known and non-negligible chance – which can be calculated statistically – of being selected for the sample.

Reflexivity The process of thinking critically about one's role as a researcher and positionality within hierarchical power relations, including in the production of knowledge.

Relational ethics Also known as an "ethics of care," it refers to how one behaves in relation to research participants and colleagues while doing research.

Representivity The degree to which the sample represents the diversity of the population.

Research Systematic study guided by clear definitions, a theoretical framework, and methodology.

Research Ethics Board (REB) Also known as an Institutional Research Board, a committee that evaluates research proposals to ensure that they conform to procedural ethics.

Research topic A general theme or issue that is the starting point for research.

Respondent-driven sampling A sampling method in which initial respondents assist the researcher with recruiting other respondents.

Sample A subset of the population that is selected to be in the study.

Sampling The process by which a researcher selects units of the population to be in the sample. Sampling can either be random or non-random.

Sampling frame A list of elements in the population from which a sample is drawn.

Scholarly ethics Principles of moral behaviour in relation to academic work.

Scholarly literature   Also known as academic literature, documents based on research that have been peer reviewed.

Secondary research   Research based on existing data and documentation.

Semi-structured interviewing   An interviewing method in which the interviewer has an interview guide or map with a list of topics and questions to be covered. However, the exact wording of a question will vary, and researchers can change the order of questions in response to what the respondent says or to follow the natural "flow" of the conversation.

Simple random sampling   A sampling method in which the researcher starts with a sampling frame and assigns a number to each unit in the sampling frame. They then randomly select numbers to identify the units that will be in their sample.

Snowball sampling   Also known as chain sampling, a technique where a researcher starts off with a certain number of participants and then asks those participants to identify other participants.

Socially constructed   Describes something that is the product of human interaction and behaviour, not objective reality.

Sound postcards   A participatory method in which participants take part in music workshops and then record "postcards" to capture memories, experiences, or significant events in audio form.

Sovereign state   A geopolitical entity that has control over a territory, a population, a government, and has relations with other states. It is often taken as the unit of analysis in international research.

Structured interviewing   Also called surveys or questionnaires, an interview method based on preset questions that need to be asked in exactly the same way and in the same order to each respondent.

Suppression of data   A violation of scholarly ethics, when a researcher deliberately ignores or destroys information that does not support their hypothesis, theory, or argument.

Survey   See **structured interviewing**.

Theory   From the Greek word "to see," a way of linking concepts and organizing data to assist with analysis.

Thick description   Coined by anthropologist Clifford Geertz, it refers to rich and contextualized details and interpretations as part of ethnographic approaches.

Transdisciplinarity The creation of a new, unified intellectual approach that goes beyond any one discipline.

Unit of analysis The who or what that is being studied.

Unlearn The process of reflecting on our own thoughts, attitudes, beliefs, behaviours, feelings, and biases.

Unstructured interviewing An interviewing method in which the interviewer has minimum control over the interview and allows respondents to express themselves in their own terms and at their own pace.

Validity The degree to which the variable actually measures or represents the concept.

Variability The different states or properties of a variable.

Variable "A measurable characteristic that can have more than one value" (O'Sullivan et al., 493).

Voluntary, informed consent The ethical principle that research participants must freely choose to take part in a study after having been informed of the research question and objectives as well as any potential harms or benefits of participation.

World Café A group-based participatory method that is used to foster dialogue and brainstorming, build relationships, and facilitate collaborative learning and knowledge through multiple rounds of discussions at small tables in a café-like setting.

World view A set of beliefs and understandings about the world and human existence.

Notes

1 Why Research across Borders?

1 "Fragile States Index Methodology," accessed 8 November 2022, https://fragilestatesindex.org/methodology/.
2 "Country Indicators for Foreign Policy," accessed 8 November 2022, https://carleton.ca/cifp/about-cifp/.
3 "States of Fragility 2022," accessed 8 November 2022, http://www.oecd.org/dac/states-of-fragility-fa5a6770-en.htm.
4 Thomas Nail, *Theory of the Border* (New York: Oxford University Press, 2016), 2.
5 Raka Shome, "Post-Colonial Reflections on the 'Internationalization' of Cultural Studies," *Cultural Studies* 23, no. 5–6 (2009): 715.
6 Danielle Jacobson and Nida Mustafa, "Social Identity Map: A Reflexivity Tool for Practicing Explicit Positionality in Critical Qualitative Research," *International Journal of Qualitative Methods* 18 (2019), https://doi.org/10.1177/1609406919870075.
7 Margaret Kovach, "Conversation Method in Indigenous Research," *First Peoples Child & Family Review: An Interdisciplinary Journal Honouring the Voices, Perspectives, and Knowledges of First Peoples through Research, Critical Analyses, Stories, Standpoints and Media Reviews* 5, no. 1 (2010): 40–8, https://doi.org/10.7202/1069060ar.
8 Shawn Wilson, *Research Is Ceremony: Indigenous Research Methods* (Black Point, NS: Fernwood Publishing, 2008), 91.
9 "Democracy Index," accessed 8 November 2022, https://www.eiu.com/topic/democracy-index.
10 "Democracy Index."
11 "Polity IV Project," accessed 8 November 2022, http://www.systemicpeace.org/polity/polity4x.htm.

12 Monty G. Marshall et al., "Polity IV, 1800–1999: Comments on Munck and Verkuilen," *Comparative Political Studies* 35, no. 1 (2002): 42.

13 "Global State of Democracy Indices," accessed 8 November 2022, https://www.idea.int/gsod-indices/#/indices/world-map.

14 "Assessing the Quality of Democracy: A Practical Guide," accessed 8 November 2022, https://www.idea.int/publications/catalogue /assessing-quality-democracy-practical-guide.

15 Donileen R. Loseke, *Methodological Thinking: Basic Principles of Social Research Design* (Los Angeles: Sage Publications, 2012), 18.

16 Victoria Maynard, Elizabeth Parker, and John Twigg, "The Effectiveness and Efficiency of Interventions Supporting Shelter Self-Recovery following Humanitarian Crises" (London: Oxfam, Feinstein International Center, UKAID, 2017), https://policy-practice.oxfam.org .uk/publications/the-effectiveness-and-efficiency-of-interventions -supporting-shelter-self-recov-620189.

17 Shahra Razavi, "Revisiting Equity and Efficiency Arguments for Gender Equality: A Principled but Pragmatic Approach," *Canadian Journal of Development Studies/Revue canadienne d'études du développement* 38, no. 4 (2017): 558–63.

18 Naila Kabeer and Luisa Natali, "Gender Equality and Economic Growth: Is There a Win-Win?," *IDS Working Papers* no. 417 (2013): 6, quoted in Shahra Razavi, "Revisiting Equity and Efficiency Arguments," 559.

2 How Is Knowledge Disciplined? The Opportunities and Challenges of Research across Disciplines and Epistemologies

1 Jeroen Gunning, "A Case for Critical Terrorism Studies?," *Government and Opposition* 42, no. 3 (2007): 363–93.

2 Jacob L. Stump and Priya Dixit, "Toward a Completely Constructivist Critical Terrorism Studies," *International Relations* 26, no. 2 (June 2012): 212.

3 Mark Youngman, "Building 'Terrorism Studies' as an Interdisciplinary Space: Addressing Recurring Issues in the Study of Terrorism," *Terrorism and Political Violence* 32, no. 5 (2020): 1091–105.

4 Émile Durkheim, *The Rules of the Sociological Method*, ed. George E.G. Catlin, trans. Sarah A. Solvay and John H. Mueller (New York: The Free Press, 1938), 2.

5 Eve Tuck and K. Wayne Yang, "Decolonization Is Not a Metaphor," *Decolonization: Indigeneity, Education & Society* 1, no. 1 (2012): 1–40.

6 Donileen R. Loseke, *Methodological Thinking: Basic Principles of Social Research Design* (Los Angeles: Sage Publications, 2012), 7.

7 Deborah McGregor, Jean-Paul Restoule, and Rochelle Johnston, eds., *Indigenous Research: Theories, Practices, and Relationships* (Toronto: Canadian Scholars' Press, 2018), 7.

8 McGregor, Restoule, and Johnston, *Indigenous Research*.

9 McGregor, Restoule, and Johnston, *Indigenous Research*, 14.

10 Denise Wilson, Alayne Mikahere-Hall, and Juanita Sherwood, "Using Indigenous Kaupapa Māori Research Methodology with Constructivist Grounded Theory: Generating a Theoretical Explanation of Indigenous Womens Realities," *International Journal of Social Research Methodology* 25, no. 3 (2022): 375–90, doi: 10.1080/13645579.2021.1897756.

11 University College London, "Happiness Equation: New Equation Reveals How Other People's Fortunes Affect Our Happiness," *Phys.Org* (blog), 14 June 2016, https://phys.org/news/2016-06-happiness -equation-reveals-people-fortunes.html.

12 Michelle Pidgeon, "Indigenous Wholistic Framework," in "More Than a Checklist: Meaningful Indigenous Inclusion in Higher Education," *Social Inclusion* 4, no. 1 (2016): 77–91, https://www.researchgate.net/figure /Indigenous-Wholistic-Framework_fig1_295839816.

13 "World of Science Research Production," accessed 8 November 2022, https://worldmapper.org/maps/science-paperspublished-2016/?sf _action=get_data&sf_data=results&_sft_product_cat=science&sf_paged=2.

14 Stephen J. Rosow, "Toward an Anti-disciplinary Global Studies," *International Studies Perspectives* 4, no. 1 (2003): 1, https://doi .org/10.1111/1528-3577.04101.

15 Renée Marlin-Bennett and David K. Johnson, "International Political Economy: Overview and Conceptualization," *Oxford Research Encyclopedia of International Studies,* 22 December 2017, https://doi .org/10.1093/acrefore/9780190846626.013.239.

16 See, for example, Rosow, "Toward an Anti-disciplinary Global Studies," 1–14.

17 Marilyn Stember, "Advancing the Social Sciences through the Interdisciplinary Enterprise," *The Social Science Journal* 28, no. 1 (1991): 1.

18 See J. Marshall Beier and Samantha L. Arnold, "Becoming Undisciplined: Toward the Supradisciplinary Study of Security," *International Studies Review* 7, no. 1 (2005): 41–61; and Rosow, "Toward an Anti-disciplinary Global Studies," 1–14.

19 Sarita Cargas and Kristina Ederbach, "Rethinking Multidisciplinarity within Human Rights Education," Open Global Rights, 3 September 2020, https://www.openglobalrights.org/rethinking-multidisciplinarity -within-human-rights-education/.

3 Ethics, Power, and Positionality

1 Nicole Behnam and Kristy Crabtree, "Big Data, Little Ethics: Confidentiality and Consent," *Forced Migration Review* 61 (2019): 4–6.

2 Courtenay R. Conrad and Jacqueline H.R. DeMeritt, "Unintended Consequences: The Effect of Advocacy to End Torture on Empowerment Rights Violations," in *Examining Torture,* ed. Tracy Lightcap and James Pfiffner (New York: Palgrave Macmillan, 2014), 159–83, https://doi .org/10.1057/9781137439161_7.

3 Nupur Singhal and Poornima Bhola, "Ethical Practices in Community -Based Research in Non-Suicidal Self-Injury: A Systematic Review," *Asian Journal of Psychiatry* 30 (2017): 127–34, https://doi.org/10.1016 /j.ajp.2017.08.015.

4 Freedom House, "Social Media Surveillance," accessed 8 November 2022, https://freedomhouse.org/report/freedom-on-the-net/2019 /the-crisis-of-social-media/social-media-surveillance.

5 Mark Christopher Navin and J.M. Dieterle, "Cooptation or Solidarity: Food Sovereignty in the Developed World," *Agriculture and Human Values* 35, no. 2 (2018): 319–29, https://doi.org/10.1007/s10460-017 -9823-7.

6 Cleophas Karooma, "Research Fatigue among Rwandan Refugees in Uganda," *Forced Migration Review* 61 (2019): 18–19.

7 Christina Clark-Kazak, "Ethical Considerations: Research with People in Situations of Forced Migration," *Refuge: Canada's Journal on Refugees/ Refuge: Revue canadienne sur les réfugiés* 33, no. 2 (2017): 11–17, https://doi .org/10.7202/1043059ar.

8 Erika Frydenlund and José Padilla, "Opportunities and Challenges of Using Computer-Based Simulation in Migration and Displacement Research: A Focus on Lesbos, Greece," in *Documenting Displacement: Questioning Methodological Boundaries in Forced Migration Research*, ed. Katarzyna Grabska and Christina Clark-Kazak (Montreal: McGill-Queen's University Press, 2022), 279–308.

9 Yandisa Sikweyiya and Rachel Jewkes, "Perceptions and Experiences of Research Participants on Gender-Based Violence Community Based Survey: Implications for Ethical Guidelines," *PLOS ONE* 7, no. 4 (2012), https://doi.org/10.1371/journal.pone.0035495.

10 Kim Anh Duong, "Doing Human Trafficking Research: Reflections on Ethical Challenges," *Journal of Research in Gender Studies* 5, no. 2 (2015): 171–90.

11 Jonathan Watts and John Vidal, "Environmental Defenders Being Killed in Record Numbers Globally, New Research Reveals," *The Guardian*, 13 July 2017, https://www.theguardian.com/environment/2017/jul/13 /environmental-defenders-being-killed-in-record-numbers-globally -new-research-reveals.

12 Neil Bilotta, "Navigating Ethical Terrains: Perspectives on 'Research Ethics' in Kakuma Refugee Camp" (PhD diss., McGill University, 2018), 134, https://escholarship.mcgill.ca/concern/theses/3t945t11k.

13 Anna Chiumento, Atif Rahman, and Lucy Frith, "Writing to Template: Researchers' Negotiation of Procedural Research Ethics," *Social Science & Medicine* 255 (2020), https://doi.org/10.1016/j.socscimed.2020.112980.

14 Marilys Guillemin and Lynn Gillam. "Ethics, Reflexivity, and 'Ethically Important Moments' in Research," *Qualitative Inquiry* 10, no. 2 (2004): 261–80, https://doi.org/10.1177/1077800403262360.

15 Sandy Gifford, "To Respect or Protect?: Whose Values Shape the Ethics of Refugee Research?," in *Values and Vulnerabilities: The Ethics of Research with Refugees and Asylum Seekers*, ed. Karen Block, Elisha Riggs, and Nick Haslam (Toowong: Australian Academic Press, 2013), 41.

16 Amy Zarzeczny and Timothy Caulfield, "Legal Liability and Research Ethics Boards: The Case of Neuroimaging and Incidental Findings," *International Journal of Law and Psychiatry* 35, no. 2 (2012): 137–45, https://doi.org/10.1016/j.ijlp.2011.12.005.

17 Virginia Held, *The Ethics of Care: Personal, Political, and Global* (New York: Oxford University Press, 2006), 13.

18 Victoria Lawson, "Geographies of Care and Responsibility," *Annals of the Association of American Geographers* 97 no 1 (2007): 1–11. https://doi.org/10.1111/j.1467-8306.2007.00520.x, p. 6.

19 Held, *Ethics of Care*, 10–11.

20 Linda Finlay, "'Reflexive Embodied Empathy': A Phenomenology of Participant-Researcher Intersubjectivity," *The Humanistic Psychologist* 33, no. 4 (2005): 271–92, http://dx.doi.org/10.1207/s15473333thp3304_4.

21 Ann Bonner and Gerda Tolhurst, "Insider-Outsider Perspectives of Participant Observation," *Nurse Researcher* 9, no. 4 (2002): 7.

22 Danielle Jacobson and Nida Mustafa, "Social Identity Map: A Reflexivity Tool for Practicing Explicit Positionality in Critical Qualitative Research," *International Journal of Qualitative Methods* 18 (2019). https://doi.org/10.1177/1609406919870075.

4 Designing a Research Project across Borders

1 Christopher Day and Kendra L. Koivu, "Finding the Question: A Puzzle-Based Approach to the Logic of Discovery," *Journal of Political Science Education* 15, no. 3 (2019): 377–86, https://doi.org/10.1080/15512169.2018.1493594.

2 The following three questions come from Day and Koivu, "Finding the Question," 384.

3 All of the quoted questions below are from Day and Koivu, "Finding the Question," 384.

4 Elizabethann O'Sullivan, Gary Rassel, Maureen Berner, and Jocelyn Taliaferro, *Research Methods for Public Administrators*, 6th ed. (New York: Routledge, 2016), 15.

5 Kevin Durrheim, "Research Design," in *Research in Practice: Applied Methods for the Social Sciences*, ed. Martin Terre Blanche, Kevin Durrheim, and Desmond Painter (Cape Town: University of Cape Town Press, 2006), 34.

6 François Pierre Gingras and Catherine Côté, "La théorie et le sens de la recherche," in *Recherche sociale. De la problématique à la collecte des données*, ed. Benoît Gauthier, 5th ed. (Montreal: Presses de l'Université du Québec, 2009), 109–34; my translations.

7 M. Neil Browne and Stuart M. Keeley, *Asking the Right Questions: A Guide to Critical Thinking*, 8th ed. (Upper Saddle River, NJ: Pearson Education, 2007), 3.

5 Measurement across Borders

1 Rachel Brett and Margaret McCallin, *Children: The Invisible Soldiers* (Stockholm, Sweden: Save the Children, 1996), 31 (emphasis added).
2 Oliver Bakewell, "Research beyond the Categories: The Importance of Policy Irrelevant Research into Forced Migration," *Journal of Refugee Studies* 21, no. 4 (2008): 432–53.
3 Roger Brubaker and Frederick Cooper, "Beyond 'Identity,'" *Theory and Society* 29, no. 1 (2000): 4, https://doi.org/10.1023/A:1007068714468.
4 Brubaker and Cooper, "Beyond 'Identity,'" 4.
5 UNICEF, *The Paris Principles: Principles and Guidelines on Children Associated with Armed Forces and Groups*, February 2007, https://childrenandarmedconflict.un.org/publications/ParisPrinciples_EN.pdf.
6 *Oxford English Dictionary*, s.v. "child," accessed 10 November 2022, https://www.oed.com/view/Entry/31619?rskey=0x2pVM&result=1&isAdvanced=false#eid.
7 *Oxford English Dictionary*, s.v. "soldier," accessed 10 November 2022, https://www.oed.com/view/Entry/184107?rskey=VTCfa4&result=1#eid.
8 Donileen R. Loseke, *Methodological Thinking: Basic Principles of Social Research Design* (Los Angeles: Sage Publications, 2012), 69.
9 Uppsala Conflict Data Program (UCDP) and Center for Studies of Civil Wars, International Peace Research Institute, Oslo (PRIO), *UCDP/PRIO Armed Conflict Dataset Codebook* (2017), 1–3, https://ucdp.uu.se/downloads/replication_data/2018_c_666956-l_1-k_ucdp-prio-acd-181-codebook.pdf.
10 Gary D. Bouma, Rod Ling, and Lori Wilkinson, *The Research Process*, 2nd ed. (Oxford: Oxford University Press, 2012), 55.
11 Elizabethann O'Sullivan, Gary Rassel, Maureen Berner, and Jocelyn DeVance Taliaferro, *Research Methods for Public Administrators*, 6th ed. (New York: Routledge, 2016), 493.
12 *UCDP/PRIO Armed Conflict Dataset Codebook*, 6
13 *UCDP/PRIO Armed Conflict Dataset Codebook*, 9.
14 Loseke, *Methodological Thinking*, 18.
15 Online Etymology Dictionary, s.v. "theory," accessed 10 November 2022, https://www.etymonline.com/word/theory#:~:text=1590s%2C%20%22conception%2C%20mental%20scheme,%22to%20see%2C%22%20which%20is.

16 This section draws on Sakiko Fukuda-Parr, "Theory and Policy in International Development: Human Development and Capability Approach and the Millennium Development Goals," *International Studies Review* 13, no. 1 (2011): 122–32.

17 Fukuda-Parr, "Theory and Policy in International Development," 123.

18 Fukuda-Parr, "Theory and Policy in International Development," 126.

19 UNDP, *Human Development Report 2001: Making New Technologies Work for Human Development* (2001), 23, https://hdr.undp.org/content/human -development-report-2001.

20 Loseke, *Methodological Thinking*, 68.

6 Case Studies in Global Context

1 "The Nobel Peace Prize 2006," NobelPrize.org, accessed 10 November 2022, https://www.nobelprize.org/prizes/peace/2006/summary/.

2 Myrto Chliova, Jan Brinckmann, and Nina Rosenbusch, "Is Microcredit a Blessing for the Poor? A Meta-Analysis Examining Development Outcomes and Contextual Considerations," *Journal of Business Venturing* 30, no. 3 (2015): 467–87, https://doi.org/10.1016/j.jbusvent.2014.10.003.

3 Christine Keating, Claire Rasmussen, and Pooja Rishi, "The Rationality of Empowerment: Microcredit, Accumulation by Dispossession, and the Gendered Economy," *Signs: Journal of Women in Culture and Society* 36, no. 1 (2010): 153–76, https://doi.org/10.1086/652911.

4 Robert K. Yin, *Case Study Research and Applications: Design and Methods* (Los Angeles: Sage Publications, 2017), 32–3.

5 Robert K. Yin, "Analytic Generalization," in *Encyclopedia of Case Study Research*, ed. Albert J. Mills, Gabrielle Eurepos, and Elden Wiebe (Los Angeles: Sage Publications, 2010), 20–2.

6 Michael Burawoy, "The Extended Case Method," *Sociological Theory* 16, no. 1 (1998): 19, https://doi.org/10.1111/0735-2751.00040.

7 Gwendolyn Alexander Tedeschi, "Overcoming Selection Bias in Microcredit Impact Assessments: A Case Study in Peru," *The Journal of Development Studies* 44, no. 4 (2008): 504–18, https://doi .org/10.1080/00220380801980822.

8 Tedeschi, "Overcoming Selection Bias," 504.

9 Tedeschi, "Overcoming Selection Bias," 505.

10 Alexander L. George and Andrew Bennett, *Case Studies and Theory Development in the Social Sciences* (Cambridge, MA: MIT Press, 2005), 31.

11 Lawrence Craig Watson and Maria-Barbara Watson-Franke, *Interpreting Life Histories: An Anthropological Inquiry* (New Brunswick, NJ: Rutgers University Press, 1985), 2 (emphasis in original).

12 Jo-ann Archibald, "An Indigenous Storywork Methodology," in *Handbook of the Arts in Qualitative Research: Perspectives, Methodologies, Examples,*

and Issues, ed. J. Gary Knowles and Ardra L. Cole (Los Angeles: Sage Publications, 2008), 373.

7 Sampling, Access, and Representation across Borders

1 Luz Garcini et al., "Effectiveness of Respondent-Driven Sampling for Conducting Health Studies among Undocumented Immigrants at a Time of Heightened Immigration Enforcement," *Journal of Immigrant Minority Health* 24, no. 1 (2022): 102–10, https://doi.org/10.1007/s10903-020-01112-4.
2 Garcini et al., "Effectiveness of Respondent-Driven Sampling," 103.
3 Garcini et al., "Effectiveness of Respondent-Driven Sampling," 103.
4 Nicole Narea, "Poll: Most Americans Support a Path to Citizenship for Undocumented Immigrants," Vox, 4 February 2021, https://www.vox.com/policy-and-politics/2021/2/4/22264074/poll-undocumented-immigrants-citizenship-stimulus-biden.
5 "Data for Progress," Vox, accessed 10 November 2022, https://www.filesforprogress.org/datasets/2021/2/dfp-vox-biden-immigration-agenda.pdf.
6 Bettina Bruns and Judith Miggelbrink, eds., *Subverting Borders: Doing Research on Smuggling and Small-Scale Trade* (Weisbaden: Springer Science & Business Media, 2011).
7 Alice Bloch, "Survey Research with Refugees: A Methodological Perspective," *Policy Studies* 25, no. 2 (2004): 146, https://doi.org/10.1080/0144287042000262215.
8 Bloch, "Survey Research," 148.
9 Georgia Robins Sadler, Hau-Chen Lee, Rod Seung-Hwan Lim, and Judith Fullerton, "Recruitment of Hard-to-Reach Population Subgroups via Adaptations of the Snowball Sampling Strategy," *Nursing & Health Sciences* 12, no. 3 (2010): 369–74, https://doi.org/10.1111/j.1442-2018.2010.00541.x.
10 Bloch, "Survey Research," 139–51.
11 Human Security Report Project, *Human Security Report 2009/2010: The Causes of Peace and the Shrinking Costs of War* (New York: Oxford University Press, 2009).
12 Gary Witham, Anna Beddow, and Carol Haigh, "Reflections on Access: Too Vulnerable to Research?," *Journal of Research in Nursing* 20, no. 1 (2015): 28–37, https://doi.org/10.1177/1744987113499338.
13 Mary Ann Powell et al., "Sensitive Topics in Social Research Involving Children," *International Journal of Social Research Methodology* 21, no. 6 (2018): 647–60, https://doi.org/10.1080/13645579.2018.1462882.
14 Wayne Stephen Coetzee, "Doing Research on 'Sensitive Topics': Studying the Sweden–South Africa Arms Deal," *Scientia Militaria: South African Journal of Military Studies* 48, no. 2 (2022): 65–85, https://doi.org/10.5787/48-2-1278.
15 Carla Suarez, "'Living between Two Lions': Civilian Protection Strategies during Armed Violence in the Eastern Democratic Republic of the

Congo," *Journal of Peacebuilding & Development* 12, no. 3 (2017): 54–67, https://doi.org/10.1080/15423166.2017.1372796.

8 Interviewing across Borders

1 Ho Ngoc Son, Dong Thi Linh Chi, and Aaron Kingsbury, "Indigenous Knowledge and Climate Change Adaptation of Ethnic Minorities in the Mountainous Regions of Vietnam: A Case Study of the Yao People in Bac Kan Province," *Agricultural Systems* 176 (2019), https://doi .org/10.1016/j.agsy.2019.102683.

2 Son, Linh Chi, and Kingsbury, "Indigenous Knowledge," 1.

3 Son, Linh Chi, and Kingsbury, "Indigenous Knowledge," 2.

4 Son, Linh Chi, and Kingsbury, "Indigenous Knowledge," 3.

5 Son, Linh Chi, and Kingsbury, "Indigenous Knowledge," 4.

6 Son, Linh Chi, and Kingsbury, "Indigenous Knowledge," 4.

7 Son, Linh Chi, and Kingsbury, "Indigenous Knowledge," 4.

8 Son, Linh Chi, and Kingsbury, "Indigenous Knowledge," 4.

9 Rachel Baker and Rachel Hinton, "Do Focus Groups Facilitate Meaningful Participation in Social Research?," in *Developing Focus Group Research: Politics, Theory and Practice*, ed. Rosaline Barbour and Jenny Kitzinger (Los Angeles: Sage Publications, 1999), 79–98, https://dx .doi.org/10.4135/9781849208857.n6.

10 Pew Research Center, "U.S. Survey Methodology," https://www .pewresearch.org/our-methods/u-s-surveys/, quoted in Daniel Druckman, *Doing Research: Methods of Inquiry for Conflict Analysis* (Thousand Oaks, CA: Sage Publications, 2005), 11.

11 David Adeloye, Neil Carr, and Andrea Insch, "Conducting Qualitative Interviews on Sensitive Topics in Sensitive Places: The Case of Terrorism and Tourism in Nigeria," *Tourism Recreation Research* 45, no. 1 (2020): 69, https://doi.org/10.1080/02508281.2019.1656872.

12 Adeloye, Carr, and Insch, "Conducting Qualitative Interviews," 69–79.

9 Ethnographic Approaches across Borders

1 Merethe Skårås, "Focused Ethnographic Research on Teaching and Learning in Conflict Zones: History Education in South Sudan,"*Forum for Development Studies* 45, no. 2 (2018): 217–38, https://doi .org/10.1080/08039410.2016.1202316.

2 Skårås, "Focused Ethnographic Research," 218.

3 Skårås, "Focused Ethnographic Research," 217.

4 Michelle H. Raheja, "Reading Nanook's Smile: Visual Sovereignty, Indigenous Revisions of Ethnography, and 'Atanarjuat (The Fast Runner),'" *American Quarterly* 59, no. 4 (2007): 1159–85.

5 Graeme Rodgers, "'Hanging Out' with Forced Migrants: Methodological and Ethical Challenges," *Forced Migration Review* 21 (2004): 48–9.

6 Clifford Geertz, "Thick Description: Toward an Interpretive Theory of Culture," in *The Cultural Geography Reader*, ed. Timothy Oaks and Patricia Price (London: Routledge, 2008), 41–51, https://doi.org/10.4324/9780203931950.

7 Joseph G. Ponterotto, "Brief Note on the Origins, Evolution, and Meaning of the Qualitative Research Concept Thick Description," *The Qualitative Report* 11, no. 3 (2006): 541, https://doi.org/10.46743/2160-3715/2006.1666.

8 Alpa Shah, "Ethnography? Participant Observation, a Potentially Revolutionary Praxis," *HAU: Journal of Ethnographic Theory* 7, no. 1 (2017): 45–59 (emphasis in original), https://doi.org/10.14318/hau7.1.008.

9 Turid Hagene, "The Power of Ethnography: A Useful Approach to Researching Politics," *Forum for Development Studies* 45, no. 2 (2018): 307, https://doi.org/10.1080/08039410.2017.1366360.

10 Onajomo Akemu and Samer Abdelnour, "Confronting the Digital: Doing Ethnography in Modern Organizational Settings," *Organizational Research Methods* 23, no. 2 (2020): 296–321, https://doi.org/10.1177/1094428118791018.

11 Leesa Costello, Marie-Louise McDermott, and Ruth Wallace, "Netnography: Range of Practices, Misperceptions, and Missed Opportunities," *International Journal of Qualitative Methods* 16, no. 1 (2017). https://doi.org/10.1177/1609406917700647.

12 Bart Barendregt, "Deep Hanging Out in the Age of the Digital; Contemporary Ways of Doing Online and Offline Ethnography," *Asiascape: Digital Asia* 4, no. 3 (2017): 307–19, https://doi.org/10.1163/22142312-12340082.

13 Costello, McDermott, and Wallace, "Netnography."

14 Marion Engin, "Research Diary: A Tool for Scaffolding," *International Journal of Qualitative Methods* 10, no. 3 (2011): 296, https://doi.org/10.1177/160940691101000308.

15 Sarah Li, "The Natural History of a Doctoral Research Study: The Role of a Research Diary and Reflexivity," in *Emotions and Reflexivity in Health & Social Care Field Research*, ed. Helen Allan and Anne Arber (Cham, Switzerland: Palgrave Macmillan, 2018), 13, http://dx.doi.org/10.1007/978-3-319-65503-1_2.

16 Government of Canada, "Tri-Council Policy Statement," 2018, https://ethics.gc.ca/eng/policy-politique_tcps2-eptc2_2018.html.

17 Leanne Townsend and Claire Wallace, "Social Media Research: A Guide to Ethics," University of Aberdeen, accessed 10 November 2022, https://www.gla.ac.uk/media/Media_487729_smxx.pdf.

18 Townsend and Wallace, "Social Media Research," 5.

19 Ryerson University, Research Ethics Board, "Guidelines for Research Involving Social Media," November 2017, 5, https://www.ryerson.ca/content/dam/research/documents/ethics/guidelines-for-research-involving-social-media.pdf.

20 For example, see María Cristina González, "The Four Seasons of Ethnography: A Creation-Centered Ontology for Ethnography," *International Journal of Intercultural Relations* 24, no. 5 (2000): 623–50, https://doi.org/10.1016/S0147-1767(00)00020-1; and Virginie Magnat, "Can Research Become Ceremony? Performance Ethnography and Indigenous Epistemologies," *Canadian Theatre Review* 151 (2012): 30–6, http://doi.org/10.1353/ctr.2012.0058.

10 Participatory Research in International, Cross-Cultural Contexts

 1 Robert Chambers, "The Origins and Practice of Participatory Rural Appraisal," *World Development* 22, no. 7 (1994): 954.
 2 V. Ernesto Méndez, Martha Caswell, Stephen R. Gliessman, and Roseann Cohen, "Integrating Agroecology and Participatory Action Research (PAR): Lessons from Central America," *Sustainability* 9, no. 5 (2017): 705–14, http://dx.doi.org/10.3390/su9050705.
 3 Méndez et al., "Integrating Agroecology," 710.
 4 Méndez et al., "Integrating Agroecology," 711.
 5 Méndez et al., "Integrating Agroecology," 713.
 6 Méndez et al., "Integrating Agroecology," 714.
 7 Méndez et al., "Integrating Agroecology," 714.
 8 Méndez et al., "Integrating Agroecology," 714.
 9 Marina Apgar and Jodie Thorpe, "What Is Participation?" Eldis, accessed 10 November 2022, https://www.eldis.org/keyissues /what-participation.
10 Sherry R. Arnstein, "A Ladder of Citizen Participation," *Journal of the American Institute of Planners* 35, no. 4 (1969): 216–24, https://doi .org/10.1080/01944366908977225.
11 "Key Principles of Participatory Learning and Action," About Participatory Methods, Institute of Development Studies, accessed 10 November 2022, https://www.participatorymethods.org/page/about -participatory-methods.
12 Cindy Peltier, "An Application of Two-Eyed Seeing: Indigenous Research Methods with Participatory Action Research," *International Journal of Qualitative Methods* 17, no. 1 (2018). https://doi.org/10.1177 /1609406918812346.
13 Budd L. Hall and Rajesh Tandon, "Decolonization of Knowledge, Epistemicide, Participatory Research and Higher Education," *Research for All* 1, no. 1 (2017): 6–19, http://dx.doi.org/10.18546/RFA.01.1.02.
14 Sara Kindon, Rachel Pain, and Mike Kesby, "Participatory Action Research: Origins, Approaches and Methods," in *Participatory Action Research Approaches and Methods: Connecting People, Participation and Place*, ed. Sara Kindon, Rachel Pain, and Mike Kesby (New York: Routledge, 2007), 35, https://doi.org/10.4324/9780203933671.

15 "Key Principles of Participatory Learning and Action."

16 Kindon, Pain, and Kesby, "Participatory Action Research," 35.

17 Méndez et al., "Integrating Agroecology," 711.

18 Caroline Wang and Mary Ann Burris, "Photovoice: Concept, Methodology, and Use for Participatory Needs Assessment," *Health Education and Behavior* 24, no. 3 (1997): 369–87, https://doi.org/10.1177/109019819702400309.

19 Caroline Wang, "Photovoice: A Participatory Action Research Strategy Applied to Women's Health," *Journal of Women's Health* 8, no. 2 (1999): 185, https://doi.org/10.1089/jwh.1999.8.185.

20 Stuart Greene, Kevin J. Burke, and Maria K. McKenna, "A Review of Research Connecting Digital Storytelling, Photovoice, and Civic Engagement," *Review of Educational Research* 88, no. 6 (2018): 844–78, https://doi.org/10.3102/0034654318794134.

21 Linda Liebenberg, "Thinking Critically about Photovoice: Achieving Empowerment and Social Change," *International Journal of Qualitative Methods* 17, no. 1 (2018). https://doi.org/10.1177/1609406918757631.

22 Robert Chambers, "Participatory Mapping and Geographic Information Systems: Whose Map? Who Is Empowered and Who Disempowered? Who Gains and Who Loses?" *The Electronic Journal of Information Systems in Developing Countries* 25, no. 1 (2006): 1–11, https://doi.org/10.1002/j.1681-4835.2006.tb00163.x.

23 Chambers, "Participatory Mapping," 1–11.

24 Christa Fouché and Glenda Light, "An Invitation to Dialogue: 'The World Café' in Social Work Research," *Qualitative Social Work* 10, no. 1 (2011): 28–48, https://doi.org/10.1177/1473325010376016.

25 Juanita Brown, "The World Café: Living Knowledge through Conversations That Matter" (PhD diss., Fielding Institute, 2002), https://st4.ning.com/topology/rest/1.0/file/get/2836607717?profile=original.

26 Katharina Löhr, Michael Weinhardt, and Stefan Sieber, "The 'World Café' as a Participatory Method for Collecting Qualitative Data," *International Journal of Qualitative Methods* 19 (2020), https://doi.org/10.1177/1609406920916976.

27 Fouché and Light, "An Invitation to Dialogue."

28 Andrea Rodríguez-Sánchez and Miguel Alonso-Cambrón, "Sound and Memory: Collaborative Reflection on Using Sound Postcards in Rebuilding Social Fabric with Victims of Forced Displacement in Colombia," in *Documenting Displacement: Inter-Disciplinary Methodologies in Forced Migration Research*, ed. Katarzyna Grabska and Christina Clark-Kazak (Montreal: McGill-Queen's University Press, 2022), 153–72.

29 Yuriko Cowper-Smith, *The Oral Defence: Speaking Back to the Community* (Vancouver: UBC Press, forthcoming).

11 Analysing Text and Images in Cross-Border Research

 1 Christina Clark-Kazak, "Representing Refugees in the Life Cycle: A Social Age Analysis of United Nations High Commissioner for Refugees Annual Reports and Appeals 1999–2008," *Journal of Refugee Studies* 22, no. 3 (2009): 302, https://doi.org/10.1093/jrs/fep012.
 2 Clark-Kazak, "Representing Refugees," 306.
 3 Clark-Kazak, "Representing Refugees," 311.
 4 Clark-Kazak, "Representing Refugees," 320.
 5 Paul Dudman, archivist from Library, Archives and Learning Services at the University of East London, personal communication with author, 21 May 2021.
 6 Jinfang Niu, "Integrated Online Access to Objects and Archives," *Archivaria* 86 (2018): 152–79.
 7 Daniela Agostinho, "Archival Encounters: Rethinking Access and Care in Digital Colonial Archives," *Archival Science* 19 (2019): 141–65, https://doi.org/10.1007/s10502-019-09312-0.
 8 Daniel Berliner, "Sunlight or Window Dressing? Local Government Compliance with South Africa's Promotion of Access to Information Act," *Governance* 30, no. 4 (2017): 641–61, https://doi.org/10.1111/gove.12246.
 9 Jennifer Rowley and John Farrow, *Organizing Knowledge: An Introduction to Managing Access to Information: Introduction to Access to Information*, 3rd ed. (London: Routledge, 2017).
10 Kevin Walby and Alex Luscombe, "Criteria for Quality in Qualitative Research and Use of Freedom of Information Requests in the Social Sciences," *Qualitative Research* 17, no. 5 (2017): 537–53, https://doi.org/10.1177/1468794116679726.
11 Laura K. Nelson, Derek Burk, Marcel Knudsen, and Leslie McCall, "The Future of Coding: A Comparison of Hand-Coding and Three Types of Computer-Assisted Text Analysis Methods," *Sociological Methods & Research* 50, no. 1 (2021): 202–37, https://doi.org/10.1177/0049124118769114.
12 Nelson et al., "Future of Coding."
13 Nelson et al., "Future of Coding," 202.
14 Christopher Lucas, Richard A. Nielsen, Margaret E. Roberts, Brandon M. Stewart, Alex Storer, and Dustin Tingley, "Computer-Assisted Text Analysis for Comparative Politics," *Political Analysis* 23, no. 2 (2015): 254–77, https://doi.org/10.1093/pan/mpu019.
15 Stuart Hall, "The Work of Representation," in *Representation: Cultural Representations and Signifying Practices*, ed. Stuart Hall (Thousand Oaks, CA: Sage Publications, 1997), 13–74.

16 Teun A. Van Dijk, "Principles of Critical Discourse Analysis," *Discourse &* *Society* 4, no. 2 (1993): 249–83 (emphasis in original), https://doi.org /10.1177/0957926593004002006.

17 Sarah Cummings et al., "Critical Discourse Analysis of Perspectives on Knowledge and the Knowledge Society within the Sustainable Development Goals," *Development Policy Review* 36, no. 6 (2018): 727–42, https://doi.org/10.1111/dpr.12296.

18 See Peter Hamilton, "Representing the Social: France and Frenchness in Post-War Humanist Photography," in *Representation: Cultural Representations and Signifying Practices*, ed. Stuart Hall (Thousand Oaks, CA: Sage Publications, 1997), 75–150; Roland Barthes, *Image, Music, Text*, trans. Stephen Heath (New York: Hill and Wang, 1977); Susan Sontag, *Regarding the Pain of Others* (New York: Picador, 2003).

19 Hamilton, "Representing the Social," 85.

20 Hamilton, "Representing the Social," 86.

21 Nandita Dogra, "'Reading NGOs Visually' – Implications of Visual Images for NGO Management," *Journal of International Development* 19, no. 2 (2007): 163, https://doi.org/10.1002/jid.1307.

22 For more information about the Displaces project, see "Educating without Borders: UEL and Friends in Calais and Beyond," accessed 10 June 2020, https://educatingwithoutborders.wordpress .com/displaces-a-project-by-gideon-mendel-and-calais-jungle -residents/.

23 Sontag, *Regarding the Pain of Others*.

24 Machiel Lamers, "Representing Poverty, Impoverishing Representation? A Discursive Analysis of a NGOs Fundraising Posters," *Graduate Journal of Social Science* 2, no. 1 (2005): 44.

25 Evi Chatzipanagiotidou and Fiona Murphy, "Exhibiting Loss: Refugee Art, Methodological Dubiety and the Responsibility (Not) to Document Loss," in *Documenting Displacement: Questioning Methodological Boundaries in Forced Migration Research*, ed. Katarzyna Grabska and Christina Clark-Kazak (Montreal: McGill-Queen's University Press, 2022), 81–103.

26 Stefanie E. Davis, "Objectification, Sexualization, and Misrepresentation: Social Media and the College Experience," *Social Media + Society* 4, no. 3 (2018), https://doi.org/10.1177/2056305118786727.

12 Presenting Research Findings across Borders

1 World Health Organization, "Timeline: WHO's COVID-19 Response," accessed 10 November 2022, https://www.who.int/emergencies /diseases/novel-coronavirus-2019/interactive-timeline/#!.

2 Francesco Bogliacino et al., "Expert Endorsement and the Legitimacy of Public Policy: Evidence from Covid19 Mitigation Strategies," *Journal of*

Risk Research 24, no. 3–4 (2021): 394–415, https://doi.org/10.1080
/13669877.2021.1881990.

3 Bogliacino et al., "Expert Endorsement,"

4 Kate L. Mandeville et al., "Academics and Competing Interests in H1N1 Influenza Media Reporting," *Journal of Epidemiological Community Health* 68, no. 3 (2014): 197–203.

5 Carmen Pérez-Llantada, Ramón Plo, and Gibson R. Ferguson, "'You Don't Say What You Know, Only What You Can': The Perceptions and Practices of Senior Spanish Academics regarding Research Dissemination in English," *English for Specific Purposes* 30, no. 1 (2011): 18–30, https:// doi.org/10.1016/j.esp.2010.05.001.

6 "Open Access," SPARC, accessed 10 November 2022, https://sparcopen .org/open-access/.

7 "Open Data," SPARC, accessed 10 November 2022, https://sparcopen .org/open-data/.

8 Peter Suber, *Open Access* (Cambridge, MA: MIT Press, 2012), 36.

9 "About the Licenses," Creative Commons, accessed 10 November 2022, https://creativecommons.org/licenses/.

10 Plain Language Association International, "What Is Plain Language?," accessed 10 November 2022, https://plainlanguagenetwork.org/plain -language/what-is-plain-language/.

11 Plain Language Association International, "What Is Plain Language?"

12 "How to Turn Your Journal Article into an Infographic," *Journal of Marketing Management*, 8 February 2017, https://www.jmmnews.com /how-to-turn-journal-article-into-infographic/.

13 Bailey J. Sousa and Alexander M. Clark, "Six Insights to Make Better Academic Conference Posters," *International Journal of Qualitative Methods* 18 (2019). https://doi.org/10.1177/1609406919862370.

14 Kunal Chaturvedi, Dinesh Kumar Vishwakarma, and Nidhi Singh, "COVID-19 and Its Impact on Education, Social Life and Mental Health of Students: A Survey," *Children and Youth Services Review* 121 (2021), https://doi.org/10.1016/j.childyouth.2020.105866.

15 Lutz Bornmann, "What Is Societal Impact of Research and How Can It Be Assessed? A Literature Survey," *Journal of the American Society for Information Science and Technology* 64, no. 2 (2013): 217–33, https://doi .org/10.1002/asi.22803.

Bibliography

Abfalter, Dagmar, Julia Mueller-Seeger, and Margit Raich. "Translation Decisions in Qualitative Research: A Systematic Framework." *International Journal of Social Research Methodology* 24, no. 4 (2021): 469–86. https://doi.org/10.1080/13645579.2020.1805549.

Adeloye, David, Neil Carr, and Andrea Insch. "Conducting Qualitative Interviews on Sensitive Topics in Sensitive Places: The Case of Terrorism and Tourism in Nigeria." *Tourism Recreation Research* 45, no. 1 (2020): 69–79. https://doi.org/10.1080/02508281.2019.1656872.

Agostinho, Daniela. "Archival Encounters: Rethinking Access and Care in Digital Colonial Archives." *Archival Science* 19, no. 2 (2019): 141–65. https://doi.org/10.1007/s10502-019-09312-0.

Ahmed, Wasim. "Using Twitter as a Data Source: An Overview of Social Media Research Tools (2021)." *LSE Impact Blog*, 18 May 2021. https://blogs.lse.ac.uk/impactofsocialsciences/2021/05/18/using-twitter-as-a-data-source-an-overview-of-social-media-research-tools-2021/.

Airoldi, Massimo. "Ethnography and the Digital Fields of Social Media." *International Journal of Social Research Methodology* 21, no. 6 (2021): 661–73. https://doi.org/10.1080/13645579.2018.1465622.

Akemu, Onajomo, and Samer Abdelnour. "Confronting the Digital: Doing Ethnography in Modern Organizational Settings." *Organizational Research Methods* 23, no. 2 (2020): 296–321. https://doi.org/10.1177/1094428118791018.

Akesson, Bree, Miranda D'Amico, Myriam Denov, Fatima Khan, Warren Linds, and Claudia A. Mitchell. "'Stepping Back' as Researchers: Addressing Ethics in Arts-Based Approaches to Working with War-Affected Children in School and Community Settings." *Educational Research for Social Change (ERSC)* 3, no. 1 (2014): 75–89.

American Anthropological Association. "American Anthropological Association's Executive Board Statement on the Human Terrain System

Project," press release, 6 November 2007, http://s3.amazonaws.com /rdcms-aaa/files/production/public/FileDownloads/pdfs/pdf /EB_Resolution_110807.pdf.

Angeles, Leonora C. "Feminist Demands, Dilemmas, and Dreams in Introducing Participatory Action Research in a Canada-Vietnam Capacity-Building Project." In *Feminist Community Research: Case Studies and Methodologies*, edited by Gillian Creese and Wendy Frisby, 37–57. Vancouver: UBC Press, 2011.

Angotti, Nicole, and Christie Sennott. "Implementing 'Insider' Ethnography: Lessons from the Public Conversations about HIV/AIDS Project in Rural South Africa." *Qualitative Research* 15, no. 4 (2015): 437–53. https://doi .org/10.1177/1468794114543402.

Araos, Malcolm, James Ford, Lea Berrang-Ford, Robbert Biesbroek, and Sarah Moser. "Climate Change Adaptation Planning for Global South Megacities: The Case of Dhaka." *Journal of Environmental Policy & Planning* 19, no. 6 (2017): 682–96. https://doi.org/10.1080/1523908X.2016.1264873.

Archibald, Jo-ann. "An Indigenous Storywork Methodology." In *Handbook of the Arts in Qualitative Research: Perspectives, Methodologies, Examples, and Issues*, edited by J. Gary Knowles and Ardra L. Cole, 371–93. Los Angeles: Sage Publications, 2008.

Archibald, Mandy M., Rachel C. Ambagtsheer, Mavourneen G. Casey, and Michael Lawless. "Using Zoom Videoconferencing for Qualitative Data Collection: Perceptions and Experiences of Researchers and Participants." *International Journal of Qualitative Methods* 18 (2019). https://doi .org/10.1177/1609406919874596.

Arnstein, Sherry R. "A Ladder of Citizen Participation." *Journal of the American Institute of Planners* 35, no. 4 (1969): 216–24. https://doi .org/10.1080/01944366908977225.

Bacon, Chris, Ernesto Mendez, and Martha Brown. "Participatory Action Research and Support for Community Development and Conservation: Examples from Shade Coffee Landscapes in Nicaragua and El Salvador." UC Santa Cruz: Center for Agroecology. Retrieved from https:// escholarship.org/uc/item/1qv2r5d8.

Baker, Rachel, and Rachel Hinton. "Do Focus Groups Facilitate Meaningful Participation in Social Research?" In *Developing Focus Group Research: Politics, Theory and Practice*, edited by Rosaline Barbour and Jenny Kitzinger, 79–98. Los Angeles: Sage Publications, 1999. https://doi .org/10.4135/9781849208857.n6.

Bakewell, Oliver. "Research beyond the Categories: The Importance of Policy Irrelevant Research into Forced Migration." *Journal of Refugee Studies* 21, no. 4 (2008): 432–53. https://doi.org/10.1093/jrs/fen042.

Balcells, Laia, and Christopher M. Sullivan. "New Findings from Conflict Archives: An Introduction and Methodological Framework." *Journal of Peace Research* 55, no. 2 (2018): 137–46. https://doi.org /10.1177/0022343317750217.

Baldwin-Edwards, Martin, Brad K. Blitz, and Heaven Crawley. "The Politics of Evidence-Based Policy in Europe's 'Migration Crisis.'" *Journal of Ethnic and Migration Studies* 45, no. 12 (2019): 2139–55. https://doi.org/10.1080/1369183X.2018.1468307.

Barendregt, Bart. "Deep Hanging Out in the Age of the Digital; Contemporary Ways of Doing Online and Offline Ethnography." *Asiascape: Digital Asia* 4, no. 3 (2017): 307–19. https://doi.org/10.1163/22142312-12340082.

Barthes, Roland. *Image, Music, Text.* Translated by Stephen Heath. New York: Hill and Wang, 1977.

Bastow, Simon, Patrick Dunleavy, and Jane Tinkler. *The Impact of the Social Sciences: How Academics and Their Research Make a Difference.* London: Sage Publications, 2014.

Behnam, Nicole, and Kristy Crabtree. "Big Data, Little Ethics: Confidentiality and Consent." *Forced Migration Review* 61 (2019): 4–6.

Beier, J. Marshall, and Samantha L. Arnold. "Becoming Undisciplined: Toward the Supradisciplinary Study of Security." *International Studies Review* 7, no. 1 (2005): 41–61. https://doi.org/10.1111/j.1521-9488.2005.00457.x.

Bennett, Kevin J., Tyrone F. Borders, George M. Holmes, Katy Backes Kozhimannil, and Erika Ziller. "What Is Rural? Challenges and Implications of Definitions That Inadequately Encompass Rural People and Places." *Health Affairs* 38, no. 12 (2019): 1985–92. https://doi.org/10.1377/hlthaff.2019.00910.

Bergen, Nicole. "Narrative Depictions of Working with Language Interpreters in Cross-Language Qualitative Research." *International Journal of Qualitative Methods* 17, no. 1 (2018). https://doi.org/10.1177/1609406918812301.

Berliner, Daniel. "Sunlight or Window Dressing? Local Government Compliance with South Africa's Promotion of Access to Information Act." *Governance* 30, no. 4 (2017): 641–61. https://doi.org/10.1111/gove.12246.

Bernard, Josef, Hana Daňková, and Petr Vašát. "Ties, Sites and Irregularities: Pitfalls and Benefits in Using Respondent-Driven Sampling for Surveying a Homeless Population." *International Journal of Social Research Methodology* 21, no. 5 (2018): 603–18. https://doi.org/10.1080/13645579.2018.1454640.

Bilotta, Neil. "Navigating Ethical Terrains: Perspectives on 'Research Ethics' in Kakuma Refugee Camp." PhD diss., McGill University, 2018. https://escholarship.mcgill.ca/concern/theses/3t945t11k?locale=en.

Bloch, Alice. "Survey Research with Refugees: A Methodological Perspective." *Policy Studies* 25, no. 2 (2004): 139–51. https://doi.org/10.1080/0144287042000262215.

Bogliacino, Francesco, Rafael Charris, Camilo Gómez, Felipe Montealegre, and Cristiano Codagnone. "Expert Endorsement and the Legitimacy of Public Policy: Evidence from Covid-19 Mitigation Strategies." *Journal of Risk Research* 24, no. 3–4 (2021): 394–415. https://doi.org/10.1080/13669877.2021.1881990.

Bonner, Ann, and Gerda Tolhurst. "Insider-Outsider Perspectives of Participant Observation." *Nurse Researcher* 9, no. 4 (2002): 7–19. https://www.researchgate.net/publication/11232650_Insider-outsider_perspectives_of_participant_observation.

Bornmann, Lutz. "What Is Societal Impact of Research and How Can It Be Assessed? A Literature Survey." *Journal of the American Society for Information Science and Technology* 64, no. 2 (2013): 217–33. https://doi.org/10.1002/asi.22803.

Bouma, Gary D., Rod Ling, and Lori Wilkinson. *The Research Process*. Oxford: Oxford University Press, 1993.

Bouvier, Gwen, and David Machin. "Critical Discourse Analysis and the Challenges and Opportunities of Social Media." *Review of Communication* 18, no. 3 (2018): 178–92. https://doi.org/10.1080/15358593.2018.1479881.

Brear, Michelle R., and Rebecca Gordon. "Translating the Principle of Beneficence into Ethical Participatory Development Research Practice." *Journal of International Development* 33, no. 1 (2021): 109–26. https://doi.org/10.1002/jid.3514.

Brett, Rachel, and Margaret McCallin. *Children: The Invisible Soldiers*. Stockholm: Save the Children, 1996.

Brewer, John D. "The Ethics of Ethical Debates in Peace and Conflict Research: Notes towards the Development of a Research Covenant." *Methodological Innovations* 9 (2016). https://doi.org/10.1177/2059799116630657.

Brigden, Noelle, and Anita R. Gohdes. "The Politics of Data Access in Studying Violence across Methodological Boundaries: What We Can Learn from Each Other?" *International Studies Review* 22, no. 2 (2020): 250–67. https://doi.org/10.1093/isr/viaa017.

Brigden, Noelle, and Miranda Hallett. "Fieldwork as Social Transformation: Place, Time, and Power in a Violent Moment." *Geopolitics* 26, no. 1 (2021): 1–17. https://doi.org/10.1080/14650045.2020.1717068.

Bright, Jonathan, and John Gledhill. "A Divided Discipline? Mapping Peace and Conflict Studies." *International Studies Perspectives* 19, no. 2 (2018): 128–47. https://doi.org/10.1093/isp/ekx009.

Brown, Courtney A., Anna C. Revette, Sarah D. de Ferranti, Holly B. Fontenot, and Holly C. Gooding. "Conducting Web-Based Focus Groups with Adolescents and Young Adults." *International Journal of Qualitative Methods* 20 (2021). https://doi.org/10.1177/1609406921996872.

Brown, Juanita. "The World Café: Living Knowledge through Conversations That Matter." PhD. diss., Fielding Institute, 2002. https://st4.ning.com/topology/rest/1.0/file/get/2836607717?profile=original.

Brown, Katherine E. "Gender, Governance, and Countering Violent Extremism (CVE) in the UK." *International Journal of Law, Crime and Justice* (2019). https://doi.org/10.1016/j.ijlcj.2019.100371.

Browne, M. Neil, and Stuart M. Keeley. *Asking the Right Questions: A Guide to Critical Thinking*. 8th ed. Upper Saddle River, NJ: Pearson Education, 2007.

Brubaker, Roger, and Frederick Cooper. "Beyond 'Identity.'" *Theory and Society* 29, no. 1 (2000): 1–47. https://doi.org/10.1023/A:1007068714468.

Bruns, Bettina, and Judith Miggelbrink, eds. *Subverting Borders: Doing Research on Smuggling and Small-Scale Trade*. Berlin: Springer Science & Business Media, 2011.

Burawoy, Michael. "The Extended Case Method." *Sociological Theory* 16, no. 1 (1998): 4–33. https://doi.org/10.1111/0735-2751.00040.

Campbell, Susanna P. "Ethics of Research in Conflict Environments." *Journal of Global Security Studies* 2, no. 1 (2017): 89–101. https://doi.org/10.1093/jogss/ogw024.

Cargas, Sarita, and Kristina Ederbach. "Rethinking Multidisciplinarity within Human Rights Education." Open Global Rights, 3 September 2020. https://www.openglobalrights.org/rethinking-multidisciplinarity-within-human-rights-education/.

Celestina, Mateja. "Between Trust and Distrust in Research with Participants in Conflict Context." *International Journal of Social Research Methodology* 21, no. 3 (2018): 373–83. https://doi.org/10.1080/13645579.2018.1427603.

Cernat, Vasile. "Roma Undercount and the Issue of Undeclared Ethnicity in the 2011 Romanian Census." *International Journal of Social Research Methodology* 24, no. 6 (2020): 761–6. https://doi.org/10.1080/13645579.2020.1818416.

Chambers, Robert. "The Origins and Practice of Participatory Rural Appraisal." *World Development* 22, no. 7 (1994): 953–69. https://doi.org/10.1016/0305-750X(94)90141-4.

– "Participatory Mapping and Geographic Information Systems: Whose Map? Who Is Empowered and Who Disempowered? Who Gains and Who Loses?" *The Electronic Journal of Information Systems in Developing Countries* 25, no. 1 (2006): 1–11. https://doi.org/10.1002/j.1681-4835.2006.tb00163.x.

Champagne-Poirier, Olivier, Marie-Ève Carignan, Marc D. David, and Tracey O'Sullivan. "Understanding and Quantifying: A Mixed-Method Study on the Journalistic Coverage of Canadian Disasters." *International Journal of Qualitative Methods* 20 (2021). https://doi.org/10.1177/1609406921990492.

Chaturvedi, Kunal, Dinesh Kumar Vishwakarma, and Nidhi Singh. "COVID-19 and Its Impact on Education, Social Life and Mental Health of Students: A Survey." *Children and Youth Services Review* 121 (2021). https://doi.org/10.1016/j.childyouth.2020.105866.

Chatzipanagiotidou, Evi, and Fiona Murphy. "Exhibiting Loss: Refugee Art, Methodological Dubiety and the Responsibility (Not) to Document Loss." In *Documenting Displacement: Questioning Methodological Boundaries in Forced Migration Research*, edited by Katarzyna Grabska and Christina Clark-Kazak, 81–103. Montreal: McGill-Queen's University Press, 2022.

Chimni, Bhupinder S. "The Birth of a 'Discipline': From Refugee to Forced Migration Studies." *Journal of Refugee Studies* 22, no. 1 (2009): 11–29. https://doi.org/10.1093/jrs/fen051.

Chiumento, Anna, Atif Rahman, and Lucy Frith. "Writing to Template: Researchers' Negotiation of Procedural Research Ethics." *Social Science & Medicine* 255 (2020). https://doi.org/10.1016/j.socscimed.2020.112980.

Chliova, Myrto, Jan Brinckmann, and Nina Rosenbusch. "Is Microcredit a Blessing for the Poor? A Meta-Analysis Examining Development Outcomes and Contextual Considerations." *Journal of Business Venturing* 30, no. 3 (2015): 467–87. https://doi.org/10.1016/j.jbusvent.2014.10.003.

Clark-Kazak, Christina. "Ethical Considerations: Research with People in Situations of Forced Migration." *Refuge: Canada's Journal on Refugees/ Refuge: Revue canadienne sur les réfugiés* 33, no. 2 (2017): 11–17. https://doi .org/10.7202/1043059ar.

– "Representing Refugees in the Life Cycle: A Social Age Analysis of United Nations High Commissioner for Refugees Annual Reports and Appeals 1999–2008." *Journal of Refugee Studies* 22, no. 3 (2009): 302–22. https://doi .org/10.1093/jrs/fep012.

Coetzee, Wayne Stephen. "Doing Research on 'Sensitive Topics': Studying the Sweden–South Africa Arms Deal." *Scientia Militaria: South African Journal of Military Studies* 48, no. 2 (2022): 65–85. https://doi .org/10.5787/48-2-1278.

Collins, Christopher S., and Carrie M. Stockton. "The Central Role of Theory in Qualitative Research." *International Journal of Qualitative Methods* 17, no. 1 (2018). https://doi.org/10.1177/1609406918797475.

Conrad, Courtenay R., and Jacqueline H.R. DeMeritt. "Unintended Consequences: The Effect of Advocacy to End Torture on Empowerment Rights Violations." In *Examining Torture*, edited by Tracy Lightcap and James Pfiffner, 159–83. New York: Palgrave Macmillan, 2014. https://doi .org/10.1057/9781137439161_7.

Cons, Jason, and Kasia Paprocki. "Contested Credit Landscapes: Microcredit, Self-Help and Self-Determination in Rural Bangladesh." *Third World Quarterly* 31, no. 4 (2010): 637–54. https://doi.org/10.1080/01436591003701141.

Copestake, James, Sonia Bhalotra, and Susan Johnson. "Assessing the Impact of Microcredit: A Zambian Case Study." *Journal of Development Studies* 37, no. 4 (2001): 81–100. https://doi.org/10.1080/00220380412331322051.

Costello, Leesa, Marie-Louise McDermott, and Ruth Wallace. "Netnography: Range of Practices, Misperceptions, and Missed Opportunities." *International Journal of Qualitative Methods* 16, no. 1 (2017). https://doi .org/10.1177/1609406917700647.

Cowper-Smith, Yuriko. *The Oral Defence: Speaking Back to the Community*. Vancouver: UBC Press, forthcoming.

Cummings, Sarah, Barbara Regeer, Leah De Haan, Marjolein Zweekhorst, and Joske Bunders. "Critical Discourse Analysis of Perspectives on Knowledge and the Knowledge Society within the Sustainable Development Goals." *Development Policy Review* 36, no. 6 (2018): 727–42. https://doi.org/10.1111/dpr.12296.

Cyr, Jennifer. "The Unique Utility of Focus Groups for Mixed-Methods Research." *PS: Political Science & Politics* 50, no. 4 (2017): 1038–42. https:// doi.org/10.1017/S104909651700124X.

Davis, Stefanie E. "Objectification, Sexualization, and Misrepresentation: Social Media and the College Experience." *Social Media + Society* 4, no. 3 (2018). https://doi.org/10.1177/2056305118786727.

Day, Christopher, and Kendra L. Koivu. "Finding the Question: A Puzzle-Based Approach to the Logic of Discovery." *Journal of Political Science*

Education 15, no. 3 (2019): 377–86. https://doi.org/10.1080/15512169.2018
.1493594.

De Hoyos, Rafael, Maurizio Bussolo, and Oscar Núñez. "Exports, Gender
Wage Gaps, and Poverty in Honduras." *Oxford Development Studies* 40,
no. 4 (2012): 533–51. http://dx.doi.org/10.1080/13600818.2012.732562.

Del Vicario, Michela, Antonio Scala, Guido Caldarelli, H. Eugene Stanley, and
Walter Quattrociocchi. "Modeling Confirmation Bias and Polarization."
Scientific Reports 7 (2017). https://doi.org/10.1038/srep40391.

Dogra, Nandita. "'Reading NGOs Visually' – Implications of Visual Images
for NGO Management." *Journal of International Development* 19, no. 2
(2007): 161–71. https://doi.org/10.1002/jid.1307.

Drawson, Alexandra S., Elaine Toombs, and Christopher J. Mushquash.
"Indigenous Research Methods: A Systematic Review." *International
Indigenous Policy Journal* 8, no. 2 (2017): 1–25. https://doi.org/10.18584
/iipj.2017.8.2.5.

Druckman, Daniel. *Doing Research: Methods of Inquiry for Conflict Analysis.*
Thousand Oaks, CA: Sage Publications, 2005.

Duong, Kim Anh. "Doing Human Trafficking Research: Reflections on Ethical
Challenges." *Journal of Research in Gender Studies* 5, no. 2 (2015): 171–90.

Durkheim, Émile. *The Rules of Sociological Method.* 8th ed. Edited by George
E.G. Catlin. Translated by Sarah A. Solvay and John H. Mueller. New York:
The Free Press, 1938. First published 1895.

Durrheim, Kevin. "Research Design." In *Research in Practice: Applied
Methods for the Social Sciences,* edited by Martin Terre Blanche, Kevin
Durrheim, and Desmond Painter, 33–59. Cape Town: University of Cape
Town Press, 2006.

Engin, Marion. "Research Diary: A Tool for Scaffolding." *International
Journal of Qualitative Methods* 10, no. 3 (2011): 296–306. https://doi
.org/10.1177/160940691101000308.

Estacio, Emee Vida, and Toni Karic. "The World Café: An Innovative Method
to Facilitate Reflections on Internationalisation in Higher Education."
Journal of Further and Higher Education 40, no. 6 (2016): 731–45. https://doi
.org/10.1080/0309877X.2015.1014315.

Evans, Megan C., and Christopher Cvitanovic. "An Introduction to Achieving
Policy Impact for Early Career Researchers." *Palgrave Communications* 4,
no. 88 (2018): 1–12. https://doi.org/10.1057/s41599-018-0144-2.

Finlay, Linda. "'Reflexive Embodied Empathy': A Phenomenology of
Participant-Researcher Intersubjectivity." *The Humanistic Psychologist* 33,
no. 4 (2005): 271–92. https://doi.org/10.1207/s15473333thp3304_4.

Fouché, Christa, and Glenda Light. "An Invitation to Dialogue: 'The World
Café' in Social Work Research." *Qualitative Social Work* 10, no. 1 (2011):
28–48. https://doi.org/10.1177/1473325010376016.

Frydenlund, Erika, and José Padilla. "Opportunities and Challenges of Using
Computer-Based Simulation in Migration and Displacement Research:
A Focus on Lesbos, Greece." In *Documenting Displacement: Questioning*

Methodological Boundaries in Forced Migration Research, edited by Katarzyna Grabska and Christina Clark-Kazak, 279–308. Montreal: McGill-Queen's University Press, 2022.

Fukuda-Parr, Sakiko. "Theory and Policy in International Development: Human Development and Capability Approach and the Millennium Development Goals." *International Studies Review* 13, no. 1 (2011): 122–32. https://doi.org/10.1111/j.1468-2486.2010.01003.x.

Gamage, Shashini, and Danesh Jayatilaka. "Life-Story Narratives, Memory Maps, and Video Stories: Spatial Narratives of Urban Displacement in Sri Lanka." In *Documenting Displacement: Inter-Disciplinary Methodologies in Forced Migration Research*, edited by Katarzyna Grabska and Christina Clark-Kazak, 138–60. Montreal: McGill-Queen's University Press, 2022.

Garcia, Gina A., and Jenesis J. Ramirez. "Proposing a Methodological Borderland: Combining Chicana Feminist Theory with Transformative Mixed Methods Research." *Journal of Mixed Methods Research* 15, no. 2 (2021): 223–41. https://doi.org/10.1177/1558689820954023.

Garcini, Luz, Thania Galvan, Juan Peña, Nellie Chen, and Elizabeth Klonoff. "Effectiveness of Respondent-Driven Sampling for Conducting Health Studies among Undocumented Immigrants at a Time of Heightened Immigration Enforcement." *Journal of Immigrant Minority Health* 24, no. 1 (2022): 102–10. https://doi.org/10.1007/s10903-020-01112-4.

Geertz, Clifford. "Thick Description: Toward an Interpretive Theory of Culture." In *The Cultural Geography Reader*, edited by Timothy Oaks and Patricia Price, 41–51. London: Routledge, 2008. https://doi.org/10.4324/9780203931950.

Georgalakis, James, Nasreen Jessani, Rose Oronje, and Ben Ramalingam, eds. *The Social Realities of Knowledge for Development: Sharing Lessons of Improving Development Processes with Evidence*. Brighton, UK: Institute of Development Studies and The Impact Initiative, 2017. https://opendocs.ids.ac.uk/opendocs/handle/20.500.12413/12852.

George, Alexander L., and Andrew Bennett. *Case Studies and Theory Development in the Social Sciences*. Cambridge, MA: MIT Press, 2005.

Gerber, Nancy, Elisabetta Biffi, Jacelyn Biondo, Marco Gemignani, Karin Hannes, and Richard Siegesmund. "Arts-Based Research in the Social and Health Sciences: Pushing for Change with an Interdisciplinary Global Arts-Based Research Initiative." *Forum Qualitative Sozialforschung/Forum: Qualitative Social Research* 21, no. 2 (2020): 30. https://doi.org/10.17169/fqs-21.2.3496.

Gifford, Sandy. "To Respect or Protect? Whose Values Shape the Ethics of Refugee Research?" In *Values and Vulnerabilities: The Ethics of Research with Refugees and Asylum Seekers*, edited by Karen Block, Elisha Riggs, and Nick Haslam, 41–59. Toowong: Australian Academic Press, 2013. https://doi.org/10.1002/j.1681-4835.2006.tb00163.x.

Gingras, François Pierre, and Catherine Côté. "La théorie et le sens de la recherche." In *Recherche sociale. De la problématique à la collecte des données*, 5th ed., edited by Benoît Gauthier, 109–34. Montreal: Presses de l'Université du Québec, 2009.

Godin, Marie, and Giorgia Donà. "Methodological and Ethical Reflections in the Displaces Participatory Photographic Project in the 'Calais Jungle.'" In *Documenting Displacement: Questioning Methodological Boundaries in Forced Migration Research*, edited by Katarzyna Grabska and Christina Clark-Kazak, 224–49. Montreal: McGill-Queen's University Press, 2022.

González, María Cristina. "The Four Seasons of Ethnography: A Creation-Centered Ontology for Ethnography." *International Journal of Intercultural Relations* 24, no. 5 (2000): 623–50. https://doi.org/10.1016/S0147-1767(00)00020-1.

Górny, Agata, and Joanna Napierała. "Comparing the Effectiveness of Respondent-Driven Sampling and Quota Sampling in Migration Research." *International Journal of Social Research Methodology* 19, no. 6 (2016): 645–61. https://doi.org/10.1080/13645579.2015.1077614.

Greene, Stuart, Kevin J. Burke, and Maria K. McKenna. "A Review of Research Connecting Digital Storytelling, Photovoice, and Civic Engagement." *Review of Educational Research* 88, no. 6 (2018): 844–78. https://doi.org/10.3102/0034654318794134.

Grek, Sotiria, and Christian Ydesen. "Where Science Met Policy: Governing by Indicators and the OECD's INES Programme." *Globalisation, Societies and Education* 19, no. 2 (2021): 122–37. https://doi.org/10.1080/14767724.2021.1892477.

Griffin, Gabriele, and Doris Leibetseder. "'Only Applies to Research Conducted in Sweden …': Dilemmas in Gaining Ethics Approval in Transnational Qualitative Research." *International Journal of Qualitative Methods* 18 (2019). https://doi.org/10.1177/1609406919869444.

Guérin, Isabelle. "Juggling with Debt, Social Ties, and Values: The Everyday Use of Microcredit in Rural South India." *Current Anthropology* 55, no. S9 (2014): S40–S50. https://doi.org/10.1086/675929.

Guillemin, Marilys, and Lynn Gillam. "Ethics, Reflexivity, and 'Ethically Important Moments' in Research." *Qualitative Inquiry* 10, no. 2 (2004): 261–80. https://doi.org/10.1177/1077800403262360.

Gunning, Jeroen. "A Case for Critical Terrorism Studies?" *Government and Opposition* 42, no. 3 (2007): 363–93. https://doi.org/10.1111/j.1477-7053.2007.00228.x.

Hagene, Turid. "The Power of Ethnography: A Useful Approach to Researching Politics." *Forum for Development Studies* 45, no. 2 (2018): 305–25. https://doi.org/10.1080/08039410.2017.1366360.

Hall, Budd L., and Rajesh Tandon. "Decolonization of Knowledge, Epistemicide, Participatory Research and Higher Education." *Research for All* 1, no. 1 (2017): 6–19. https://doi.org/10.18546/RFA.01.1.02.

Hall, Johanna, Mark Gaved, and Julia Sargent. "Participatory Research Approaches in Times of Covid-19: A Narrative Literature Review." *International Journal of Qualitative Methods* 20 (2021). https://doi.org/10.1177/16094069211010087.

Hall, Stuart. "The Work of Representation." In *Representation: Cultural Representations and Signifying Practices*, edited by Stuart Hall, 13–74. Thousand Oaks, CA: Sage Publications, 1997.

Hamilton, Peter. "Representing the Social: France and Frenchness in Post-War Humanist Photography." In *Representation: Cultural Representations and Signifying Practices*, edited by Stuart Hall, 75–150. Thousand Oaks, CA: Sage Publications, 1997.

Harris, La Donna, and Jacqueline Wasilewski. "Indigeneity, an Alternative Worldview: Four R's (Relationship, Responsibility, Reciprocity, Redistribution) vs. Two P's (Power and Profit). Sharing the Journey towards Conscious Evolution." *Systems Research and Behavioral Science* 21, no. 5 (2004): 489–503. https://doi.org/10.1002/sres.631.

Harrison, Helena, Melanie Birks, Richard Franklin, and Jane Mills. "Case Study Research: Foundations and Methodological Orientations." *Forum Qualitative Sozialforschung/Forum: Qualitative Social Research* 18, no. 1 (2017): 19. https://doi.org/10.17169/fqs-18.1.2655.

Held, Virginia. *The Ethics of Care: Personal, Political, and Global*. New York: Oxford University Press, 2006.

Henne-Ochoa, Richard. "Sustaining and Revitalizing Traditional Indigenous Ways of Speaking: An Ethnography-of-Speaking Approach." *Language & Communication* 62 (2018): 66–82. https://doi.org/10.1016/j.langcom.2018.07.002.

Holdsworth, Clare, and Georgina Brewis. "Volunteering, Choice and Control: A Case Study of Higher Education Student Volunteering." *Journal of Youth Studies* 17, no. 2 (2014): 204–19. https://doi.org/10.1080/13676261.2013.815702.

Hordge-Freeman, Elizabeth. "'Bringing Your Whole Self to Research': The Power of the Researcher's Body, Emotions, and Identities in Ethnography." *International Journal of Qualitative Methods* 17, no. 1 (2018). https://doi.org/10.1177/1609406918808862.

Hruschka, Daniel J., Beverley Cummings, Daphne Cobb St. John, Janet Moore, Gertrude Khumalo-Sakutukwa, and James W. Carey. "Fixed-Choice and Open-Ended Response Formats: A Comparison from HIV Prevention Research in Zimbabwe." *Field Methods* 16, no. 2 (2004): 184–202. https://doi.org/10.1177/1525822X03262663.

Huesca, Robert. "Social Aspects of Labor Organizing: *Maquiladora* Workers in a Grassroots Development Effort." *Journal of Developing Societies* 19, no. 2–3 (2003): 227–67. https://doi.org/10.1177/0169796X0301900205.

Human Security Report Project. *Human Security Report 2009/2010: The Causes of Peace and the Shrinking Costs of War*. New York: Oxford University Press, 2009.

Jacobson, Danielle, and Nida Mustafa. "Social Identity Map: A Reflexivity Tool for Practicing Explicit Positionality in Critical Qualitative Research." *International Journal of Qualitative Methods* 18 (2019). https://doi.org/10.1177/1609406919870075.

Jones, Briony, and Ulrike Lühe. "Knowledge for Peace: Transitional Justice and the Politics of Knowledge in Theory and Practice." In *Knowledge for Peace: Transitional Justice and the Politics of Knowledge in Theory and Practice*, edited by Briony Jones and Ulrike Lühe, 1–20. Cheltenham, UK: Edward Elgar Publishing, 2021.

Jull, Janet, Audrey Giles, and Ian D. Graham. "Community-Based Participatory Research and Integrated Knowledge Translation: Advancing the Co-creation of Knowledge." *Implementation Science* 12, no. 1 (2017): 1–9. https://doi.org/10.1186/s13012-017-0696-3.

Kabeer, Naila, and Luisa Natali. "Gender Equality and Economic Growth: Is There a Win-Win?" *IDS Working Papers*, no. 417 (2013).

Kapoor, Kawaljeet Kaur, Kuttimani Tamilmani, Nripendra P. Rana, Pushp Patil, Yogesh K. Dwivedi, and Sridhar Nerur. "Advances in Social Media Research: Past, Present and Future." *Information Systems Frontiers* 20, no. 3 (2018): 531–58. https://doi.org/10.1007/s10796-017-9810-y.

Karaffa, Cynthia A. "The Social Construction of Terrorism." In *Terrorism and Counterterrorism Today (Sociology of Crime, Law and Deviance, Volume 20)*, 67–87. Bingley, UK: Emerald Group Publishing, 2015.

Karooma, Cleophas. "Research Fatigue among Rwandan Refugees in Uganda." *Forced Migration Review* 61 (2019): 18–19.

Keating, Christine, Claire Rasmussen, and Pooja Rishi. "The Rationality of Empowerment: Microcredit, Accumulation by Dispossession, and the Gendered Economy." *Signs: Journal of Women in Culture and Society* 36, no. 1 (2010): 153–76. https://doi.org/10.1086/652911.

Keikelame, Mpoe Johannah. "'The Tortoise under the Couch': An African Woman's Reflections on Negotiating Insider-Outsider Positionalities and Issues of Serendipity on Conducting a Qualitative Research Project in Cape Town, South Africa." *International Journal of Social Research Methodology* 21, no. 2 (2018): 219–30. https://doi.org/10.1080/13645579.2017.1357910.

Khan, Mohsin Hassan, Hamedi Mohd Adnan, Surinderpal Kaur, Rashid Ali Khuhro, Rohail Asghar, and Sahira Jabeen. "Muslims' Representation in Donald Trump's Anti-Muslim-Islam Statement: A Critical Discourse Analysis." *Religions* 10, no. 2 (2019): 115. https://doi.org/10.3390/rel10020115.

Kindon, Sara, Rachel Pain, and Mike Kesby. "Participatory Action Research: Origins, Approaches and Methods." In *Participatory Action Research Approaches and Methods: Connecting People, Participation and Place*, edited by Sara Kindon, Rachel Pain, and Mike Kesby, 9–18. London: Routledge, 2007. https://doi.org/10.4324/9780203933671.

Komil-Burley, D. "Conducting Research in Authoritarian Bureaucracies: Researcher Positionality, Access, Negotiation, Cooperation, Trepidation, and Avoiding the Influence of the Gatekeepers." *International Journal of Qualitative Methods* 20 (2021). https://doi.org/10.1177/1609406921996862.

Kovach, Margaret. "Conversation Method in Indigenous Research." *First Peoples Child & Family Review: An Interdisciplinary Journal Honouring the Voices, Perspectives, and Knowledges of First Peoples through Research, Critical Analyses, Stories, Standpoints and Media Reviews* 5, no. 1 (2010): 40–8. https://doi.org/10.7202/1069060ar.

Lamers, Machiel. "Representing Poverty, Impoverishing Representation? A Discursive Analysis of a NGOs Fundraising Posters." *Graduate Journal of Social Science* 2, no. 1 (2005): 37–74.

Landolt, Patricia, Luin Goldring, and Paul Pritchard. "Decentering Methodological Nationalism to Survey Precarious Legal Status Trajectories." *International Journal of Social Research Methodology* 25, no. 2 (2022): 183–95. https://doi.org/10.1080/13645579.2020.1866339.

Lata, Lutfun Nahar. "Negotiating Gatekeepers and Positionality in Building Trust for Accessing the Urban Poor in the Global South." *Qualitative Research Journal* 21, no. 1 (2021): 76–86. https://doi.org/10.1108/QRJ-03-2020-0017.

Lavorgna, Anita, and Lisa Sugiura. "Direct Contacts with Potential Interviewees When Carrying Out Online Ethnography on Controversial and Polarized Topics: A Loophole in Ethics Guidelines." *International Journal of Social Research Methodology* 25, no. 2 (2022): 261–7. https://doi.org/10.1080/13645579.2020.1855719.

Lawson, Victoria. "Geographies of Care and Responsibility." *Annals of the Association of American Geographers* 97, no. 1 (2007): 1–11. https://doi.org/10.1111/j.1467-8306.2007.00520.x.

Li, Sarah. "The Natural History of a Doctoral Research Study: The Role of a Research Diary and Reflexivity." In *Emotions and Reflexivity in Health & Social Care Field Research*, edited by Helen Allan and Anne Arber, 13–37. Cham, Switzerland: Palgrave Macmillan, 2018. http://dx.doi.org/10.1007/978-3-319-65503-1_2.

Liebenberg, Linda. "Thinking Critically about Photovoice: Achieving Empowerment and Social Change." *International Journal of Qualitative Methods* 17, no. 1 (2018). https://doi.org/10.1177/1609406918757631.

Linnemayr, Sebastian, Larissa Jennings Mayo-Wilson, Uzaib Saya, Zachary Wagner, Sarah MacCarthy, Stewart Walukaga, Susan Nakubulwa, and Yvonne Karamagi. "HIV Care Experiences during the COVID-19 Pandemic: Mixed-Methods Telephone Interviews with Clinic-Enrolled HIV-Infected Adults in Uganda." *AIDS and Behavior* 25, no. 1 (2021): 28–39. https://doi.org/10.1007/s10461-020-03032-8.

Liu, Xu. "Interviewing Elites: Methodological Issues Confronting a Novice." *International Journal of Qualitative Methods* 17, no. 1 (2018). https://doi.org/10.1177/1609406918770323.

Löhr, Katharina, Michael Weinhardt, and Stefan Sieber. "The 'World Café' as a Participatory Method for Collecting Qualitative Data." *International Journal of Qualitative Methods* 19 (2020). https://doi.org/10.1177/1609406920916976.

Lokot, Michelle. "Whose Voices? Whose Knowledge? A Feminist Analysis of the Value of Key Informant Interviews." *International*

Journal of Qualitative Methods 20 (2021). https://doi.org/10.1177 /1609406920948775.

López-Marrero, Tania, and L. Annie Hermansen-Báez. *Participatory Listing, Ranking, and Scoring of Ecosystem Services and Drivers of Change.* Gainesville, FL: USDA Forest Service, Southern Research Station, 2011. https://changingroles.interfacesouth.org/projects/el-yunque/guides /El%20Yunque%20HTG1%20English.pdf.

Loseke, Donileen R. *Methodological Thinking: Basic Principles of Social Research Design.* Los Angeles: Sage Publications, 2012.

Lucas, Christopher, Richard A. Nielsen, Margaret E. Roberts, Brandon M. Stewart, Alex Storer, and Dustin Tingley. "Computer-Assisted Text Analysis for Comparative Politics." *Political Analysis* 23, no. 2 (2015): 254–77. https://doi.org/10.1093/pan/mpu019.

Mac Ginty, Roger. "Complementarity and Interdisciplinarity in Peace and Conflict Studies." *Journal of Global Security Studies* 4, no. 2 (2019): 267–72. https://doi.org/10.1093/jogss/ogz002.

MacLeod, Miles, and Michiru Nagatsu. "What Does Interdisciplinarity Look Like in Practice: Mapping Interdisciplinarity and Its Limits in the Environmental Sciences." *Studies in History and Philosophy of Science* 67 (2018): 74–84. https://doi.org/10.1016/j.shpsa.2018.01.001.

MacNamara, Noirin, Danielle Mackle, Johanne Devlin Trew, Claire Pierson, and Fiona Bloomer. "Reflecting on Asynchronous Internet Mediated Focus Groups for Researching Culturally Sensitive Issues." *International Journal of Social Research Methodology* 24, no. 5 (2021): 553–65. https://doi.org /10.1080/13645579.2020.1857969.

Magnat, Virginie. "Can Research Become Ceremony? Performance Ethnography and Indigenous Epistemologies." *Canadian Theatre Review* 151 (2012): 30–6. http://doi.org/10.1353/ctr.2012.0058.

Makhoul, Jihad, Maysam Alameddine, and Rema Afifi. "'I felt that I was benefiting someone': Youth as Agents of Change in a Refugee Community Project." *Health Educational Research* 27, no. 5 (2012): 914–26. https://doi .org/10.1093/her/cyr011.

Mandeville, Kate L., Sam O'Neill, Andrew Brighouse, Alice Walker, Kielan Yarrow, and Kenneth Chan. "Academics and Competing Interests in H1N1 Influenza Media Reporting." *Journal of Epidemiological Community Health* 68, no. 3 (2014): 197–203. https://doi.org/10.1136 /jech-2013-203128.

Marlin-Bennett, Renée, and David K. Johnson. "International Political Economy: Overview and Conceptualization." *Oxford Research Encyclopedia of International Studies.* 22 December 2017. https://doi.org/10.1093 /acrefore/9780190846626.013.239.

Marshall, Monty G., Ted Robert Gurr, Christian Davenport, and Keith Jaggers. "Polity IV, 1800–1999: Comments on Munck and Verkuilen." *Comparative Political Studies* 35, no. 1 (2002): 40–5. https://doi.org /10.1177/001041400203500103.

Maynard, Victoria, Elizabeth Parker, and John Twigg. "The Effectiveness and Efficiency of Interventions Supporting Shelter Self-Recovery following Humanitarian Crises." London: Oxfam, Feinstein International Center, UKAID, 2017. https://policy-practice.oxfam.org.uk/publications/the-effectiveness-and-efficiency-of-interventions-supporting-shelter-self-recov-620189.

Mayoux, Linda, and Robert Chambers. "Reversing the Paradigm: Quantification, Participatory Methods and Pro-Poor Impact Assessment." *Journal of International Development* 17, no. 2 (2005): 271–98. https://doi.org/10.1002/jid.1214.

McAvoy, Libby. "Centring the 'Source' in Open Source Investigation." Open Global Rights. 21 January 2021. https://www.openglobalrights.org/centering-the-source-in-open-source-investigation/.

McGregor, Deborah, Jean-Paul Restoule, and Rochelle Johnston, eds. *Indigenous Research: Theories, Practices, and Relationships.* Toronto: Canadian Scholars' Press, 2018.

Mendez, Jennifer Bickham. "Gender and Citizenship in a Global Context: The Struggle for Maquila Workers' Rights in Nicaragua." *Identities: Global Studies in Culture and Power* 9, no. 1 (2002): 7–38. https://doi.org/10.1080/10702890210364.

– "Organizing a Space of Their Own? Global/Local Processes in a Nicaraguan Women's Organization." *Journal of Developing Societies* 18, no. 2–3 (2002): 196–227. https://doi.org/10.1177/0169796X0201800209.

Méndez, V. Ernesto, Martha Caswell, Stephen R. Gliessman, and Roseann Cohen. "Integrating Agroecology and Participatory Action Research (PAR): Lessons from Central America." *Sustainability* 9, no. 5 (2017): 705–14. https://doi.org/10.3390/su9050705.

Milligan, Paul, Alpha Njie, and Steve Bennett. "Comparison of Two Cluster Sampling Methods for Health Surveys in Developing Countries." *International Journal of Epidemiology* 33, no. 3 (2004): 469–76. https://doi.org/10.1093/ije/dyh096.

Montreuil, Marjorie, Aline Bogossian, Emilie Laberge-Perrault, and Eric Racine. "A Review of Approaches, Strategies and Ethical Considerations in Participatory Research with Children." *International Journal of Qualitative Methods* 20 (2021). https://doi.org/10.1177/1609406920987962.

Nagoda, Sigrid, and Andrea J. Nightingale. "Participation and Power in Climate Change Adaptation Policies: Vulnerability in Food Security Programs in Nepal." *World Development* 100 (2017): 85–93. https://doi.org/10.1016/j.worlddev.2017.07.022.

Nail, Thomas. *Theory of the Border.* New York: Oxford University Press, 2016.

Nasheeda, Aishath, Haslinda Binti Abdullah, Steven Eric Krauss, and Nobaya Binti Ahmed. "Transforming Transcripts into Stories: A Multimethod Approach to Narrative Analysis." *International Journal of Qualitative Methods* 18 (2019). https://doi.org/10.1177/1609406919856797.

Navin, Mark Christopher, and J.M. Dieterle. "Cooptation or Solidarity: Food Sovereignty in the Developed World." *Agriculture and Human Values* 35, no. 2 (2018): 319–29. https://doi.org/10.1007/s10460-017-9823-7.

Nelson, Laura K., Derek Burk, Marcel Knudsen, and Leslie McCall. "The Future of Coding: A Comparison of Hand-Coding and Three Types of Computer-Assisted Text Analysis Methods." *Sociological Methods & Research* 50, no. 1 (2021): 202–37. https://doi.org/10.1177 /0049124118769114.

Niu, Jinfang. "Integrated Online Access to Objects and Archives." *Archivaria* 86 (2018): 152–79.

Nolte, Sandra, Richard H. Osborne, Sarah Dwinger, Gerald R. Elsworth, Melanie L. Conrad, Matthias Rose, Martin Härter, Jörg Dirmaier, and Jördis M. Zill. "German Translation, Cultural Adaptation, and Validation of the Health Literacy Questionnaire (HLQ)." *PLOS ONE* 12, no. 2 (2017). https://doi.org/10.1371/journal.pone.0172340.

Nooraie, Reza Yousefi, Joanna E.M. Sale, Alexandra Marin, and Lori E. Ross. "Social Network Analysis: An Example of Fusion between Quantitative and Qualitative Methods." *Journal of Mixed Methods Research* 14, no. 1 (2020): 110–24. https://doi.org/10.1177/1558689818804060.

Nyumba, Tobias O., Kerrie Wilson, Christina J. Derrick, and Nibedita Mukherjee. "The Use of Focus Group Discussion Methodology: Insights from Two Decades of Application in Conservation." *Methods in Ecology and Evolution* 9, no. 1 (2018): 20–32. https://doi.org/10.1111/2041-210X.12860.

Oda, Anna, Adnan Al Mhamied, Riham Al-Saadi, Neil Arya, Mona Awwad, Oula Hajjar, Jill Hanley, et al. "Ethical Challenges of Conducting Longitudinal Community-Based Research with Refugees: Reflections from Peer Researchers." In *Documenting Displacement: Questioning Methodological Boundaries in Forced Migration Research*, edited by Katarzyna Grabska and Christina Clark-Kazak, 29–55. Montreal: McGill-Queen's University Press, 2022.

Onghena, Patrick, Bea Maes, and Mieke Heyvaert. "Mixed Methods Single Case Research: State of the Art and Future Directions." *Journal of Mixed Methods Research* 13, no. 4 (2019): 461–80. https://doi.org /10.1177/1558689818789530.

O'Sullivan, Elizabethann, Gary Rassel, Maureen Berner, and Jocelyn DeVance Taliaferro. *Research Methods for Public Administrators*. 6th ed. New York: Routledge, 2016.

Panter-Brick, Catherine, Rana Dajani, Dima Hamadmad, and Kristin Hadfield. "Comparing Online and In-Person Surveys: Assessing a Measure of Resilience with Syrian Refugee Youth." *International Journal of Social Research Methodology* 25, no. 5 (2022): 703–9. https://doi.org /10.1080/13645579.2021.1919789.

Parashar, Swati. "Research Brokers, Researcher Identities and Affective Performances: The Insider/Outsider Conundrum." *Civil Wars* 21, no. 2 (2019): 249–70. https://doi.org/10.1080/13698249.2019.1634304.

Peltier, Cindy. "An Application of Two-Eyed Seeing: Indigenous Research Methods with Participatory Action Research." *International Journal of Qualitative Methods* 17, no. 1 (2018). https://doi.org/10.1177/1609406918812346.

Pelzang, Rinchen, and Alison M. Hutchinson. "Establishing Cultural Integrity in Qualitative Research: Reflections from a Cross-Cultural Study." *International Journal of Qualitative Methods* 17, no. 1 (2018). https://doi.org/10.1177/1609406917749702.

Pérez-Llantada, Carmen, Ramón Plo, and Gibson R. Ferguson. "'You Don't Say What You Know, Only What You Can': The Perceptions and Practices of Senior Spanish Academics regarding Research Dissemination in English." *English for Specific Purposes* 30, no. 1 (2011): 18–30. https://doi.org/10.1016/j.esp.2010.05.001.

Peticca-Harris, Amanda, Nadia deGama, and Sara R.S.T.A. Elias. "A Dynamic Process Model for Finding Informants and Gaining Access in Qualitative Research." *Organizational Research Methods* 19, no. 3 (2016): 376–401. https://doi.org/10.1177/1094428116629218.

Phillippi, Julia, and Jana Lauderdale. "A Guide to Field Notes for Qualitative Research: Context and Conversation." *Qualitative Health Research* 28, no. 3 (2018): 381–8. https://doi.org/10.1177/1049732317697102.

Piazza, James A. "Rooted in Poverty?: Terrorism, Poor Economic Development, and Social Cleavages." *Terrorism and Political Violence* 18, no. 1 (2006): 159–77. https://doi.org/10.1080/095465590944578.

Pischke, Erin C., Jessie L. Knowlton, Colin C. Phifer, Jose Gutierrez Lopez, Tamara S. Propato, Amarella Eastmond, Tatiana Martins de Souza, et al. "Barriers and Solutions to Conducting Large International, Interdisciplinary Research Projects." *Environmental Management* 60, no. 6 (2017): 1011–21. https://doi.org/10.1007/s00267-017-0939-8.

Ponterotto, Joseph G. "Brief Note on the Origins, Evolution, and Meaning of the Qualitative Research Concept Thick Description." *The Qualitative Report* 11, no. 3 (2006): 538–49. https://doi.org/10.46743/2160-3715/2006.1666.

Powell, Mary Ann, Morag McArthur, Jenny Chalmers, Anne Graham, Tim Moore, Merle Spriggs, and Stephanie Taplin. "Sensitive Topics in Social Research Involving Children." *International Journal of Social Research Methodology* 21, no. 6 (2018): 647–60. https://doi.org/10.1080/13645579.2018.1462882.

Proulx, Craig. "Colonizing Surveillance: Canada Constructs an Indigenous Terror Threat." *Anthropologica* (2014): 83–100.

Pulker, Claire Elizabeth, Georgina S.A. Trapp, Jane Anne Scott, and Christina Mary Pollard. "Global Supermarkets' Corporate Social Responsibility Commitments to Public Health: A Content Analysis." *Globalization and Health* 14, no. 1 (2018): 1–20. https://doi.org/10.1186/s12992-018-0440-z.

Raghuram, Parvati. "Race and Feminist Care Ethics: Intersectionality as Method." *Gender, Place & Culture* 26, no. 5 (2019): 613–37. http://dx.doi.org/10.1080/0966369X.2019.1567471.

Raheja, Michelle H. "Reading Nanook's Smile: Visual Sovereignty, Indigenous Revisions of Ethnography, and 'Atanarjuat (The Fast Runner).'" *American Quarterly* 59, no. 4 (2007): 1159–85. https://doi.org/10.1353/aq.2007.0083.

Rankin, Janet. "Conducting Analysis in Institutional Ethnography: Guidance and Cautions." *International Journal of Qualitative Methods* 16, no. 1 (2017). https://doi.org/10.1177/1609406917734472.

Razavi, Shahra. "Revisiting Equity and Efficiency Arguments for Gender Equality: A Principled but Pragmatic Approach." *Canadian Journal of Development Studies/Revue canadienne d'études du développement* 38, no. 4 (2017): 558–63. https://doi.org/10.1080/02255189.2017.1376624.

Reed, Mark S., Rosalind Bryce, and Ruth Machen. "Pathways to Policy Impact: A New Approach for Planning and Evidencing Research Impact." *Evidence & Policy: A Journal of Research, Debate and Practice* 14, no. 3 (2018): 431–58. https://doi.org/10.1332/174426418X15326967547242.

Richards, Eve, Paola Simeti, Catherine Drolet, Bintou Faye, and Alyssa Peyton. Proposition MÉSI. Course Presentation, ECH 2720, Fall 2020.

Robards, Brady, and Siân Lincoln. "Uncovering Longitudinal Life Narratives: Scrolling Back on Facebook." *Qualitative Research* 17, no. 6 (2017): 715–30. https://doi.org/10.1177/1468794117700707.

Rodgers, Graeme. "'Hanging Out' with Forced Migrants: Methodological and Ethical Challenges." *Forced Migration Review* 21 (2004): 48–9.

Rodriguez-Garavito, Cesar. "Scientists and Activists Collaborate to Bring Hard Data into Advocacy." Open Global Rights, 21 November 2017. https://www.openglobalrights.org/scientists-and-activists-collaborate-to-bring-hard-data-into-advocacy/.

Rodríguez-Sánchez, Andrea, and Miguel Alonso-Cambrón. "Sound and Memory: Collaborative Reflection on Using Sound Postcards in Rebuilding Social Fabric with Victims of Forced Displacement in Colombia." In *Documenting Displacement: Inter-Disciplinary Methodologies in Forced Migration Research*, edited by Katarzyna Grabska and Christina Clark-Kazak, 153–72. Montreal: McGill-Queen's University Press, 2022.

Rojas, Lucero Ibarra. "On Conversation and Authorship: Legal Frameworks for Collaborative Methodologies." *International Journal of Qualitative Methods* 20 (2021). https://doi.org/10.1177/1609406921993289.

Rosow, Stephen J. "Toward an Anti-disciplinary Global Studies." *International Studies Perspectives* 4, no. 1 (2003): 1–14. https://doi.org/10.1111/1528-3577.04101.

Rowley, Jennifer, and John Farrow. *Organizing Knowledge: An Introduction to Managing Access to Information: Introduction to Access to Information.* 3rd ed. London: Routledge, 2017.

Ruedin, Didier. "The Role of Language in the Automatic Coding of Political Texts." *Swiss Political Science Review* 19, no. 4 (2013): 539–45. https://doi.org/10.1111/spsr.12050.

Sadler, Georgia Robins, Hau-Chen Lee, Rod Seung-Hwan Lim, and Judith Fullerton. "Recruitment of Hard-to-Reach Population Subgroups via Adaptations of the Snowball Sampling Strategy." *Nursing & Health Sciences* 12, no. 3 (2010): 369–74. https://doi.org/10.1111/j.1442-2018.2010.00541.x.

Schuster, Caroline E. "Reconciling Debt: Microcredit and the Politics of Indigeneity in Argentina's Altiplano." *PoLAR: Political and Legal Anthropology Review* 33, no. 1 (2010): 47–66. https://doi.org/10.1111/j.1555-2934.2010.01092.x.

Schwirplies, Claudia. "Citizens' Acceptance of Climate Change Adaptation and Mitigation: A Survey in China, Germany, and the US." *Ecological Economics* 145 (2018): 308–22. https://doi.org/10.1016/j.ecolecon.2017.11.003.

Seehawer, Maren Kristin. "Decolonising Research in a Sub-Saharan African Context: Exploring Ubuntu as a Foundation for Research Methodology, Ethics and Agenda." *International Journal of Social Research Methodology* 21, no. 4 (2018): 453–66. https://doi.org/10.1080/13645579.2018.1432404.

Shah, Alpa. "Ethnography? Participant Observation, a Potentially Revolutionary Praxis." *HAU: Journal of Ethnographic Theory* 7, no. 1 (2017): 45–59. https://doi.org/10.14318/hau7.1.008.

Shamrova, Daria P., and Cristy E. Cummings. "Participatory Action Research (PAR) with Children and Youth: An Integrative Review of Methodology and PAR Outcomes for Participants, Organizations, and Communities." *Children and Youth Services Review* 81 (2017): 400–12. https://doi.org/10.1016/j.childyouth.2017.08.022.

Sharp, Joanne. "A Subaltern Critical Geopolitics of the War on Terror: Postcolonial Security in Tanzania." *Geoforum* 42, no. 3 (2011): 297–305. https://doi.org/10.1016/j.geoforum.2011.04.005.

Shome, Raka. "Post-Colonial Reflections on the 'Internationalization' of Cultural Studies." *Cultural Studies* 23, no. 5–6 (2009): 694–719. https://doi.org/10.1080/09502380903132322.

Sikweyiya, Yandisa, and Rachel Jewkes. "Perceptions and Experiences of Research Participants on Gender-Based Violence Community Based Survey: Implications for Ethical Guidelines." *PLOS ONE* 7, no. 4 (2012). https://doi.org/10.1371/journal.pone.0035495.

Singh, Deepshikha. "Gender Relations, Urban Flooding, and the Lived Experiences of Women in Informal Urban Spaces." *Asian Journal of Women's Studies* 26, no. 3 (2020): 326–46. https://doi.org/10.1080/12259276.2020.1817263.

Singhal, Nupur, and Poornima Bhola. "Ethical Practices in Community-Based Research in Non-Suicidal Self-Injury: A Systematic Review." *Asian Journal of Psychiatry* 30 (2017): 127–34. https://doi.org/10.1016 /j.ajp.2017.08.015.

Skårås, Merethe. "Focused Ethnographic Research on Teaching and Learning in Conflict Zones: History Education in South Sudan." *Forum for Development Studies* 45, no. 2 (2018): 217–38. https://doi.org/10.1080 /08039410.2016.1202316.

Smith, Karen, Kirsten Holmes, Debbie Haski-Leventhal, Ram Cnaan, Fedima Handy, and Jeffrey Brudney. "Motivations and Benefits of Student Volunteering: Comparing Regular, Occasional, and Non-Volunteers in Five Countries." *Canadian Journal of Nonprofit and Social Economy Research* 1, no. 1 (2010): 65–81.

Son, Ho Ngoc, Dong Thi Linh Chi, and Aaron Kingsbury. "Indigenous Knowledge and Climate Change Adaptation of Ethnic Minorities in the Mountainous Regions of Vietnam: A Case Study of the Yao People in Bac Kan Province." *Agricultural Systems* 176 (2019). https://doi .org/10.1016/j.agsy.2019.102683.

Sontag, Susan. *Regarding the Pain of Others*. New York: Picador, 2003.

Sousa, Bailey J., and Alexander M. Clark. "Six Insights to Make Better Academic Conference Posters." *International Journal of Qualitative Methods* 18 (2019). https://doi.org/10.1177/1609406919862370.

Stein, Arlene. "Sex, Truths, and Audiotape: Anonymity and the Ethics of Exposure in Public Ethnography." *Journal of Contemporary Ethnography* 39, no. 5 (2010): 554–68. https://doi.org/10.1177/0891241610375955.

Stember, Marilyn. "Advancing the Social Sciences through the Interdisciplinary Enterprise." *The Social Science Journal* 28, no. 1 (1991): 1–14. https://doi.org/10.1016/0362-3319(91)90040-B.

Stewart, David W., and Prem Shamdasani. "Online Focus Groups." *Journal of Advertising* 46, no. 1 (2017): 48–60. https://doi.org/10.1080/00913367 .2016.1252288.

Stoecker, Randy, and Elisa Avila. "From Mixed Methods to Strategic Research Design." *International Journal of Social Research Methodology* 24, no. 6 (2021): 627–40. https://doi.org/10.1080/13645579.2020.1799639.

Stump, Jacob L., and Priya Dixit. "Toward a Completely Constructivist Critical Terrorism Studies." *International Relations* 26, no. 2 (2012): 199–217. https://doi.org/10.1177/0047117811404720.

Suarez, Carla. "'Living between Two Lions': Civilian Protection Strategies during Armed Violence in the Eastern Democratic Republic of the Congo." *Journal of Peacebuilding & Development* 12, no. 3 (2017): 54–67.

Subedi, Binaya. "Recognizing Respondents' Ways of Being and Knowing: Lessons Un/Learned in Researching Asian Immigrant and Asian-American Teachers." *International Journal of Qualitative Studies in Education* 20, no. 1 (2007): 51–71. https://doi.org/10.1080/09518390600924352.

Suber, Peter. *Open Access*. Cambridge, MA: MIT Press, 2012.

Sumiala, Johanna Maaria, and Minttu Tikka. "Broadcast Yourself – Global News! A Netnography of the 'Flotilla' News on YouTube." *Communication, Culture & Critique* 6, no. 2 (2013): 318–35. https://doi .org/10.1111/cccr.12008.

"Syrian Refugees in Jordan: A Protection Overview," Jordan INGO Forum, January 2018, https://reliefweb.int/sites/reliefweb.int/files/resources /JIFProtectionBrief-2017-Final.pdf.

Tedeschi, Gwendolyn Alexander. "Overcoming Selection Bias in Microcredit Impact Assessments: A Case Study in Peru." *The Journal of Development Studies* 44, no. 4 (2008): 504–18. https://doi.org/10.1080/00220380801980822.

Thaler, Gregory M. "Ethnography of Environmental Governance: Towards an Organizational Approach." *Geoforum* 120 (2021): 122–31. https://doi .org/10.1016/j.geoforum.2021.01.026.

Thaler, Kai M. "Reflexivity and Temporality in Researching Violent Settings: Problems with the Replicability and Transparency Regime." *Geopolitics* 26, no. 1 (2021): 18–44. https://doi.org/10.1080/14650045.2019.1643721.

Thambinathan, Vivetha, and Elizabeth Anne Kinsella. "Decolonizing Methodologies in Qualitative Research: Creating Spaces for Transformative Praxis." *International Journal of Qualitative Methods* 20, no. 1 (2021). https://doi.org/10.1177/16094069211014766.

Tomaszewski, Lesley Eleanor, Jill Zarestky, and Elsa Gonzalez. "Planning Qualitative Research: Design and Decision Making for New Researchers." *International Journal of Qualitative Methods* 19 (2020). https://doi.org /10.1177/1609406920967174.

Tuck, Eve, and K. Wayne Yang. "Decolonization Is Not a Metaphor." *Decolonization: Indigeneity, Education & Society* 1, no. 1 (2012): 1–40.

Tucker, Karen. "Unraveling Coloniality in International Relations: Knowledge, Relationality, and Strategies for Engagement." *International Political Sociology* 12, no. 3 (2018): 215–32. https://doi.org/10.1093/ips/oly005.

Van der Geest, Sjaak. "Lying in Defence of Privacy: Anthropological and Methodological Observations." *International Journal of Social Research Methodology* 21, no. 5 (2018): 541–52. https://doi.org/10.1080/13645579 .2018.1447866.

Van Dijk, Teun A. "Principles of Critical Discourse Analysis." *Discourse & Society* 4, no. 2 (1993): 249–83. https://doi.org/10.1177/0957926593004002006.

Van Dyke, Ruth. "Investigating Human Trafficking from the Andean Community to Europe: The Role of Goodwill in the Researcher–Gatekeeper Relationship and in Negotiating Access to Data." *International Journal of Social Research Methodology* 16, no. 6 (2013): 515–23. https://doi.org/10 .1080/13645579.2013.823280.

Walby, Kevin, and Alex Luscombe. "Criteria for Quality in Qualitative Research and Use of Freedom of Information Requests in the Social Sciences." *Qualitative Research* 17, no. 5 (2017): 537–53. https://doi .org/10.1177/1468794116679726.

Walter, Maggie, and Michele Suina. "Indigenous Data, Indigenous Methodologies and Indigenous Data Sovereignty." *International Journal of Social Research Methodology* 22, no. 3 (2019): 233–43. https://doi.org/10.1080/13645579.2018.1531228.

Walton, Janet B., Vicki L. Plano Clark, Lori A. Foote, and Carla C. Johnson. "Navigating Intersecting Roads in a Mixed Methods Case Study: A Dissertation Journey." *Journal of Mixed Methods Research* 14, no. 4 (2020): 436–55. https://doi.org/10.1177/1558689819872422.

Wang, Caroline. "Photovoice: A Participatory Action Research Strategy Applied to Women's Health." *Journal of Women's Health* 8, no. 2 (1999): 185–92. https://doi.org/10.1089/jwh.1999.8.185.

Wang, Caroline, and Mary Anne Burris. "Empowerment through Photo Novella: Portraits of Participation." *Health Education Quarterly* 21, no. 2 (1994): 171–86. https://doi.org/10.1177/109019819402100204.

– "Photovoice: Concept, Methodology, and Use for Participatory Needs Assessment." *Health Education and Behavior* 24, no. 3 (1997): 369–87. https://doi.org/10.1177/109019819702400309.

Watson, Lawrence Craig, and Maria-Barbara Watson-Franke. *Interpreting Life Histories: An Anthropological Inquiry*. New Brunswick, NJ: Rutgers University Press, 1985.

Watts, Jonathan, and John Vidal. "Environmental Defenders Being Killed in Record Numbers Globally, New Research Reveals." *Guardian*, 13 July 2017. https://www.theguardian.com/environment/2017/jul/13/environmental-defenders-being-killed-in-record-numbers-globally-new-research-reveals.

Wilkinson, Catherine, and Samantha Wilkinson. "Doing It Write: Representation and Responsibility in Writing Up Participatory Research Involving Young People." *Social Inclusion* 5, no. 3 (2017): 219–27. https://doi.org/10.17645/si.v5i3.957.

Williams, Matthew L., Pete Burnap, Luke Sloan, Curtis Jessop, and Hayley Lepps. "Users' Views of Ethics in Social Media Research: Informed Consent, Anonymity, and Harm." In *The Ethics of Online Research*, edited by Kandy Woodfield, 27–52. Bingley, UK: Emerald Publishing, 2018.

Williams, Rebecca J. "Silence Is Not Always Golden: Reciprocal Peer Interviews as a Method to Engage Youth in Discussion on Violence in Honduras." *International Journal of Social Research Methodology* 24, no. 4 (2021): 453–67. https://doi.org/10.1080/13645579.2020.1801601.

Wilson, Denise, Alayne Mikahere-Hall, and Juanita Sherwood. "Using Indigenous Kaupapa Māori Research Methodology with Constructivist Grounded Theory: Generating a Theoretical Explanation of Indigenous Women's Realities." *International Journal of Social Research Methodology* 25, no. 3 (2022): 375–90. https://doi.org/10.1080/13645579.2021.1897756.

Wilson, Elena, Amanda Kenny, and Virginia Dickson-Swift. "Ethical Challenges in Community-Based Participatory Research: A Scoping

Review." *Qualitative Health Research* 28, no. 2 (2018): 189–99. https://doi
.org/10.1177/1049732317690721.

Wilson, Ian, Sharon R.A. Huttly, and Bridget Fenn. "A Case Study of
Sample Design for Longitudinal Research: Young Lives." *International
Journal of Social Research Methodology* 9, no. 5 (2006): 351–65. https://doi
.org/10.1080/13645570600658716.

Wilson, Shawn. *Research Is Ceremony: Indigenous Research Methods.* Black
Point, NS: Fernwood Publishing, 2008.

Windsong, Elena Ariel. "Incorporating Intersectionality into Research
Design: An Example Using Qualitative Interviews." *International Journal
of Social Research Methodology* 21, no. 2 (2018): 135–47. https://doi.org
/10.1080/13645579.2016.1268361.

Witham, Gary, Anna Beddow, and Carol Haigh. "Reflections on Access: Too
Vulnerable to Research?" *Journal of Research in Nursing* 20, no. 1 (2015):
28–37. https://doi.org/10.1177/1744987113499338.

Yaylacı, Şule. "Utility of Focus Groups in Retrospective Analysis of Conflict
Contexts." *International Journal of Qualitative Methods* 19 (2020). https://
doi.org/10.1177/1609406920922735.

Yeong, May Luu, Rosnah Ismail, Noor Hassim Ismail, and Mohd Isa
Hamzah. "Interview Protocol Refinement: Fine-Tuning Qualitative
Research Interview Questions for Multi-Racial Populations in
Malaysia." *The Qualitative Report* 23, no. 11 (2018): 2700–13. https://doi
.org/10.46743/2160-3715/2018.3412.

Yin, Robert K. "Analytic Generalization." In *Encyclopedia of Case Study
Research*, edited by Albert J. Mills, Gabrielle Eurepos, and Elden Wiebe,
20–2. Thousand Oaks, CA: Sage Publications, 2010.

– *Case Study Research and Applications: Design and Methods.*
Los Angeles: Sage Publications, 2017.

Youngman, Mark. "Building 'Terrorism Studies' as an Interdisciplinary
Space: Addressing Recurring Issues in the Study of Terrorism."
Terrorism and Political Violence 32, no. 5 (2020): 1091–105. https://doi
.org/10.1080/09546553.2018.1520702.

Zarzeczny, Amy, and Timothy Caulfield. "Legal Liability and Research
Ethics Boards: The Case of Neuroimaging and Incidental Findings."
International Journal of Law and Psychiatry 35, no. 2 (2012): 137–45. https://
doi.org/10.1016/j.ijlp.2011.12.005.

Zimbalist, Zack. "Bystanders and Response Bias in Face-to-Face Surveys in
Africa." *International Journal of Social Research Methodology* 25, no. 3 (2022):
361–77. https://doi.org/10.1080/13645579.2021.1886397.

Index

Page numbers in italics represent illustrations with *f* denoting figures and *t* denoting tables.